Conceiving Carolina ∾

Conceiving Carolina ~

Proprietors, Planters, and Plots, 1662–1729

L.H. Roper

CONCEIVING CAROLINA
© L.H. Roper, 2004

First published 2004 by
PALGRAVE MACMILLAN™
175 Fifth Avenue, New York, N.Y. 10010 and
Houndmills, Basingstoke, Hampshire, England RG21 6XS
Companies and representatives throughout the world

PALGRAVE MACMILLAN is the global academic imprint of the Palgrave Macmillan division of St. Martin's Press, LLC and of Palgrave Macmillan Ltd. Macmillan® is a registered trademark in the United States, United Kingdom and other countries. Palgrave is a registered trademark in the European Union and other countries.

ISBN 1–4039–6479–3 hardback

Library of Congress Cataloging-in-Publication Data
Roper, L.H. (Louis, H.)
    Conceiving Carolina : proprietors, planters, and plots, 1662–1729 / L.H. Roper.
        p. cm.
    Includes bibliographical references and index.
    ISBN 1–4039–6479–3
        1. South Carolina—History—Colonial period, ca. 1600–1775.
    2. South Carolina—Politics and government—To 1775. 3. Landowners—South Carolina—Political activity—History—17th century.
    4. Landowners—South Carolina—Political activity—History—18th century. 5. South Carolina—Race relations. 6. South Carolina—Relations—Great Britain. 7. Great Britain—Relations—South Carolina.
    8. Great Britain—Colonies—America—Administration—History—17th century. 9. Great Britain—Colonies—America—Administration—History—18th century. I. Title.

F272.R68 2004
975.7'02—dc22   2003060754

A catalogue record for this book is available from the British Library.

Design by Newgen Imaging Systems (P) Ltd. Chennai, India.

First edition: April 2004
10 9 8 7 6 5 4 3 2 1

Printed in the United States of America.

Contents

Acknowledgments   vii

Introduction   1

Prologue   15

1.   Genesis   21

2.   Blueprint   29

3.   Birthpangs   41

4.   The Rise of the Goose Creek Men   51

5.   Plots   69

6.   Stuarts Town   83

7.   Treachery   95

8.   Tests   117

9.   Consternation   133

10. Conclusions   143

Abbreviations   159
Notes   161
Index   209

Acknowledgments

The pursuit of historical inquiry results, happily, in the accrual of many debts and the emergence of this book grants me the opportunity to acknowledge these. I would like to thank staff at the South Carolina Department of Archives and History, the South Carolina Historical Society, the Public Record Office of Great Britain, the British Library (Early Modern Printed and Manuscript Collections), the National Archives of Scotland, the National Library of Scotland, the Edinburgh City Archives, the Department of Western Manuscripts of the Bodleian Library at the University of Oxford, the Pepys Library at Magdalene College, University of Cambridge, the Gloucestershire Record Office, the Guildhall Library, and, last but by no means least, the Interlibrary Loan Department at Sojourner Truth Library at the State University of New York at New Paltz for their assistance in helping with my enquiries and producing documents and other materials. I would like to thank His Grace, the duke of Beaufort, for permission to quote from documents in his possession at Badminton, Gloucestershire, and Mrs. Margaret Richards, librarian at Badminton, for arranging the temporary transfer of those records to the Gloucestershire Record Office.

I would like to especially thank Bertrand Van Ruymbeke who, with his wife, Meredith, gave me a place to stay in Charleston while I undertook research in South Carolina. He also applied his considerable knowledge of the sources and of proprietary South Carolina to his reading of the manuscript and he continues to engage me in ongoing discussions about the proprietors and their world. I should also like to thank Evan Haefeli, Sarah Barber, Warren Billings, Randy Sparks, Louise Yeoman, and an anonymous reader for the press for their encouragement and insights. My thanks also to Brendan O'Malley and the staff at Palgrave for their enthusiastic support and their assistance in bringing this project to fruition. Finally, I would also like to thank Charles Lesser for his continuing interest in this project and helpful references.

Various fragments of this work have already appeared in public. An article appeared in the 1996 number of *The Historian*.[1] I also subjected audiences at the International Seminar on the History of the Atlantic World at the Charles Warren Center for the Study of American History at Harvard University, the annual meeting of the South Carolina Historical Association, the Society of Early Americanists Conference, the Annual Meeting of the Organization of American Historians, the Annual Meeting of the American Historical Association, and the Fifth Omohundro Institute of Early American History and Culture Conference to my efforts to think out the various problems that this book tries to address and I would like to thank those who participated in those sessions. Finally, I would like to express my gratitude for the financial support from the John Carter Brown Library, the Office of Academic Affairs at the State University of New York at New Paltz, and United University Professions, which subsidized research trips and conference appearances.

Finally, I would like to thank the Department of History at the University of Rochester for awarding me assistantships/fellowships for the four years I spent as a student there. More particularly, I would like to acknowledge the unpayable debt I owe to my mentors. From Perez Zagorin, I gained a deep understanding of early modern Europe. I gained—and continue to gain—from the wisdom afforded me by Mary Young. Finally, John Waters gave me a priceless education, not only about the pre-industrial world (including early America), but how to be a mentor, a historian, and a friend. I have tried in a feeble way to apply their advice, both in particular and in general, in my own labors in the vineyard. The mistakes that remain are, of course, my own.

As for everything else, I would like to simply thank my spouse, Rosemarie Frisone, for making it all possible and I dedicate this volume to her.

Introduction ∿

This book, in the first instance, offers a new history of South Carolina from the formation of the proprietorship that founded the colony in late 1662 to the statutory buy-out of the Lords Proprietors in 1729. In doing so, it adopts the now fashionable "Atlantic" perspective on events and behavior.[2] But, it does not track the movement of people to a "New World," the environment of which purportedly compelled social and cultural adaptation on their part or seek to plot the formation of a "new" colonial society, let alone a "unique plantation regime."[3] Instead, it focuses, perhaps unfashionably, on the central roles of politics and contingency in the creation of Carolina since it was the pursuit of political interests and a common understanding of how to pursue them that bridged the ocean: on the one hand, these phenomena provided a common milieu for men on the make in the later Stuart period; on the other, colonial political figures, in pursuit of power, wealth, and status in accordance with the prevailing transatlantic view of how the world worked, cultivated associations with patrons in England. The results generated significant social and political results in both the colony and the metropolis.

Thus, the book offers a proposal for reconfiguring our approach to the study of colonial British America. Since the rise of the "new social history" a generation ago, early Americanists have devised a number of strategies to develop a new framework for understanding their subject in the trail generated by an explosion of work from diverse geographical and social perspectives, with admittedly indifferent success. Many peers regard the development of the field since World War II as "liberating," while others have expressed concern that the sheer quantity of work threatens to render prospects for a common comprehension problematic.[4]

Ironically and significantly, this self-styled historiographical new broom has not effected an alteration in the fundamental approach taken by the field: the eternal quest to find the "origins" of American society—with at least part of an eye on American independence and the "American Revolution"—in the mixture of "Old World" (European and African) and "New" (landscape, including "Indians"). This phenomenon has endured even in the recent signs that have emerged of a new offensive on the notion of American "exception-alism," undertaken generally in tandem with an attempt to reconsider the history of the British Empire.[5]

The history you are about to read, then, constitutes a contribution, in part, to this assault. And the dates of the proprietorship facilitate the place-ment of South Carolina's early history outside of the long shadows cast both by American independence and by the Jamestowns and Plymouths of Anglo-American colonization. It does, though, decline Joyce Chaplin's invitation to employ theory (particularly of the "post-colonial stripe") as the primary means to bridge the gap between metropolitan and colonial history.[6]

Instead, while casting aside the perennial question of "old" versus "new" (recast in faddish "Atlantic" terms) as a red herring, it suggests that the clear-est perspective for examining and understanding motives and behavior, as well as colonial development, comes from a thorough grounding in the context which spawned South Carolina and from emphasizing the enduring links—especially in terms of orientation, personalities, ideas, and politics—in the English-speaking "Atlantic World." In providing this reconsideration the volume considers the settlement of this province in accordance with what we know of the social, political, and religious history of early modern (espe-cially late seventeenth-century) England as well as, where appropriate, that of Scotland and Ireland.

By carefully reviewing the character of the "Old World" that gave birth to South Carolina and by assessing relevant developments and phenomena on both sides of the Atlantic, we learn that, although marked differences certainly came to exist between the colony and England, these arose naturally from historical (including, of course, geographical) circumstances: this colony, just as Cornwall, Ireland, New England, and Virginia before it, came to constitute a distinct, yet clearly connected, part of the Anglo-American world—one variation upon a theme.

By no means does the adoption of this approach diminish the importance of either American Indians or of Africans to the narrative. Proprietary South Carolina's often shabby and occasionally sordid story encompassed Scotland, Ireland, Bermuda, New England, the West Indies, Virginia, and the forests of southeastern North America, as well as London, Charles Town, and West Africa. Yet, English colonizers and colonists, for better or for worse, laid out the social and political stakes in the province—as their counterparts did in other parts of the empire—which constituted the parameters of behavior for non-English, as well as European, historical actors.

Obviously, and unfortunately, the Indians and Africans who found them-selves the objects of this behavior correspondingly found themselves in a position from which it was exceedingly problematical for them to express their feelings on the character of reality, although they, and the social schemes the planters devised in their attempt to recreate an English-style hierarchy, certainly came to affect both those schemes and the mindset that gave rise to them. One of the great tragedies of all this is the great, practically impossible, difficulty in obtaining evidence of African and Indian behavior in South Carolina prior to the founding of *The South Carolina Gazette* in 1732.[7] The present study, then, makes no attempt to discuss Africans and Indians per se or the impact of the "new world" created for these people by Europeans but does seek to offer an account of the world in which the diverse inhabitants of the Carolina Lowcountry interacted after 1670.[8]

Since South Carolina arose out of a context notoriously pervaded by cynicism, failure, exploitation, plotting, treachery, and disingenuousness—the England of Charles II and his successors—naturally, perhaps even inevitably, these social and political qualities readily transplanted to the province. Still, the unattractive behavior of many of the historical actors—we shall meet them in chapter 4—involved here endlessly fascinates, both in the academic and in the general sense. The endemic schemes to overthrow governments, to destroy rivals, and to betray neighbors—murder, kidnap, blackmail, battery, and theft, sometimes perpetrated under the rule of law—as well as epidemic disease, American and European war, and seemingly endless finger-pointing make for compelling reading. They also overwhelmed the intentions of the Lords Proprietors for their colony just as the "Popish Plot" (1682), the "Rye-House Plot" (1683), and similar activities convulsed the metropolis, as we shall see in chapter 5.

The salacious nature of the proprietary period does not mean, though, that the proprietorship, the problems the venture sought to address, the plans the Lords devised, and the difficulties, both more or less apparent, they and their colonists faced should hold no further interest for students of British North America. For although, by the early eighteenth century, the colony's Church of England clergy, for example, collectively regarded the place as a Godforsaken backwater, a continuous trickle of European arrivals did make their way to South Carolina. In this important sense, failure—of the province to attract and keep sufficient numbers of people from Western Europe during the proprietary period—bred, on the one hand, success for the white planters in terms of property accumulation and accompanying status in the customary way, but, on the other, further failure in terms of the acute anxieties generated by the slave system they devised, in part, to meet their labor demands. And, of course, South Carolina came to play an extraordinary role in the subsequent history of the United States; a better understanding of its proprietary period provides a surer platform for understanding this purportedly peculiar colony/state.

A fresh study of the history of the colony also enables us to determine the nature of the changes that took place at its genesis and to consider this history in terms of early modern English colonization generally. In turn, this examination must entail, given present predilections, addressing "modernization" in both the metropolitan and colonial contexts. Did, for instance, the early colonization of South Carolina lay the foundations for the "developmental model" of "modernization"—the increasing pervasiveness of the market economy and accompanying celebration of the individual by early modern British society (even as the state governing that society continued to build its power)—postulated as having taken place in the Lowcountry—and everywhere else in the "first British Empire"—after 1710?[9] Did it offer "an exceptionally promising field for the pursuit—and realization—of collective as well as individual aspirations" that resulted in a "special place that deviated sharply from the Old World societies of Europe?"[10] Did its political and social character emerge as a consequence of the adaptations demanded by the American environment of "Old World" systems of belief?[11] Or, instead, did the cut of this colony's social cloth run out, perhaps more mundanely, in the wake of the internecine political behavior of leading Carolinians and other less controllable factors?

It may seem that we already know as much as we can know about early South Carolina. The textbook account goes as follows. After 1669, the Lords Proprietors, especially the first earl of Shaftesbury (in conjunction with their secretary, John Locke), codified an agrarian sociopolitical system in their Fundamental Constitutions of Carolina, but proprietary intentions and interests almost immediately ran afoul of the notorious faction of "Goose Creek men" (named after the location of their plantations on a tributary of the Cooper River), who purportedly consisted primarily of "Barbadian Anglicans." Early on, the numerically superior Barbadians purportedly scored a significant triumph by securing proprietary approval for counting slaves as "servants" for purposes of determining headrights to land grants. This "coup," accompanied by the ultimately successful establishment of rice and other staple commodities, along with South Carolina's malarial climate, competition from other colonies—especially Pennsylvania after its founding in 1682—and the leveling off of the English population after 1650, gave rise to a colonial society preoccupied with its "black majority" after 1708. It also encouraged South Carolina's initial development, in Peter Wood's famous phrase, as "the colony of a colony": the Carolinians immediately directed their economic activity, notably cattle ranching, to servicing Barbados rather than fulfilling proprietary expectations that they plant staple crops.

Subsequently, this "anti-proprietary" group repeatedly ignored proprietary instructions, rejected the Fundamental Constitutions, refused to pay quitrents, harbored pirates, ignored pleas to settle in towns and plant staple crops, broke proprietary control of the Indian trade, and generally opposed the efforts of the Lords to secure a profit from their colonial investment.

Their behavior resulted in proprietary disgust with and disinterest in the project. In 1704, the Goose Creek men switched sides and allied themselves with the Lords against Carolina's Dissenters. This maneuver succeeded primarily in alienating the colonial party who had supported the proprietors having been attracted to the province by the promise of religious toleration. When the Lords proved ineffective in dealing with crises brought on by the Yamassee War (1715–16), pirates (1718), and continuing French encroachment in the west, the creole descendants of the Goose Creek men, in conjunction with newer arrivals from England built on the "anti-proprietary" sentiment that "had existed in the colony almost from the beginning" to overthrow the Lords. The proprietors contributed to their own demise by disallowing a series of laws—to place duties on imports, to further regulate the Indian trade, to retire outstanding bills of credit, and to permit the issuance of paper money—compounded by their insistence on keeping lands seized from the defeated Yamassees for themselves and disregarding the colonists' plans to attract new migrants to those territories.

Historians then have generally supported the verdict that the Carolinians rendered on the proprietary regime in 1719: their rebellion "ended the remnants of Shaftesbury's faded dream: a utopian society flourishing under the benign auspices of the proprietors." Yet, even "if South Carolina had not become utopia, it was becoming more English." Although "the revolution [against the proprietors] was not much of a revolution" in terms of its violence or the significance of constitutional issues, it had cast off the "anomaly" of proprietary government.[12]

In political terms, then, the prevailing view has remained essentially one of conflict: between proprietors and their opponents, between, Indian traders and planters, between "Anglicans" and Dissenters. Most recently, Meaghan N. Duff has sought to demonstrate proprietary inability to implement a "land program" thanks to colonial intransigence, while Gary L. Hewitt has styled the 1719 rebellion against the proprietary government as the triumph of planters against mercantile interests.[13]

In social terms, the political activity of the Goose Creek men generated the social result of a world that "was neither England nor Barbados, though it embodied elements of both." The Carolinian "model was Barbados," in terms of creating "an exploitative society in which free whites prospered on black slave labour," although the mainland planters "never committed themselves to one crop as exclusively as Barbadians did." By the end of the proprietary period, the planters "had passed through the first of what has been identified as the three principal stages in the socio-cultural development of most colonies: simplification, elaboration, and replication."[14] The "relatively egalitarian social structure" of the early settlement gave way as "the population and the economy grew," Carolinians imported more slaves, and "local institutions became more complex and elaborate." Widening gaps appeared in the social structure and the arrival of more blacks "enlarged the gulf between men who were—or would become—free and those who were not. At the same time the racial division masked the increasing complexity of white society." Such "differences from England made local society unique," notwithstanding "numerous ties" between South Carolina and the rest of the British Empire.[15]

Just how "unique" was it, though, in what passed for the British Empire in the late seventeenth and early eighteenth centuries? Notoriously, slavery played an inordinate role in South Carolina, both in terms of the size of its population of African descent (at least in terms of the mainland colonies) and with respect to involvement in the Indian slave trade. Yet, these apparently distinctive phenomena demonstrate, in actuality, that the province experienced normative development: even in the teeth of arguable "modernization," it, like the rest of the Anglo-American Atlantic World, retained a demonstrably agrarian and, correspondingly, hierarchical character. Race-based slavery, already entrenched in the West Indies and in the Chesapeake by the time of Carolina's founding, slipped all-too-easily onto the Lowcountry landscape.

But how did this happen? We have known for over a century that the various incarnations of the Goose Creek men provided the impetus for the early development of South Carolina. We have also known the importance of the shadowy Indian slave trade to the character of proprietary South Carolina.[16] Yet, a great deal has remained unknown. In the first place, scholarship has not yielded a full disclosure of the activities of these "dealers in Indians," which has shrouded, in turn, a better appreciation of their *raison d'être* and the motivations for their behavior. This fog has had the further effect of shrouding the motives and behavior of the proprietors, the nominal opponents of the Goose Creek men.

My investigation has yielded a significantly different understanding of what happened. In the first place, the well-publicized connection between the West Indies, especially Barbados, and South Carolina, while certainly significant, has been overstated. Migrants from the islands did comprise a sizeable element in the colony's population from its inception and the mainland province did adopt the Barbadian approach to "managing" slave labor.[17]

Yet, most of the leading Goose Creek men, including their longtime chief, Maurice Mathews, came from England. They appear to have had no direct experience with slavery or slaves prior to their arrival in America; certainly, no manifestation of a desire on their part to build a slaveholding society per se in South Carolina appears in the historical record.[18]

Identifying early Carolinians as "Barbadian" or "American," as distinct from "English" can be misleading, certainly in this case. The "weightier sort" of migrant—those expected to govern Carolina—maintained presences in various parts of England's Atlantic empire. These people—Mathews, the Colleton family, Sir John Yeamans, Andrew Percival, Robert Quarry, James Moore, James Morton, Seth Sothell, Sir Nathaniel Johnson and his son, Robert, and son-in-law, Thomas Broughton, William Rhett, Job How, and Nicholas Trott—and their peers held political and commercial interests in and had familiarity with places on both sides of the ocean, physically and mentally. Thus, we should regard them (as they did themselves) more as inhabitants of an Anglo-Atlantic world rather than as denizens of an "Old World" or a "New."[19]

The realization that West Indians did not play a controlling role in South Carolina's early history forces further revisions in terms of proprietary-era politics. Although conflict did predominate the political scene, the Goose Creek men did not constitute an anti-proprietary faction. Reconsidering the record reveals that if any consistency exists in the history of proprietary South Carolina it exists in the perpetually cynical behavior of this faction. They involved themselves in the Indian trade—either initiating or adding considerable fuel to an already present cycle of war and enslavement—almost immediately after the founding of the colony in 1670. Then, a series of diplomatic efforts and wars enabled them to dispose successfully of their rival, Dr. Henry Woodward, and his trading partners, the Westos, between 1677 and 1680. In 1686, it was the turn of Henry Erskine, third Baron Cardross, and his seemingly promising Scottish settlement. Fourteen years later, they had rather less luck in removing their longtime Spanish competitors from St. Augustine—although they did succeed in teetering South Carolina on the brink of bankruptcy; in 1707, Sir Nathaniel Johnson drove his enemy, the reform-minded trader Thomas Nairne into temporary exile in London.

Throughout, they continually opposed constitutional government (baffling the Lords) and reforms that might have placed their activities under unbearable scrutiny. They also cultivated powerful friends to cement their position when the situation suited them, be they proprietary, such as John, Lord Granville, Sothell, and John Archdale, or otherwise, such as the Royal Navy Captain Thomas Spragg, the Board of Trade functionary Edward Randolph, or their Spanish neighbors. When circumstance suited, they cooperated with the proprietors: Archdale, for instance, successfully collected the quitrents when he assumed personal charge of the government in 1695—but Randolph, supplied with information from Goose Creek, accused him of permitting pirates to anchor at Charles Town. Yet, when it did not suit, they did not cooperate.

Thus, we must regard the characterization of factions as "anti-proprietary" and "proprietary"—and even the whole issue of proprietary attempts to control the colony—as misleading. While the younger sons of aristocracy and gentry may have competed for land in seventeenth-century Virginia and Barbados (and elsewhere), the demographic character of proprietary South Carolina meant that few white males, regardless of their background, went without land, although we should note that the dearth of records prevents the sort of analysis James Horn has provided for the Chesapeake.[20] Moreover, unlike in Virginia and Barbados, succeeding generations of Carolina planters did not move to overthrow the preceding generation.

Instead, the political activity of the Goose Creek men revolved around their enslavement of Indians, a lucrative part of South Carolina's lucrative trade with indigenous folk. Their ferocious defense of their trading interests continually disrupted the Carolina political scene, had a significantly adverse impact on European migration to the colony, and provoked war. Clearly the behavior of this faction—much more so than anything the proprietors did (or did not) do—triggered the crises that resulted in the overthrow of the proprietary regime as the Lords and a number of planters recognized at the time. Most particularly, the "dealers in Indians," having wrecked the colony's economy by issuing worthless paper currency (necessitated by the disastrous attempt to capture St. Augustine in 1702) and having brought the colony to the brink of destruction by warring with the Yamassees and their confederates—who had attacked out of fear of being enslaved and transported to the Caribbean—the Carolinians came to see salvation in royal rule from an admittedly overwhelmed proprietorship: they did not rest easily, though, until the Crown and Parliament bought the Lords out ten years after the "revolution." For all of the recent historiographical ink spilled on early English "state formation," the government of George I proved in no hurry to place Carolina under its direct authority.

Ultimately, the proprietors, as they themselves well knew, could not do much to bring such a vigorous group as the Goose Creek men to heel. The limits of early modern government, aggravated in the case of a smaller, private operation such as the proprietorship, compounded by the reality of a 3,000-mile ocean voyage, meant that the Lords would always have to remain dependent upon the efforts of their settlers to maintain good order in their province. Indeed, the Fundamental Constitutions that they devised under-scored this recognition by expressly delegating primary governmental responsibilities to those on the colonial scene with the experience and means to deal with colonial issues. Furthermore, the proprietors consistently reminded their settlers of their respective positions in their letters. The admitted lack of interest of some later proprietors, such as the second duke of Beaufort, the minority of others, and the distractions presented by metro-politan affairs further weighted direct responsibility for the proprietary administration towards Charles Town.

In retrospect then, the Carolina proprietors sought to govern their province in ways that made sense to themselves and made sense with respect to the general understanding of politics and society as it existed in the England of the late seventeenth and early eighteenth centuries. In this context, the proprietors, over the almost 70-year history of their government, were not generally ignorant, inept, or impotent.[21]

Nor were they overly concerned with securing a financial return from their province. Except for the Colleton family (who kept their lands until independence) and, briefly, the first earl of Shaftesbury, none of the Lords ever operated their own plantations in the colony. They did give themselves a limited monopoly over the Indian trade, but primarily, as they said, in order to facilitate frontier peace; a peace which, as we shall see, their agents promptly shattered for their own pecuniary and political reasons—not to break proprietary control over the trade. Moreover they haggled with the Goose Creek men over the quitrent payments designed to pay government officials—unsurprisingly, since the latter usually consisted of opponents to the "dealers in Indians." Yet, the proprietors did not necessarily expect for Carolina to yield a profit for themselves—not to say that they would have objected to receiving one; they certainly hoped for a return on their investment—nor did they ever seek to "impose" themselves on their colonists. Rather, they began and maintained the venture primarily for public purposes, as the seventeenth century defined the term.

Some of the Lords did devote attention to promoting migration, establishing a government, and putting the colony on a sound economic footing. Others, for various reasons, especially as the proprietorship came to an end, maintained relatively little interest in the colony. And why should they have had, considering the treatment many Carolinians had accorded the Fundamental Constitutions and the general proprietary effort to facilitate orderly government and settlement in the colony over 50 years? In any event, the proprietors never regarded the difficulties they had in terms of "who was going to have the predominant voice in the colony." Instead, and consistently, they intended for a balance to exist between the voices of colonizers and colonists; this intention appears formally in the language of the Fundamental Constitutions and informally throughout their correspondence. That elements among the province's "weightier sort" often acted in illegitimate and unforeseen ways cannot really be blamed on the Lords, except for an ill-advised intervention in the Establishment controversy of 1704–06.[22]

In the broader scheme of things, the factional convulsions that beset early South Carolina scarcely made the province unique in an empire where factions defined politics. A glance at the histories of the various colonies quickly confirms this: rebellions against Lord Baltimore in Maryland,

Leisler's Rebellion (and response) in New York, Bacon's Rebellion, infighting in New Jersey and Pennsylvania, and the 1710 murder of Governor Daniel Parke of the Leeward Islands by irate planters.[23] The colonial struggle between factions, in turn, as Bernard Bailyn has argued in a seminal essay, may even have defined early American societies since, at least in early Virginia, it generated both a "divergence between political and social leadership" and a social structure that was "by European standards strangely shaped."[24]

Building upon these insights, it has become a commonplace of the historiography of the first British Empire that the social formation of Anglo-American elites demonstrates that the colonial experience, especially the availability of land, played a central role in furthering sociopolitical transformation in British North America by providing new individual opportunities—for investment as well as livelihood—that were supposedly unavailable in the metropolis. Indeed, the European settlement of North America has come to mark the transfer of European cultural baggage to a place "where the premodern world became modern and where Europeans became Americans."[25]

This metamorphosis purportedly began when European migrants, already alienated from their traditional backgrounds, arrived in the "New World," bringing with them a previously acquired individualistic and acquisitive bent. Transplanted to North America—"a place of vast unoccupied or under-utilized spaces where the inhabitants of the Old World could escape its trammels and form a distinctive new social order in which the inhibiting conditions and rules governing the Old World would not apply"—"the ideal of the pursuit of happiness by independent people" came to provide the genesis of American ideals albeit, curiously, while the colonies, at the same time, began increasingly to resemble the "Old World."[26]

The character of proprietary South Carolina follows this conception of Americanization to some degree. For instance, the provincial elite took advantage of American opportunities and of the natural fluidity of infant societies to rise to positions of prominence from non-aristocratic origins, just as its counterparts—the Livingstons, Delanceys, Phillipses, and Van Cortlandts in New York, the Codringtons, Modyfords, and Draxes on Barbados, and the Lees, Harrisons, Carters, and Byrds in Virginia—in other colonies did.

Moreover, the planters, almost immediately upon landing at Ashley River, became accustomed to governing themselves. Certainly, like other colonists, they competed vigorously for power and status in their colonial backwater. Certainly also, the distress wrought by this competition—especially in terms of its effects on migration and settlement—resulted in a "strangely shaped" version of the early modern English hierarchy.[27]

Yet, the now-classic characterization of the change of metropolitan politics and society into new forms does not seem to provide an especially apt framework in which to fit South Carolina's development. In the first place, the record demonstrates that all of the members of Carolina's political nation, no matter what side they were on, continually looked to the metropolis for connections, for support, and as the model upon which to base their own political system—and did so from the moment the "first fleet" assembled in the Downs in 1669 through the final success of appeals for royal takeover in 1729.

Furthermore, "early Americans" scarcely held a monopoly on factional strife in the early modern period. Colonists such as the Goose Creek men behaved very much as their counterparts in England did. Those who found themselves out of power on both sides of the Atlantic often adopted the language of liberty against the alleged oppressions of officialdom. At the same time, patronage, with its components of reciprocity, deference, and condescension, played as significant a part in the colonists' view of the world just as it did for their counterparts on the make in the metropolis: London remained the home of their patrons and, correspondingly, the sun around which South Carolina clients orbited, although the greater distance between themselves and the capital enabled them to pursue individual, petty agendas with greater impunity than their counterparts in Ireland and in the English shires could. Notwithstanding the intermittent attentions of the proprietors, the Carolinian elite remained linked, psychologically, as well as politically with metropolitan realities.

Then, in terms of social values, there cannot be much question that those Europeans who migrated, either freely or as servants, to South Carolina (at least) did so for the most part because they believed (insofar as they had any positive purpose in migrating) that their estates, to use the early modern term, would improve thereby bringing "independence" as opposed to "opportunity" or "happiness" in a general sense. It seems quite significant that the colony's promoters continued to emphasize the relative availability of landed estates to prospective immigrants—as opposed to "vast unoccupied or underutilized spaces"—furthered by a benevolent meteorological and governmental climate, and the continued equation by promoters and settlers of landed property with status and power—a belief they shared, of course, with their counterparts back in England and elsewhere in the English Empire. Furthermore, the Fundamental Constitutions, designed to protect stakes in society, although never officially ratified by the colonists, remained a symbol, even at the end of the proprietary period, of this enduring belief in landed estates as the proper barometer of status and power and in the corresponding belief in the desirability of a landed aristocracy, entitled or otherwise, as the independent anchors of a commonwealth. At the same time, the failure to fully transplant particular English ideas—which had been undertaken on more formal basis in Carolina than in other colonies—occurred primarily because of the perennial shortage of Western European migrants, particularly servants, in the province.[28]

Indeed, the record gives us a good idea as to why people did not migrate to Carolina. Scots pondering relocation in the 1680s, determined that the colony was not the "covenanted" land. Then, a number of prospective English migrants at the end of the reign of Charles II had more important tasks—assassination and insurrection—to which to attend. For still others, the shockingly repellant behavior of the Carolinians served both as a deterrent for would-be migrants and, for those with the misfortune to have already found themselves there, as an incentive to depart. Malaria, dysentery, competition from other colonies, and the abiding threat of Spanish and Indians rounded off the unhappy scene.

In the end, slavery, as we are all painfully aware, provided an all-too-easy solution to these difficulties and, in a tragic paradox, was used as early as 1682, as an incentive for those seeking "independence" to move to Carolina. Already favored by merchants and other English folk around the Atlantic World by 1675, including, of course, Barbadian *émigrés*, Goose Creek men, and other planters (it may be an exaggeration to consider Carolinian enthusiasm for the "peculiar institution" as evidence that the colony served as a "cultural hearth" of the island plantation society), slave labor provided the pragmatic means to translate the "blank slate" of the "New World" into those benchmark landed estates that self-styled persons of substance pursued on both sides of the ocean.[29]

In 1808—126 years after Shaftesbury's death—the Patriot-historian David Ramsay could reflect that South Carolina contained, for his practical purposes, four groups: planters, farmers, cottagers, and squatters. To the transplanted Pennsylvanian landed estates—in conjunction, of course, with slave labor—remained, as they had a century before, the barometer of sociopolitical position and new written constitutions now existed to protect those estates. Although people of color and white women inevitably failed to register in Ramsay's account, enslavement, of course, permeated the entire character of reality in South Carolina by the beginning of the nineteenth century. It is certainly possible to characterize this system as a manifestation of the pursuit of opportunity that, we have been told, was inherent in Anglo-American colonization; an extension, in turn, of the individualistic and acquisitive *mentalité* that became increasingly prevalent in early modern Europe. The system certainly brought Charles Town's planters greater wealth than the rest of George III's North American subjects.[30]

On the other hand, the increasingly heavy dependence on slavery and slaves in South Carolina may have reflected the ongoing addiction of the planters to the pursuit of status, derived, of course, from landed wealth, even in the continuing face of adverse demographics—caused, paradoxically, by increased dependence during the eighteenth century upon income generated by cultivating rice in the swampy Lowcountry that whites could and did largely avoid.[31] Certainly, *pace* analyses of early modern affirmations of American exceptionalism, the seemingly unhinged behavior of Americans such as South Carolina's "dealers in Indians" and the obnoxious slavery-based societies these people produced gave rise to eighteenth-century concerns over the deleterious effects of America on European "civilization."[32]

Certainly, also South Carolina, and perhaps Anglo-America in general, at the end of the seventeenth century, does not appear to have held any particular attraction for the English. Although we have no precise figures of departures or arrivals, the population figures provided in 1709 indicate that relatively few people made the transatlantic trek to Charles Town, even considering the effects of epidemic disease on the colony's population.[33] The promotional promises of large land grants and religious toleration, in general, seem not to have outweighed a stagnant English population, fear of an ocean voyage and of the "wilderness," and the dubious political scene of the province. By 1729, South Carolina enjoyed commercial activity and wealth generated by the cultivation of staples, to be sure, but continued to suffer from scanty demographics and community formation. This result provoked twinned efforts by the province's leaders after 1730 to correct what they regarded as dangerously unbalanced demographics and to impose increasingly stringent controls on the movement and behavior of the province's black inhabitants.[34]

The history of proprietary South Carolina may enable us to draw connections between political, intellectual, and social history, but it also reminds us that such connections can often be accidental and can arise as much from cynicism, mistake, irrationality, and felony as they do for other reasons. Had, for instance, Mathews and his associates not seen off the Scots in 1686, as detailed in chapters 6 and 7, would race-based slavery have become so peculiarly predominant in South Carolina? We, of course, cannot know, but, for what it is worth, the proprietors certainly thought that things would have turned out rather differently for their province, at least in the short term.[35]

Prologue ∿

O n October 31, 1662, Sir Robert Harley wrote to his brother that he had had the pleasure of an encounter with George Monck, duke of Albemarle, one of the most powerful men in England. Harley reported that Albemarle along "with some others" had embarked on a new colonization project and were in the process of taking out a patent from the monarch for land between Virginia and Spanish Florida. Armed with favorable reports on the prospects for the territory in question, the duke and his associates were ready to commence colonization.

Sir Robert accorded Albemarle's offer of the governorship of the planned province due deference even though doubts presented themselves. In the first place, he expressed skepticism about commitment of the patentees, who also included Sir George Carteret, the Treasurer of the Navy: they initially hoped to attract some 3,000 colonists from Virginia and New England, but had yet to put any money forward to further the venture. In addition, the neighboring presence of Spanish and Indians posed worries.

Yet, the proposal had much to recommend it, although Sir Robert ultimately declined the duke's offer. Carolina, it seemed, offered prospects for cultivating many commodities which, as Harley observed to his brother, combined with its proximity to England's other colonies could make the place a center of the already lucrative intercolonial trade.[36]

Sir Robert's letter helps to shed light on the initial formation and intentions of the Carolina proprietorship. Historians have argued, without supplying much in the way of evidence, that the impetus for colonizing Carolina came from Barbados. They point to the direct involvement of the Barbadian planter Sir John Colleton in the project and that island's need both for a place to divert part of its overwhelming population, as well as to provide food for a place whose agricultural production had been almost wholly given over to sugar by 1660.[37]

It is quite possible that Colleton, along with another proprietor, Sir William Berkeley, the longtime governor of Virginia who had striven since the 1640s to expand that colony southward, did spark Albemarle's interest in America.[38] But Harley's letter makes it apparent that the duke took a lead sometime in the autumn of 1662. His direct involvement, in turn, would have attracted the other members of the undertaking: Anthony Ashley Cooper (later, Lord Ashley and first earl of Shaftesbury) had partnered Albemarle on the Cromwellian Council of State and in the Army during the Interregnum; while John Berkeley, Baron Berkeley of Stratton and Sir William's brother, William, first earl of Craven, as well as Carteret, had all manifested an interest in England's overseas trade and settlement as part of a palpable increase in thought about empire and colonization that had germinated under the Cromwellian regime. The most likely reason behind the formation of this unlikely proprietorship seems to have been a mixture of Sir William Berkeley's goals for Virginia and the needs of Barbados (probably conveyed directly to Albemarle by his kinsman, Sir Thomas Modyford and Colleton) meshing with the "improving urges" of Ashley, Baron Berkeley, and Carteret.[39]

We can only speculate as to the reasons behind the inclusion of the eighth member. Edward Hyde, the constant companion and advisor of Charles II during the dark days of the Interregnum, who became earl of Clarendon and Lord Chancellor of England at the Restoration, nominally seconded the proprietorship. Clarendon seems to have shared in the initial enthusiasm for overseas expansion expressed at the accession of his protégé to his three thrones in 1660; indeed, his enemies charged at his impeachment in 1667 that "he had gotten great sums of money indirectly and corruptly from plantations."[40]

Yet, beset by the gout, preoccupied with affairs of state, and having a low opinion of some of his new partners, he can only have been a lukewarm participant, at best. Possibly, he lent his name as part of the government's anti-Spanish foreign policy of the moment (this would also explain the timing of the Carolina grant). In response to Spanish reluctance to concede the English possession of Dunkirk and Jamaica at the Restoration, Clarendon (and Albemarle) vigorously prosecuted an alliance with the newly independent Portuguese monarchy. This policy, the centerpiece of which was the marriage of Charles II to Catherine of Braganza in April 1662, involved sending troops to support Portugal's war with Spain in 1663 as the Carolina charter passed the seals. Creating a new colony headed by the most prominent military man in England (Albemarle, who, like Clarendon, had benefited from Portuguese liberality) and the government's chief minister on the borders of Spanish Florida could, at least in the minds of the English, have sent an additional message to Felipe IV.[41] In any event, Carolina receives no mention in the lengthy and bitter memoirs Clarendon composed in exile.

On the one hand, the makeup of the proprietorship makes sense: it included at least one member, Sir William Berkeley, directly on the American scene and another, Colleton, with considerable resources on Barbados. Albemarle provided the focus, Clarendon lent his name, the rest contributed such expertise and other resources they could. Yet, the membership also reflected the generally patchwork nature of English politics following the accession of Charles II. While Albemarle and Ashley had served on the Protector's Council of State, Clarendon, Craven, Carteret, and John Berkeley dreamt of the overthrow of the Protectorate as the king's wretched court-in-exile limped from the Spanish Netherlands to France and back during the Interregnum. Ashley's trimming—his service to Cromwell had not prevented him from hurrying to the quay to greet the restored monarch—had raised many eyebrows; Clarendon, from the forced repose of exile, particularly noted his "slippery humour."[42] Furthermore, the embittered and rancorous atmosphere that surrounded the defeated monarch bred enmity among the faithful. John Berkeley developed a deep and personal loathing of Clarendon, which the Chancellor reciprocated.[43]

Such concerns, though, remained in the background when the undertaking was launched. The new proprietors, "being excited with a laudable and pious zeal for the propagation of the Christian faith, and the enlargement of our empire and dominions" received the king's American lands between 36 and 30 degrees north latitude along with the delegation of wide governmental powers, in accordance with the standard "bishop-of-Durham" clause in their charter, to create laws and civic institutions, levy taxes, build fortifications, recruit migrants, and grant land as those medieval prelates had done on the Scottish frontier.[44]

Initially, expectations were high, although a couple of problems had to be ironed out. The first of these were two legal claims—one brought by the duke of Norfolk and the other by a London merchant, Samuel Vassall—who claimed a prior right to Carolina by virtue of acquisition of a grant that Charles I had made to his attorney general, Sir Robert Heath in 1632.[45] The new proprietors had to beat these challenges off before the Privy Council and receive a second charter that quieted all potentially rival claimants.[46] Second, and potentially more troublesome, a group of New Englanders had settled in the Cape Fear area. However, they came to regard the prospects at that location as unpromising and began making public noises to that effect. This adverse publicity threatened to strangle the Carolina project immediately after its conception.

Happily, though, for its backers, Albemarle had received several letters reporting the interest of a number of Barbadians in moving to the mainland. The duke wrote to Lord Willoughby, governor of the island, that this inclination would suit both colonies: settlers in Carolina would produce commodities that would complement, rather than compete with, those grown on Barbados.[47]

Thus, flush with purpose, the proprietors (minus Clarendon) set to work. Two months after their charter passed the seals, they convened on May 23, 1663 (Sir William Berkeley had returned to Virginia to set up the government and open the land office). They each contributed £25 to a fund under the control of Sir John Colleton, their cashkeeper, and published their terms for settling Carolina.[48]

Green shoots emerged quickly: a settlement was established along the Chowan River and negotiations commenced with prospective migrants from New England. Sir William, in light of these developments, was to get to work on the Carolina end, although flexibility remained paramount as it would throughout the history of the venture. As the proprietor on the scene, Berkeley, his partners reminded him would be in the best position to determine what courses of action to pursue. Thus, they left the charge of the enterprise in his hands.[49]

Things were also looking up on the West Indian front. On August 12, 1663, the Lords received a set of proposals from "Barbados Adventurers" who had engaged William Hilton and a crew on a seven-month voyage to the Carolina coast. Having received Hilton's favorable report, but concerned not to absorb further colonizing costs, the West Indians now sought an understanding with the proprietors.

The Barbadians, who included a number of experienced planters, knew the requirements of building a new settlement. For their part, they sought "sole power" for governing the colony, a proposal that met with approval: it fit proprietary aims of encouraging American-oriented migration and of delegating colonial authority (as much as possible) and the costs of settlement to local agents. Thus, the problems of distance and expense would be largely solved.[50]

Correspondingly, the colonists were to have the power, but at their own expense, to build fortifications, to present nominees to the proprietors for the governorship and the council, to select their own governmental representatives, and to construct public buildings on proprietary lands. The Lords also provided for religious toleration, headrights and "freedom dues," as well as customs relief for any useful commodities for seven years, in exchange for the payment of quitrents.[51]

On January 11, 1665, the proprietors and the Adventurers ratified "Articles of Agreement" under which the Lords agreed to provide firearms and powder, along with the means for building and maintaining a fort near Port Royal. They also covenanted to defray the costs of this settlement and appointed, based upon favorable reports received by Sir John Colleton, the prominent Barbadian, Sir John Yeamans to govern the colony.[52]

The Articles ensured that everybody knew where they stood. The agreement provided that the first colonists would receive 150 acres and another

150 acres for each male servant who came armed with a musket, powder, and shot. Servants who reached the end of their terms were entitled to 75 acres. The articles further provided that the governor was to choose a council and that registers and surveyors were to be appointed at proprietary pleasure by either the Lords themselves or the governor. They also stipulated religious toleration.

The colonists, as agreed, held primary responsibility for the government (as Carolinians would throughout the proprietary period) so long as they did not act against the interests of the proprietors or liberty of conscience. Their laws were to receive the approval of the Lords after 18 months, and their assemblies, in conjunction with the governor, had the further powers to set up courts, levy taxes, set out parishes and hundreds or equivalent localities (in accordance with the needs and wishes of the freemen), build forts, train the militia, naturalize foreigners (as in England), lay out freedom dues for freed servants, and pay official salaries. The articles also provided detailed terms, including headrights and payment of quitrents, for granting land to migrants in order to promote settlement.[53]

With the relationship between colonizers and colonists codified and the Adventurers ready to undertake the colonization of the place, Carolina seemed poised for success. Instead, it soon ran into the sand. Two months after the agreement on the Articles, to the shock of many members of its own government, England declared war on the United Provinces. The conflict started well for the English but required the marshalling of considerable resources—ships, of course, but also naval stores and seamen, many of whom were pressed to fill quotas.[54] In terms of Carolina it presented a distraction as the necessity of securing funding devolved on Ashley, the de facto Lord Treasurer in lieu of his superannuated father-in-law, the earl of Southampton. The war also commandeered the attentions of Albemarle, still the kingdom's military leader, Carteret, the Navy Treasurer, Baron Berkeley, who served on the Committee of the Admiralty, and Craven, another prominent officer. Then the plague, one of the worst in the capital's history, broke out in London in the summer carrying off thousands and forcing the court (although Albemarle, for one, remained in the city) to retire to the countryside. In April 1666, the duke, "desperate for active service," received joint command of the fleet. The summer saw him in constant action. Then, on September 2, the Great Fire consumed the City. Dealing with this catastrophe required the return of Albemarle from sea duty, while Ashley, among others, could be found in the middle of the blaze leading the fight against it.[55]

The combination of war, plague, and fire—on top of the ordinary duties of government—obviously prevented the proprietors from properly attending to their colony. Moreover, the devotion of English maritime resources to the war meant that opportunities for communication—with either Carolina or Barbados—were slim. The Second Anglo-Dutch War, which came to involve the French, also obliged Sir William Berkeley in Virginia and the government of Barbados to adopt defensive measures.[56] Indeed, the Dutch seizure of Surinam and the French capture of St. Christopher put the English West Indies and shipping throughout the English Empire on alert.[57]

Peace with the Dutch and French, punctuated by the spectacular attack by de Ruyter on the English fleet at its anchor in the Medway on May 27, 1667, did not bring respite for the proprietors. The government required a scapegoat for this series of disasters and Clarendon, in the eyes of the king, had outlived his usefulness: he was dismissed from office on August 30. With the knives out, he fled to embittered exile in France. More crucially for the Carolina enterprise, Albemarle became enfeebled and retired from public life. Sir John Colleton had died earlier the same year. Three of the original eight Lords had departed the scene within five years of the start of their venture.

All of these setbacks allowed problems to fester at Cape Fear. A storm prevented Sir John Yeamans from putting his Port Royal commission into effect and swamped most of the provisions the proprietors had sent, including the arms, powder, and equipment provided for the colony's defense.[58] Disputes over the terms of land sales and rentals between Sir John and other settlers surfaced as early as June 1665; news of these disagreements apparently soured Carolina in the minds of those who had intended to move there from Virginia. Subsequent arguments over the Articles of Agreement led the inhabitants to quit the colony, although once peace was secured, the Lords tried to redress the grievances of their colonists. But it was too late: Cape Fear had joined the line of wrecks by the roadside of Anglo-American colonization—Roanoke, Saghedoc, Providence Island, and Newfoundland.[59]

Thus, at the end of 1668, the outlook for the Carolina proprietorship appeared quite gloomy. Albemarle and Colleton, its original leading lights, had departed the scene (along with Clarendon). In addition, the stigma of failure now haunted the endeavor. The Barbadian Adventurers cannot have looked back on their experience with fondness. Yet, instead of dying off, the proprietary venture received new vigor under the leadership of Anthony Ashley Cooper, Lord Ashley.[60]

In acting to resuscitate their enterprise, the remaining proprietors, along with other interested parties, agreed to turn their attentions toward the more southerly part of the proprietary grant. Robert Sandford, accompanied by some of the leaders of the Cape Fear settlement, had reconnoitered the region near Port Royal in the summer of 1666. His relation of that voyage recommended the friendly Indians, promising soil, impressive woods, deep harbors, and all sorts of flora and fauna of that "Excellent Country." Port Royal's climate and seemingly secure location, he enthused, would insure independence for settlers and vastly increase England's trade.[61] Ashley and his associates were ready to make this prophesy a reality.

Chapter 1 ∼

Genesis

On October 19, 1666, John Harrison, Esquire, steward on the Benham Valente, Berkshire estate of the earl of Craven, convened the court leet and court baron for the manor. The completion of the harvest and the corresponding *ritard* in the pre-industrial rhythms of the English agricultural year once again allowed the members of this agrarian community to turn to the matters that required their collective attention. To undertake a fuller comparison of social behavior between the "Old World" and the "New" requires a clearer understanding of the character of this sort of institution that continued to provide the basis of order for so many English people even after the Civil Wars.[62]

These manorial courts functioned to regulate the behavior—for the greater good—of the inhabitants of the estate within the hierarchy recognized by most early modern English folk as the proper way of managing affairs in a "world we have lost." Those who neglected their neighborly obligations risked communal sanction: the Benham Valente court, at its 1669 convening, ordered Jeffrey Brett, Richard Hill, and other commoners to fix their boundaries around a common field and legislated against swine feeding in the marsh between Shrovetide and the corn. In 1673, it required all tenants and other manor residents to repair their ditches, boundaries, and gates and forbade the cutting of turf on the commons. In 1698, it banned the collection of "Cow Clotts in the Common Marsh," prescribing a fine of 12 shillings for each offense.

This court was not "feudal." Rather, it primarily served as a main point of contact, an avenue of reciprocity, between Craven and his dependents. Significantly, its jurisdiction extended to oversight of the responsibilities of the lord as well as his tenants. Although Craven himself apparently never attended these proceedings, the jury "desired" him, in 1668 and again in 1670, to undertake the clearing of a "Watercourse."

The lord commanded the deference of his tenants who provided the labor for the estate. This deference however, was not supposed to be unconditional: the lord had to condescend to undertake certain responsibilities, not the least of which was protection of his "people," as the *quid pro quo*. The manorial court provided a key mechanism to ensure that everybody did what they were supposed to do in early modern England and consequently manifested the social character of reality at this time.

It, then, provided a means for resolving the local concerns of those who inhabited the wider end of the society of orders. Yet, the pastoral images of swine running loose and watercourses being drained that these court records evoke can not crowd out the reality that England, in the latter half of the seventeenth century, was not, generally speaking, an orderly place and that pressure, often intense, continued to come to bear on the world of Benham Valente and similar communities.

Discontent, often violent, simmered throughout the period from the "Henrician Reformation" of the 1530s (and, of course, earlier) through the Reform Bill of 1832 and outright rebellion broke out at regular instances. The uprisings that occurred in 1536, 1549, 1556, 1569, 1601, 1617, and 1635, the Civil Wars of 1642–51 and the rule of Cromwell, the various plots against the person of Charles II, the "Glorious Revolution" of 1688–91 (famously "bloodless" in England, but scarcely so in Ireland and Scotland), the Jacobite incursions in 1715 and again in 1745, the Wilkesite troubles of the 1760s and the Gordon Riots of 1780 provided the headlines. But manifestations of disaffection—in terms of religion, government, and economics during this time—lurked beneath the surface. A rapidly increasing population and the takeover of common lands by landlords led to a corresponding decline in the ability of people to maintain livelihoods in the countryside, thereby compelling the migration of such folk to the nation's cities, particularly London.[63]

There, to the alarm of some observers, their new situations seemed to prod many arrivals, wrenched from their familiar surroundings, toward Tyburn or potters' field, although after the Restoration long-range migration of the poor seems to have slowed somewhat. Living in open sewers surrounded by human and animal waste without the skills that would appeal to prospective employers and without recourse to family or the parish, these migrants often turned to debauchery and crime to support themselves and they were carried off by disease—smallpox, dysentery, typhus, the plague—in appalling numbers.[64] Inevitably, disaffection found a haven amongst the impoverished. This perceived collective threat to the nation—in terms of its physical, social, and governmental health—had to be addressed, commentators warned, or else all sorts of calamities would occur: the "idle" and "indolent" were carted back to their parishes of origin and whipped. A number of writers, notably Richard Hakluyt, arguing from the reign of Elizabeth I, claimed that colonization provided a means of draining off this perpetual source of discontent while it augmented England's overseas ambitions.[65]

By the time of the formation of the Carolina proprietorship, the Civil Wars and the Interregnum, of recent memory, had caused greater shock and dismay among English people. On the one hand, the king had gone to the block, episcopacy had been rousted out "root-and-branch," the House of Lords abolished, destruction unknown in England since the fifteenth century arrived in the wake of the rival armies, and Royalists were exiled or compelled to retire to the countryside. All of this tumult, in turn, saw the emergence of all sorts of new sects—Diggers, Levellers, Quakers, Muggletonians—while Cromwell and his Army, dominated by "godly" elements, had assumed power. For some, the world truly seemed to have turned upside down and it was not a pretty sight. For others, the wars against the monarchy and its supporters had come to be perceived as the first stage in a march to greater glory—the Kingdom of God—translated into the "Good Old Cause" after the disappointment of the Restoration. Happily, for most, the deep fissures that had developed in the English political nation in the 1650s had been papered over with the return of monarch, House of Lords, and bishops in 1660.[66]

Although mid-seventeenth century English folk could hold violently different beliefs on the particulars of government and religion, they could, at the same time, share certain basic attitudes. In the first place, many still preferred the sort of land-based hierarchical relationship between the various elements of society that the manorial court discussed above reflected. Again, we can scarcely style these relationships "feudalism," not only since the term was not used until the nineteenth century, but also because the once-essential military aspect of the landlord–tenant relationship had fallen into disuse, especially with the Civil Wars. They were, however, certainly agrarian and communal. Even after the Restoration, before the further population explosion of the late eighteenth century (which provoked Malthus, for one, to lament the future of the world in 1799) rendered it inadequate, and even though commerce and, later, industry, came to occupy greater importance in the economy, most English folk continued to believe that a society based upon land ownership was the norm and, correspondingly, that land ownership translated into an individual's status in society.[67]

Moreover, since the Crown still lacked the resources and initiative to undertake so much of what we regard as governmental responsibility today, it continued to make a practice of delegating responsibility for various programs and for maintaining authority to the most prominent local landowners who were correspondingly recognized by titles granted by the monarch. Carolina itself constituted one of the links in the "Great Chain of

Being" that connected social strata and defined their relationships with each other: the proprietors, by virtue of their charter, stood in the king's shoes and the provincial aristocracy took the place of their "Old World" counterparts in assuming governmental responsibilities. It was by no means a perfect system nor was it codified in England. The combination of civil war, religious uncertainty, and continuing demographic upheaval had placed it under great strain even by the 1660s. Yet, the ownership of land meant security, ideally for both the lord and his "people"; those who had become alienated from the agrarian system often faced grim prospects and, consequently in the minds of officialdom, posed a serious threat to order.[68]

Correspondingly, early modern English society, according to the view from the top of the social pyramid, fell into two essential categories: "producers" and "drains." "Producers" included aristocrats or, at least, gentlemen—people who contributed to the well-being of the realm by maintaining themselves through their landed estates. Most folk, however, fell under the "drain" rubric as tenant farmers, copyholders, wage laborers, journeymen artisans, apprentices, and indentured servants, with the indigent crushed under the weight of the whole system. According to many of their "betters," these sorts of people, at best, filled the regrettable need for manual labor in the kingdom; at worst, they represented a seething lawless element ever ready to fall sway to the criminal seductions of outlaws or "phanaticakall" preachers. The explosion of the English population between 1500 and 1650 magnified the danger of popular unrest in the eyes of social and political leaders; demographic constraints, sometimes aggravated by increasingly commercial agricultural practices, obliged more and more "drains" to remove themselves from their parishes of origin and move about the countryside looking for more tenable situations. Inevitably, many of these individuals found themselves in the ports nearest their origins—Bristol, Norwich, Plymouth—or, ultimately, London whose population had burst through the city's medieval walls into the Middlesex and Surrey countryside by the end of the sixteenth century.[69]

The authorities employed both carrot and stick in their efforts to bring the movement of people to heel: parliamentary statute (the Poor Law of 1593 provided the basis for the distribution of poor relief for 250 years) to provide a modicum of assistance; floggings and prison for impoverished persons found outside the boundaries of their parishes without license; and, eventually, transportation of petty convicts and felons to overseas colonies, as Hakluyt and his followers advocated.[70]

Then, although many members of the elite regarded their less fortunate compatriots with a mixture of contempt and fear, landowners had no choice but to rely on tenants, servants, and wage laborers as the sources for agricultural workers. A gentleman, by definition, lived off of the income produced by his estates without having, literally, to get his hands dirty. Someone, though, had to dirty their hands or estates would produce no income. No income, in turn, would mean no wealth and no status. Being a "gentleman" thus required reciprocity: in exchange for the deference of "dependents," the lord was obliged to render judgment on their concerns, provide them with casks of ale and roasted bullocks at Christmas, and to hear their grievances in miniature of the monarch's entertaining of the grievances of the subject in parliament.

The concept of "estate" provided the benchmark for position in the society of orders. Those who hoped to climb the ladder endeavored to parley their positions, through careful husbandry, shrewd land management practices (such as enclosing common land to support larger sheep herds whose wool would provide more income), and taking advantage of the rising population (and corresponding shortage of landed opportunity) to raise the obligations of their tenants. Prosperous merchants who lacked sizeable landholdings and were, consequently, the objects of aristocratic disdain, often moved to translate their liquid wealth into landed estates. The acquisition of a stake in society gave them *entrée* to political power and social status; only then, could they command the deference of "inferiors" and involve themselves in government.[71]

This widespread search for greener pastures transformed small towns into raucous centers of international commerce. The "saga of Western man's restless expansion across the globe," as one historian has termed the movement of early modern European peoples, was generated by overpopulation and a corresponding shortage of resources, as well as the general inability and, perhaps, unwillingness of communities—from the parish to the state—to handle these twinned phenomena. As migrants traveled further and further from their roots, they shed their local skins and came to identify themselves more as "English," "French," or "Spanish" and less as "Cornish," "Gascon," or "Catalan." Self-interest, rather than traditional community values— *Gesellschaft* as opposed to *Gemeinschaft*—began to control the behavior of these "new" Europeans while "neighborhood," in a temporary sense, rather than kinship formed the new basis of their social relationships. These developments, we have been told, translated easily to the American environment.[72]

Yet, if the promotional literature disseminated to attract migrants to Carolina and other colonies provides any indication, early modern English folk continued to stress the importance of income-producing landed estates—with suggestions of commodities to grow to generate that income— to one's social and political status. Such estates constituted stakes driven into the soil of the community by the landholder that, at least in theory, announced a commitment to its prosperity and security. Consequently, acquisition of estates elevated an owner to an "independent" status or, if the income they brought was sufficient, to that of "gentleman" in a way that fungible wealth never could.[73]

At least in part, Ashley viewed Carolina as an experimental vehicle for turning the problems brought on by demographic increase into imperial advantages. Like Hakluyt before him, he believed that America could provide both a drain for surplus population and a source of valuable commodities, notably "wines, oyles, and silkes."[74] Ashley, though, went further in both colonial theory and practice; first, by noting the need for a landed gentry to establish themselves as colonial leaders if overseas establishments were to survive and, then devising a system of government in writing that would serve, by offering estates and the guarantees to preserve them that would attract and keep the weightier sort on the scene. The "psychology of colonization" (to use Jack P. Greene's term) of Ashley and his fellow proprietors—further manifested in the promotional literature for the colony— also required the movement of "drains," both to provide bound labor for estates and to alleviate the perceived population boom in the metropolis.[75] The result would, indeed, bring happiness for all concerned. The commodities produced by the estates of the weightier sort would, in the public sense, remove English dependency upon unreliable foreign suppliers and bring customs revenue for the Crown. In the private sense, it would generate the requisite income for masters to maintain their sociopolitical independence and status. The elite, in turn, would then provide security for their dependents in a "New World" recreation of the Benham Valente system.

For their province, the proprietors envisioned that the presence of the weightier sort and their "improvement" of the "wilderness" would draw merchants, artisans, and servants in their wake. Limited liberty of conscience, naturalization for foreigners, and guarantee of land titles would provide further attractions. For the Lords, accustomed to viewing reality from the top down, prosperity for the upper orders would, through the cultivation of estates and towns, insure security and happiness for all. Thus, Carolina's promoters invariably tuned their appeals to a frequency that would appeal to those who sought independent status and who were willing to undertake the customary reciprocal responsibilities, albeit in a faraway place.

To encourage the movement of gentlemen, the Lords initially offered 100-acre headrights to every free person who migrated to Carolina, with an additional 100 acres granted for every male servant who accompanied the planter. Those aspiring to a higher position, who "with a little industry might better themselves," also suited the colony's needs admirably: initially, as servants; then, after paying off their indentures and acquiring "freedom dues," by becoming "considerable men." Ex-servants would receive their 100 acres at the expiration of their terms.[76]

All of Carolina's other enumerated advantages trickled down from land ownership. Promoters recognized that the prospect of vast tracts of Carolina land alone would not, in itself, generate status nor would empty acres lure producers of wealth to the colony. Estates on either side of the Atlantic were worth nothing to their owners unless they were accompanied by the political freedoms enjoyed by the beneficiaries of the English system of government, as well as by a readily accessible pool of agricultural laborers.[77]

In order to acquire and maintain significant estates in America (and, by extension, plant a successful colony), as both colonizers and colonists had realized by 1670, the weightier sort had to resort to the cultivation of commodities for which a demand existed in the metropolis. This reality, on the face of things, gave imperial and commercial perspectives a foothold in the older way of thinking since it gave rise to musings about the colonial production of commodities, especially naval stores, that would reduce the dependency of the metropolis upon potential enemies, and legislation, in the form of the Navigation Acts, which, in theory, codified this sentiment. The maritime traffic and the wealth generated by staple agriculture also encouraged, by definition, mercantile activity. Yet, those who conceived of an English empire in the seventeenth century, at least in terms of Carolina, did not express demands for a further breakdown, for instance, of the world of the manor. Rather, they continued to view the opportunities purportedly afforded by colonization very much from the perspective that sought to maintain or retrieve the manorial sense of community.[78]

We should also recall that Ashley and his cohort did not separate activities such as colonization into public and private undertakings.[79] In terms, then, of incorporating their own interests with those of the "public," the proprietors continually reserved lands for themselves from the beginning of their enterprise. Some of them did set up plantations where they or their agents experimented with various crops and engaged in the Indian trade with an eye to generating American wealth. It does not appear, though, that the Lords primarily regarded Carolina as an opportunity to make money neither did they hold out any particular expectations for their American estates.

In the first place, as the Lords noted repeatedly, the income that the colony generated, in terms of quitrents paid and from the sale of public lands, was supposed to go toward the maintenance of the government and their own rents due to the Crown. Moreover, they may well have known that, over a generation previously, Sir Francis Bacon had cautioned that profit from a new plantation venture could require up to a 20-year wait for investors; if they had not read Bacon, one of their early officeholders might have taken the opportunity to fill them in.[80] In terms of personal experience, Ashley had owned a plantation on Barbados where Sir John Colleton remained a prominent figure there; Sir John Berkeley and Carteret partnered another proprietary venture in New Jersey at the same time as Carolina; Albemarle and Clarendon also had American connections. Most importantly, Sir William Berkeley had governed Virginia off an on for almost 40 years where his physical presence combined with the perquisites of office enabled him to acquire substantial wealth and power.

By Bacon's yardstick and considering the hazards that had befallen other enterprises, as well as the general fragility of existence in early modern England, only the sunniest of optimists would have predicted that the Carolina undertaking would bear fruit within the lifetimes of the original proprietors. By 1663, all of the Lords, except the 43-year-old (but sickly) Ashley, had already surpassed the life expectancy of the time: for instance, both Albemarle and Clarendon (both of whom also had chronic health problems) were 55, while Carteret was 65. Thus, considering their respective ages and knowledge, the proprietors, in terms of private interest, had to place Carolina under the category of "estate planning." Any dividends that their venture might yield would fall to their descendants, although foresight of this kind was *de rigeur* for landowning families in Stuart England.[81]

As experienced servants of the Crown, however, with, perhaps for their tastes, too great a familiarity with the religious, constitutional, and demographic problems of Stuart England, the proprietors obviously regarded colonization as a means of generating wealth and prosperity for the kingdom. Some of them may also have regarded a colony as a laboratory for improving the social relations of their times, relations that the recent Civil Wars had nearly rendered asunder. In the seventeenth century, the personal enrichment of royal servants and the good of the kingdom went hand in hand. Thus, the proprietary plan for settlement was a public service: it intended to drain people from older, more crowded colonies, instead of further depleting the metropolitan population, to their new plantation where, through their industry (and ideally, with minimal direct help from and cost to the proprietors), they would create and improve estates by producing commodities that would generate wealth for the settlers and, via the customs, for the proprietors and the Crown. As they pointed out themselves, "ye business is yd kings & nations more than our owne."[82]

Chapter 2 ⌇

Blueprint

The Fundamental Constitutions of Carolina, a copy of which accompanied the "first fleet," constituted the centerpiece of the proprietary plan to encourage settlement after 1669—from England or wherever in the empire—and to address concerns over English society in the aftermath of the Civil Wars.[83] More formal than the 1665 Articles of Agreement with the Barbados Adventurers, these written Constitutions set forth in some detail the powers and responsibilities of the Lords and of their colonists. Moreover, recognizing the problems presented by distance as well as by the distractions posed by metropolitan affairs, the Lords specifically and formally delegated most of their authority to the leaders of the settlement. The "fundamentals" represents the most formal attempt to provide a governmental and social framework in the history of Anglo-American colonization.[84]

Yet, our understanding of the proprietors and their Fundamental Constitutions remains anchored to the belief that the Lords intended to maintain direct oversight over the region "south and west of Cape Fear" and that, correspondingly, South Carolinians chafed at proprietary efforts, such as the Constitutions, purportedly made to keep them in line, *viz.*, "being the proprietors' prescription, [the Constitutions] epitomized the unilateral imposition of outside authority on the people of South Carolina" and "[had] the document gone into effect, it would have permanently relegated most local leaders to a subordinate and relatively passive role in the polity."[85]

The *ex post facto* vantage point of non-ratification offers a misleading perspective of the Constitutions and their suitability as a framework for encouraging colonial development. By considering the document and its history within their context rather than jumping ahead to the end of the tale, a rather different understanding of the Constitutions, their creators and their opponents emerges. Instead, it seems that the architects were not out of touch with reality, and that their scheme, considered from the perspective from which it was set, made good sense.

The whole reformation of the venture and the subsequent attempts of its members to sort it out indicate that the Lords never conceived of their proprietary status as the equivalent of some medieval fiefdom nor did they envision their colony as some sort of utopian "citty on a hill" to serve as an example for the metropolis. Indeed, it seems that the proprietors, throughout the history of the proprietorship, never intended to play an active role in governing the province. To do so would have been impractical: an ocean separated the colonizers from their colonists (the voyage across it could take up to ten weeks), important matters at home preoccupied them, and they lacked immediate knowledge of American affairs. To govern the colony for the king, contribute to the wealth and power of the realm and, possibly, collect some personal return seems to have generally constituted the extent of their ambitions.

Nevertheless, colony-building required colonists as well as proprietary care, and South Carolina, as the bulk of the documentation for this period again illustrates, did receive attention from its Lords. Most obviously, the proprietors needed to recruit migrants, particularly those who belonged to the weightier sort or who sought to become gentlemen by acquiring American estates. Less than 15 years after the end of the Civil Wars and a continent away from the center of authority, Ashley and his associates would have known that prospective migrants would require clear guarantees of liberties and security for estates. To insure such protection and recognize the preeminence of landowners—the holders of the stakes in early modern English society—while preventing the emergence of tyranny in Carolina, the Lords devised their written Constitutions.[86] This created organs of government that properly balanced liberty and order. It also created the privileges and dignities of a hereditary aristocracy—the social, military, and political backbone of the province—and it provided for religious toleration. Everybody would have known where he or she stood in their various degrees.[87]

With assurances of rights and privileges in writing and in advance, the weightier sort would surely flock to Carolina where, in turn, they would implement the Constitutions and take their place atop the society. The resulting order would provide the basis for acquiring and maintaining estates (and pursuing commerce) as well as achieving prosperity that, again in turn, would attract even more migrants seeking to better themselves in Carolina. This cycle would generate happiness and prosperity for all (excepting slaves). "There is nothing," the Lords observed in 1699, "contributes more to [the] peopling of a Countrey than an Impartiall Administration of Justice nothing encourages Trade more for it's hardly to be Imagined that men will take labour & run great hazard to gett an estate if they have not some assurance of being protected by Law."[88]

Indeed, all of the proprietary promotional efforts advertised the Fundamental Constitutions among Carolina's attractions. Samuel Wilson's "Account of the Province of Carolina" (1682) prominently extolled the document, particularly its grant of liberty of conscience and care to provide even-handed justice that would, the author noted, assure the security of settlers and their estates.[89] The very same year, "R.F." also lauded the Constitutions, especially its provisions for a parliament and a court system, as a guarantor of the estates and rights of the Carolinians.[90]

A written constitution also provided a helpful means of spanning the ocean that separated the proprietors from the colony. Distance between the center of government and the localities remained a fundamental problem in seventeenth-century England and a network of offices—from justices of the peace, sheriffs, and members of parliament to constables and hog reeves—connected Whitehall to the shires. In the transatlantic context, such delegation of authority to local officials was mandatory. Thus, the Fundamental Constitutions conferred responsibility for government upon deputies, office-holders, and aristocrats—landgraves and cassiques created under Section 9—as the points of contact between the Lords Proprietor and Carolina.[91]

In theory, the Constitutions reserved considerable power to the proprietors: they created the aristocracy (Section 10). They also comprised the membership of the "palatine's court" that summoned parliaments, pardoned offenders, selected officers, created ports, controlled the public treasury, and held a veto over acts passed by the grand council and parliament (Section 33). They headed the eight "supreme" courts with retinues of councillors (Sections 28, 35, 38, 39, 41, 43, 44, 45); held the highest military offices (Sections 34, 42); served as the speaker of the parliament (Section 37). And they controlled, with their appointees, the grand council and, thereby, the introduction of legislation into parliament (Sections 50, 51).

In reality, though, most of these powers were to be exercised by leaders on the scene; proprietors, by all means, if they happened to be present (as in Section 59, for instance, which provides that the eldest proprietor in residence "shall of course be the palatine's deputy") but, if not, then by deputies appointed pursuant to Section 56. Under this latter provision, a deputy, during the absence from the province of the proprietor who had appointed him, enjoyed "the same power, to all intents and purposes, as he himself who deputes him" except for confirming acts of parliament (Section 76) and in creating landgraves and cassiques (Section 10). In exercising proprietary powers, deputies were to serve at the pleasure of their patron or for a maximum term of four years.

Just as the Lords recognized the problems of colonization and of their own mortality, they also knew that the likelihood of any of them soon visiting, let alone taking up residence in, Carolina was exceedingly slim.

The evidence offers no indication that any of the proprietors themselves seriously considered a trip to their colony prior to 1695 and only two of them actually lived in the province during the entire history of the proprietorship. The Lords, therefore, had to intend for the deputies, along with the other landgraves and cassiques, to exercise routinely the judicial and executive powers nominally held by the proprietors until their peers began living in the province, as some did by the end of the seventeenth century.

Of course, the Lords expected their appointees to act in accordance with instructions and in the proprietary interest, just as the government in England expected local officials to do their duty. The nature of Carolina's intended framework, though, compounded by distance and by proprietary recognition of geography, gave deputies and other officers considerable latitude. Letters to the colony's leaders underscore this desire to delegate. Time and again, the proprietors instructed their officeholders, such as Sir Nathaniel Johnson in 1702, "to follow such Rules as we have given in our Fundamentall Constitutions Temporary Laws and Instructions to our former Governours" but "to be guided by the same or soe many Articles thereof as shall *in your Judgment* seeme most fitt to be put in Practice" (emphasis added).[92]

In addition to providing the structure of their government, the Lords also used the Fundamental Constitutions to provide socioeconomic encouragement to the would-be aristocrats and officeholders they needed to put their model into practice. Thus, the Constitutions went to great lengths in setting forth the dignities of landgraves and cassiques who were entitled to four and two baronies of 12,000 acres, respectively, "hereditarily and unalterably annexed to and settled upon the said dignity" (Section 9). The aristocracy were to share, under Section 10, in the responsibility of nominating additions to their numbers as the colony grew. Correspondingly, they were to serve as councillors and assistants to the proprietors' courts (Sections 28, 29), as members of the grand council (as both deputies and in their own right, Section 50) and of parliament in their respective houses (Section 71).

Landgraves and cassiques, as well as the lords of manors, also received control over the "leet-men" who were to work on their estates. The Constitutions created this latter status for people who wanted to bind themselves and their descendants voluntarily to a signory, barony or manor without "liberty to go off from the land of their particular lord, and live anywhere else, without license" from their lord (Section 22). The document also gave the power to manor lords to hold "courts-leet" to handle cases (from which leet-men had no appeal) arising on their estates (Sections 16, 24).

The inclusion of these "feudal" concepts still bewilders historians. Why did "enlightened" thinkers like Locke and Ashley seek to institute a version of hereditary serfdom especially at a time when that institution had practically died out in England?[93] Some writers have noted that Ashley and Locke were concerned about the perceived overpopulation of England in 1670 and perhaps believed that the urban poor, whose situation was particularly cruel, might have considered binding themselves out to American lords to be preferable to continuing in a marginal existence in the "Old World."[94]

Ashley, for one, certainly thought that the status of leet-man on his personal plantation offered "a comfortable living" to the desperate in both England and America. The Fundamental Constitutions themselves provided that when leet-men and leet-women married, they were to receive ten acres to hold for the rest of their lives in exchange for one-eighth of the year's revenue from that land (Section 26). On Ashley's own plantation at St. Giles Edisto, after serving their time as servants, "Every Originall Leetman" could expect a house in a town along with 60 acres as a copyhold together with common land sufficient to accommodate three or four cows, along with two cows, two sows, and 15 bushels of corn. Then, in order to encourage the "posterity" of leet-men to settle on his lands, Ashley proposed to give them at least ten more acres at their marriage. In exchange, each leet-man was "to pay 1/8 yearly of the value of the Land to be lett & 1/3 Calve till I have Received 3 yearlings for every Cow he hath had of me & the same proportion of Sow pigs att two months old." He believed that this arrangement would not only attract the "worthy poor"; it would also encourage the construction of towns vital to defense and to commerce.[95]

In a philosophical sense, the intended situation of leet-men may have seemed a masterstroke. It gave the impoverished a stake in society thereby binding them to the commonwealth and ensuring order in a "Harringtonian" sense while maintaining the hierarchy that Ashley and most of his contemporaries regarded as essential for a properly balanced society. At the same time, it further ensured order by preventing leet-men from clogging the provincial courts with landlord problems.[96]

Thus, the notion of English folk enrolling as leet-men in Carolina is not quite so far-fetched as it may, at first, seem. Indeed, this arrangement would not really have deprived impoverished migrants of any sort of social and political rights. Prospective leet-men would almost certainly have lacked the 40-shilling freehold necessary to hold the franchise in England. The landless neither voted nor held any place in an English political nation that, correspondingly, offered them no protection. Such people would have had no rights to surrender in the first place had they enrolled themselves as leet-men.

In fact, had the impoverished of late seventeenth-century England transported themselves to Carolina they not only would have gained the material advantages and security offered by leet status, they would actually have acquired formal avenues to pursue grievances. A poor migrant who became a leet-man in Carolina, just as his weightier counterpart who became a landgrave or cassique, would have been the recipient of unprecedented written guarantees. In exchange for offering the labor of themselves and their progeny to lords and, in the "feudal" sense, serving in the militia, leet-men would have been protected by the manorial system.

Thus, to call the proprietors and Locke to task for trying to "recreate serf-dom" misses the point of the Fundamental Constitutions.[97] Of course, they believed that the proper scheme of things required that men with estates rule over those without. Such an attitude was scarcely unique to the thought of James Harrington and it permeated the Constitutions, which restricted access to the province's various courts to freemen (Section 22), required jury-men to own at least 50 acres (Section 68) and members of parliament to own 500 acres (Section 71), and limited the franchise to freeholders (Section 75, but without the 40-shilling threshold required in England). However, the creation of hereditary leet-men did nothing in itself to "ensure" further the predominance of gentlemen; otherwise why make enrolling in this status voluntary?

Moreover, the people who poured from the shires into early modern English cities in search of livelihood had become detached from the reci-procity afforded by "traditional" society. The Fundamental Constitutions offered a restoration of the channels through which lords and their depen-dents discharged their respective obligations (and Section 24 of the August 1682 version offered further protection by mandating that the registrations of leet-men take place "in Open Court"[98]) under the sort of system sketched at the beginning of chapter 1.

Even in the latter half of the seventeenth century, security for tenants—as well as, of course, income for the lord—remained a primary purpose of the estate system. Thus, the establishment of courts-leet, a key element in this system, did not reflect some sort of ambition of the Lords to sit in pomp rendering judgment over colonial vassals nor did it demonstrate the inherent unsuitability of "Old World" values for America or an underlying naiveté concerning the nature of colonization on the part of the proprietors. The courts of the sort set up in Sections 16 and 22 of the Fundamental Constitutions were not designed to oppress. Rather, they were intended to serve as conduits for addressing local concerns in an orderly fashion and for the preservation of communal rights, in accordance with local customs; a forum where the lord, in early modern fashion, condescended to hear the grievances of his tenants. They were also designed to maintain the connection— again as it was recognized at the time—between those granted power by virtue of their landholdings and those who, because they did not own land, would otherwise have remained voiceless and powerless. Of course, their labor, as "drains," would be exploited. This was the way of the English world where "inferiors" had to work to support their "superiors," in exchange theoretically for protection and redress of grievances, as well as themselves and their families.

The proprietors thus expected that their province would be "peopled" by proprietors, landgraves, cassiques, manor lords, freemen, leet-men, and slaves.[99] Thus, the respective attractions of land, labor, religious toleration, limited government, and security all spelled out in the Fundamental Constitutions would make Carolina a difficult venue for prospective European migrants of all backgrounds to resist. Upon arrival, they would settle on their "signories," "baronies," and "manors," assume their respective stations, build their communities, and start producing the commodities that would bring prosperity for all (excluding slaves who, under Section 109, were placed under the complete authority of their masters). Although the names might have changed, the essence of "Old World" relationships and "Old World" issues would remain the same. Hogs ran loose, watercourses required "scowring," and people "cutt turf" from the commons and such things had to be regulated. Those best suited to do the regulating were the people who lived on the estates—the jurymen, the haywards, and other such officials— just as they did in Berkshire. Thus, Ashley and Locke (and any unknown associates) fitted the largely commercial character of a colonial society (by seventeenth-century definition created to generate exports) into an agrarian framework, and their Fundamental Constitutions bridged the Restoration debate over whether Harringtonian-style classical republicanism or a "modern" liberal society best suited a commonwealth.[100]

Promotional authors, such as "R.F." and Wilson, hastened to provide reassurance on these points. They observed that the climate of Carolina presented a special opportunity for landed income by allowing for the production of sun-drenched staple crops to rainy England but with the advantages of English-style government, underscored by the unique written constitution prepared by benevolent proprietors. Thus, the Lords had designed a government properly balanced between the aristocracy (in the Grand Council), the commons, and the proprietors (as agents of the monarch) that would prevent any unwarranted encroachment on the liberties of the people.[101]

For those concerned about a shortage of "drains" to provide the requisite labor and the requisite status for Carolina planters, pamphleteers pointed out that African slaves had become an acceptable, for some even preferred, alternative to indentured servants just ten years after the establishment of Charles Town.[102] In the minds of at least some planters by 1680, slaves were more loyal and better workers than the traditional alternative and, unlike servants, they could never legally depart their situations.[103] These incentives, combined with religious toleration for Dissenters and headrights for planters (later reduced to 50 acres), South Carolina had proven auspicious for the prosperity of migrants.[104]

Again, English people at this time looked beyond wealth to status that landed income, not money, provided. Indeed, by the end of the seventeenth century, Carolina had even developed its own nascent hereditary aristocracy. Landgraves and cassiques, such as Thomas Smith, Joseph Morton, and Daniel Axtell, who built up their plantations and served as the political leaders—governors, members of the council and assembly, judges, receivers, sheriffs—of the colony just as their counterparts did in England. However, although a recognizable metropolitan-style pyramid had started to emerge by the first decade of the eighteenth century, several factors combined to hamper the emergence of the province as a precise mirror of early modern English society.

Demographics constituted the most important of these phenomena. First, as we know, even as glowing pictures of life in the province left the presses, Carolinians were dealing with an extraordinarily high mortality rate driven by swampy surroundings and malaria imported from West Africa. The population of the colony, both black and white, failed to reproduce itself during the colonial period.[105]

At the same time, by the last half of the seventeenth century, as we also know, the demand for labor in the English colonies generally outstripped the supply provided by migration from England. The metropolitan population, which had risen steadily between 1500 and 1650, leveled off—demography no longer acutely pressured people to move very long distances, especially across the ocean—while the Caroline government as well as private individuals had taken concrete steps to improve the lot of England's poor.[106]

Furthermore, Carolina had to compete with other colonies, notably Pennsylvania with a more benign environment, for this declining migrant pool. The English population had not only become static in terms of numbers by 1660, but the long-range subsistence movement of the poorer sort that had predominated for the previous century and a half subsided after 1660. The evidence suggests that poor folk still moved about constantly, but that the movement tended to be more localized—usually within the same shire or region. The general stagnation of population meant less competition for the necessities of life. At the same time, towns and cities, again, most spectacularly, London, whose apprenticeship and other employment prospects continued to attract most migrants, usually "in response to cyclical trade booms" rather than demand created by epidemics, which had begun to diminish by 1669. An estimated 69,000 people emigrated from England to its colonies during the 1630s and 1640s and a further 10,000 departed in the 1650s. However, in the decade following the Restoration, the number of American departures plummeted almost 30,000 from that peak figure.

Although over 50,000 people emigrated in the 1670s, the numbers never again approached their highest figure—in the final decade of the seventeenth century, only some 30,300 people took ship, considerably less than half of the 69,100 estimate we have for 1630–39.[107]

Yet, "push" factors still operated to a degree. In Norfolk, landlords increasingly turned to sheep-raising at the expense of their corn-growing tenants, resulting in a collapse of traditional agrarian relationships, conflict, depopulation, and, in the eighteenth century, the demise of open-field agriculture. Most of the displaced, however, removed to nearby "wood-pasture" areas where they found more favorable conditions rather than taking ship. They concentrated on raising livestock for urban markets and involved themselves in the woolen industry.[108]

Other phenomena contributed to the shift in migration dynamics. A palpable shift from servants-in-residence to day laborers occurred at this time that reduced the mass movement of servants at the end of their terms. Also, parish vestries and commissioners of the poor generally adopted a firmer attitude toward the movement of the poorer sort; people found outside their parishes of origin without a certificate continued to be whipped, branded, and "shunted back and forth from one county to another for months on end" while alehouses, way stations for migrants, came under strict regulation. On the other hand, local authorities began, either voluntarily or in answer to orders from above, to spend more on poor relief.[109]

The movement—for marriage or apprenticeship, generally—of the weightier sort, the perennial targets of promotion, tended to involve short distances prior to the Civil Wars. But between 1660 and 1730, migrating members of the upper orders began to travel further on the whole than their poorer counterparts. However, aristocrats, the gentry, and members of mercantile families tended to travel for pleasure, often to London or a provincial capital or county town. With improved estates and transport facilities in England, the wealthy had even less incentive to cross the ocean.

Thus, Ashley and other promoters were unwittingly devising solutions to a demographic problem that was already solving itself—at least until after 1750. In New England and, later, Pennsylvania, the nature of migration and a relatively healthful climate encouraged demographics. This result meant that dependents—spouses, children, and, more occasionally, servants—constituted the core labor force, just as they did for yeomanry in England. In South Carolina, the far less-organized movement of people, including, vitally, women, meant far less certainty about where the workers would come from—and, by extension, how "independence" and the acquisition of estates would play out.

The effects of the colony's unsettled political climate on the growth of settlement have remained less clear. Most particularly, the notorious Goose Creek men engineered the destruction of a promising Scottish colony near Port Royal and harassed their opponents, generally planters, and fought the establishment of constitutional government for almost 30 years. Thus, the proprietors observed in 1691, "few have come to you since [1684] but the French nor will people come there untill things are better settled."[110] Conversely, while Ashley subsequently engaged in the most cynical attacks on his enemies— employing perjury, hysteria, innuendo, and sham plots to drag the earl of Danby, Samuel Pepys, and others to the Tower and send Oliver Plunket, Catholic archbishop of Armagh, to the block (to which the government responded in kind)—he and his partners seem not to have expected their settlers to engage in the same sort of behavior. However, the Carolinians found fraud, deceit, and character assassination ready tools in their political battles as their counterparts did in England. The Fundamental Constitutions became a leading casualty.

The continuing shortage of migrants (again excluding slaves) remained the greatest obstacle to the complete implementation of the Constitutions and to the sociopolitical concepts that underpinned them. In the meantime, the Lords delayed the implementation of their scheme, recognizing that the colony's minute population made the document's elaborate provisions impractical and they created temporary laws for their government. Copies of the original July 1669 draft and the more formal March 1670 edition of the Constitutions circulated in Carolina but carried no official sanction.[111]

Yet, subsequently, whenever the proprietors presented them for ratification, certain Carolinians demurred.[112] Far from forcing the Constitutions down the throats of their colonists, however, the proprietors, albeit reluctantly, always withdrew the scheme in the face of provincial objections while warning their colonists about the future of the colony as long as its government remained unsettled. In 1691, they observed that, despite their efforts "to Invite people to goe there that ye Strength and Security might be Increased, and great numbers of People Invited by the amendments wee had made In our Constitutions," the refusal to ratify had caused prospective migrants to change their minds "nor will people come there untill things are better settled, nor can wee with honour or a good conscience Invite men to come amongst you for wee will not deale disingenuously with any man upon any consideration whatsoever." Since they lacked the power "to compell men to come and live and continue under a government they do not like or amongst persons the unquietness of whose tempers will allow of no peace of settlement," the Lords remarked prophetically, that "your numbers will by degree be soe diminished that you will be easily cut off by the Indians or pyrates which we leave to be considered by you that you may know the consequence of hearkening to men of unquiet and factious spirits."[113]

Promoters of the colony did their best to sweep these problems under the carpet. But they also had to combat the enduring belief that long-range permanent migration, to people of early modern England, generally meant failure in the first instance, a recognition that a person or a family lacked the necessary means (of whatever nature) to survive where they were and had to move on to a destination probably unknown. Removal to America, moreover, meant risking the horrors of an ocean voyage and, in all probability, never seeing family, friends, and familiar surroundings (no matter how lowly or discouraging) again: better perhaps to die (the ultimate leveler and the inevitable fate of all humanity, in any event) in the gutter in Spitalfields than to risk being blown overboard in an Atlantic tempest, falling prey to corsairs, convulsing in agony from some mysterious, murderous pestilence, "massacr'd" by Indians, or falling into the clutches of some sadist "to be used like some damn'd slave." At least in Pennsylvania or the Jerseys, an arrival, provided she or he arrived in one piece, could expect better treatment from the colonists and less risk from disease and "savages."

It is no accident, then, that the Carolina elite quickly came to be dominated by people sent to the colony to manage the interests of others. Still others—those who found the religious and political climate unhealthy in the early 1680s, for instance—came to find life in this backwater more desirable than in the metropolis. Others came from the West Indies with the means to advance themselves already in hand. These were people with compelling reasons to take up residence in America. Some migrants followed the formula, set forth in the pamphlets and now time-honored, of taking passage as servants, receiving land at freedom, improving themselves, and becoming gentlemen, but they provided the exception to the rule. Most European arrivals came in clusters, like those in the first fleet, the Cardross settlers via Glasgow, Huguenots via London, and the Irish from Belfast, or in the wake of masters. In sum, while we can identify young, single males as the main component of English migration to the Cheseapeake and the West Indies and family groups as the primary element the settlement of New England and the "Middle Colonies," the movement of Europeans to South Carolina defies ready categorization.[114]

Otherwise, the combination of remoteness, unhealthy climate, and dubious inhabitants more than cancelled out the incentives advertised by the proprietors. Generally, if Carolina crossed the minds of the late seventeenth-century general public of England, Scotland, and Ireland, it generated negative connotations. This certainly was the opinion of James Butler, duke of Ormonde, and the greatest Irish political figure of the latter half of the seventeenth century. After almost 50 years of devoted service to the Stuart family, Ormonde fell victim to the plotting of his enemies and found himself unceremoniously turned out to pasture by James II in 1686. Suddenly compelled to rent accommodation in England and cut back drastically on his household, the depressed and embittered old man wrote his agent in Ireland of his continuing disbelief "that it was possible that in this King's or his brother's reign I should be put to seek for a habitation or retreat out of the country where my fortune lies." Incredibly, he lamented, "it is so far come to pass that I had rather live and die in Carolina than in Ireland."[115]

Thus, in 1709, 40 years after the first fleet arrived in South Carolina, the province reported a population of 9,580 souls with just 1,360 freemen, the core around which the colony was to form.[116] This shortfall certainly provided greater opportunities and corresponding status for the 1,360 who had cleared the bar that separated the independent from the dependent. English self-styled superiority, however, combined with West Indian experience and the perceived need of the planters to maintain and improve their estates to all-too-easily relegate Africans and Indians to perpetual dependency. This merger produced a racially based American twist in which masters brutally commanded the deference of their "servants" and, at least in their own minds, condescended to provide for their needs, ultimately achieving full-blown paternalism after independence from Britain in 1783.

Migration to colonial British America—presuming it was undertaken in answer to the knock of "New World" opportunities—did not manifest, at least consciously, a modern desire to free oneself "of encrusted burdens and ancient obligations." Rather, what Bernard Bailyn has termed the "peopling [sic] of British North America" comprised an extension of the early modern English sociopolitical worldview across the Atlantic. Put simply, English folk who sought to better themselves in the seventeenth and eighteenth centuries did seek the "Rank" or "quality" of "independence"; but they invariably sought the income-producing lands that supported it while accepting the accompanying social and political responsibilities as Henry Laurens, for instance, did as late as the 1770s.

Although the formal notion of a hereditary aristocracy in South Carolina never took hold, the apparently modern—that is, again, egalitarian—outcome remained firmly grounded in premodern societal belief: the more land one owned, the greater one's status. Certainly those who took up the largest Carolina land grants in the proprietary period thought they had climbed to the top of their hill and they took steps, through marriage and inheritance, to maintain and augment their position creating an aristocracy in all but name. The continued domination of the Pinckneys, Middletons, Laurens, Manigaults, and other landed families after 1710—and the twisted version of Benham Valente over which they had come to preside—indicates that the creation of an "American" society may not have occurred as rapidly or in as modern a fashion as we have been told.[117]

Chapter 3 ∽

Birthpangs

S uch eventualities, of course, remained beyond the horizon when the proprietors met on April 26, 1669, at Ashley's apparent behest, to reinvigorate their venture. Concentrating on Port Royal rather than the failure-tainted Cape Fear, they agreed to subscribe money to outfit a settlement voyage from England while Ashley, in conjunction with Locke, began devising the Fundamental Constitutions. When the fleet was assembled two months later under the leadership of Joseph West, the proprietors issued their temporary instructions for government, defense, establishing trade, laying out land grants, and planning settlement, including reserving 12,000-acre baronies for themselves and encouraging the development of townships. They also issued a draft of the Fundamental Constitutions.[118]

The three ships and their occupants waited in the Downs for a month for a favorable wind before embarking for Port Royal. On the way, they called at Kinsale where several servants seized the chance to avoid American opportunities, Bermuda, where most of the colony's provisions were lost through shipwreck, and Barbados, where the settlers refit their spirits. Arriving off the Carolina coast, after an eleven-month voyage, a misadventure with some Spaniards obliged them to change their landfall to Oyster Point on the west bank of the Ashley River.

The settlers' initial reports of wonderful environment, continued interest in migration from Barbados and other colonies, the establishment of friendly relations with the neighboring Indians, and an established population of 406 inhabitants gave cause for cautious optimism.[119] Together with Governor West's reported good judgment, everything pointed to an early achievement of the vital goal of economic self-sufficiency. Of course, this policy would reduce the proprietary outlay on the colony but it also best suited Ashley River. As Ashley well knew (if the colonists needed reminding), the longer transatlantic dependency remained in place the more dangerous the predicament of the settlers: war and other disaster might suddenly intervene and leave the migrants without readily available food and other necessities as had happened with Cape Fear.[120] In the meantime, the proprietors took prompt steps from their end to insure the provisioning of the colony through the following May when, they and their secretary, Locke, believed its own crops would start ripening.[121]

Unfortunately, almost immediately after landing, bickering between the colonists developed, much of it centering on the commanding and controversial personality of Sir John Yeamans. Irritation between the Lords and their settlers also developed, primarily over what Ashley regarded as too-frequent recourse on the part of the latter to the proprietary storehouse and too-little attention to their crops. At the same time, migrants continued to make their way to the new Charles Town from the West Indies and elsewhere, trade with Indians and other colonies developed encouragingly, and slavery became established, while the colonists continually offered hopes for the production of various "staples." The small size of the original settlement meant that the Fundamental Constitutions remained moribund so the proprietors put Temporary Laws into effect instead. In 1674, Ashley, now first earl of Shaftesbury, apparently exasperated with the lack of progress at Ashley River, convinced his partners to stump up one last time to put the colony on a secure footing while, at the same time, he moved to create an independent plantation that would provide an American income for himself and an example to the uncooperative Carolinians.[122]

It remains unclear, though, why Ashley decided to take charge of the proprietorship in 1668–69, why migrants decided—or even if they had the choice in the matter—to relocate to Carolina, why Yeamans failed to meet the expectations the Lords had of him, why the new Carolinians immediately developed the habit of quarreling among themselves and complaining about each other to the Lords, and, why correspondingly, the political scene remained unsettled for most of the proprietary period. In the absence of direct indications, we must glean what we can from the circumstantial evidence. In terms of proprietary motives, we have been told that Ashley's move to the forefront, along with the creation of the Fundamental Constitutions, may have occurred as "the result of his narrow escape from death" following a carriage accident, that his commitment of "much time and emotional energy to the project makes one suspect that he saw the colony as his ticket to immortality," as evidenced by the naming of the Ashley and Cooper Rivers.[123]

While this might serve, absent a plausible alternative, to explain Ashley's annoyance at colonists who seemed to prefer proprietary handouts to planting their own food and who repeatedly ignored proprietary interests while furthering their own, we should note that practical reasons—and Ashley was nothing if not pragmatic—did exist to explain his behavior. First, although certainly ambitious and arguably keen to make his lasting mark on history, no evidence exists to suggest that Ashley regarded his "Darling" colony as the vehicle to further such aspirations: it was far away, distracting, and expensive to maintain. Significantly, he seems not to have had any illusions about his contemporaneous involvement in the Bahamas, informing Sir Thomas Lynch, governor of Jamaica, that he planned "to throw away some money in making some experiments there."[124] Happily, the birth of a grandson on February 26, 1671, six months after the departure of the first fleet, alleviated the far more tangible issues, in terms of "legacy," presented by his chronically poor health and his "lumpish" heir.[125] We do not know, for that matter, who took the initiative in naming the rivers.

Ashley did believe in the benefits of colonization for England both in terms of trade, including significantly, the slave trade, and to attract population to English colonies from foreign parts: Carolina, in terms of territory and, conceivably in 1669, commodities, certainly offered an opportunity. The crucial question was how to ensure its future as much as possible. As a famous proponent of the essential sociopolitical role for landholding aristocrats and, thus, undoubtedly aware of the necessity to attract and maintain such an order in the colony, as well as having been a veteran of the debates over the nature of government and society that raged during the Civil Wars, it requires a minimal stretch, as we saw in chapter 2, to imagine Ashley (in conjunction with Locke) devising a model of government that would best serve the colony while, at the same time, suggesting solutions to social problems for the metropolis.[126]

Despite the promotion of this model, together with the corresponding prospects for Carolina estates, it remains entirely unclear whether or not anyone ever read any of this literature, not to mention the tomes on natural law and empire generated by seventeenth-century intellectuals in this "Golden Age" of political thought, let alone was convinced by it to take ship for Charles Town. Circumstantial evidence, again, must suffice to provide clues as to why early modern Europeans moved to Carolina: overcrowding on Barbados, distressed situations in England, or simply to see if the proverbial grass was greener across the ocean. We can only imagine what was going on in the minds of those trapped aboard ship in the Downs awaiting that easterly wind to convey them to America. Although the colonists had a draft of the Fundamental Constitutions, none wrote of packing the works of Grotius, Pufendorf, Hakluyt, Harrington, or anybody else into their intellectual baggage in preparation for this chapter in English colonization, while the warnings issued by the Lords to keep a close watch on the servants—and the escapes made good in Ireland—hint that not everyone shared great expectations of the new colony. However, paradoxically, the consistent references in the promotional literature to the availability of landed estates protected by

English laws along with religious toleration suggest that authors at least hoped that readers regarded these concepts as inducements to migrate.

Whatever the migrants thought, practically as soon as they landed at Ashley River after their 11-month odyssey, they unleashed a stream of reports extolling the potential of the country and applauding prospects for trade, especially with the Indians, and for substantial migration from other provinces. These glowing accounts, though, were invariably accompanied by complaints about other settlers and fear that such behavior would fatally injure the colony: food shortages, dishonest land distribution policies, political favoritism, incompetence, blame, and counter-blame.[127]

The belated arrival of Yeamans in the colony after finishing his duties as negotiator for the Crown with the French over boundaries on St. Christopher considerably clouded the colony's horizon. Sir John and West had an immediate falling out over precedence in the government and the leading colonists chose sides, with West and his supporters particularly careful to keep open the lines of communication with the proprietors. Coupled with the continued inability of the colony to feed itself, this political division, for which Yeamans largely took the blame in proprietary minds, raised red flags. On November 27, 1672, Ashley (now first earl of Shaftesbury) expressed fear that the colony might be "strangled in its infancy by those into whose hands we commit it." Reportedly, Yeamans had made a habit of providing the colonists' provisions at low prices while charging them exorbitant rates for everything else. The result, Shaftesbury told Sir Peter Colleton, successor to his father's proprietary interest and the Barbadian's chief backer, had cut short the Carolinians' drive to provide for themselves and had, instead, kept them dependent upon the proprietary storehouse.[128]

The partisan nature of most of the record generated in early Carolina makes it practically impossible to gauge its veracity in terms of what was actually going on. It does appear, though, that Sir John Yeamans constituted a convenient whipping boy for the colony's ills both for the Carolinians and the proprietors. Unsurprisingly, then, Sir John has had to shoulder the historiographical burden for the problems at Ashley River.

The charges levied against Yeamans included: declining to accept initially the proprietary commission as governor and appointing the elderly and "crazed" William Sayle in his place; engrossing the colony's food supply after he did arrive and forcing the inhabitants to pay his price thereby threatening a replay of the Cape Fear fiasco; seeking to subject Carolina's interests to those of Barbados; and, most significantly, representing the archetypal aggressive Barbadian of the sort who made up a substantial proportion of the early Carolinians and who served as the purported progenitors of the Goose Creek men. These experienced and "relatively wealthy" planters "exercised a disproportionate influence on the government" and "they often pursued self-interest most assiduously." Shaftesbury certainly came to regard Yeamans as a disappointment: in the summer of 1674, the proprietors removed Sir John as governor and replaced him with West.[129]

More crucially, however, too much importance has been placed on Sir John particularly and on Barbadian social and political influence on Carolina generally. West, whose first term as governor Yeamans and his associates made miserable, did identify his enemies as a "Barbados party."[130] A glance, though, at the membership of this "party" reveals that it consisted of Maurice Mathews, William Owen, William Scrivener, and Florence O'Sullivan, all direct arrivals from England, along with Thomas Gray and John Godfrey, Sir John's agents from Barbados.[131]

Ironically, given the historiographical emphasis that has been placed on overcrowding on their island as a prime motive for Barbadian involvement in Carolina colonization, the greatest impact of Barbadians on South Carolina's early history may have come through their creation of an Indian slave trade for the West Indian market and a corresponding policy of fomenting wars among indigenous folk to acquire slaves. In the first place, it is conceivable that Yeamans, or, at least, his men, Gray and Godfrey, all acquainted with the socioeconomic situation on the island, envisioned the mainland as a new source for slaves and so became involved in this practice. Mathews, charged by Shaftesbury with responsibility for handling provincial Indian affairs, if unaware of the dynamics of slavery and the trade in human beings when he departed London, soon became aware of the lucre on offer and allied himself with Gray, Godfrey, and the others. Significantly, at a time when the colony's survival remained dependent on the neighborly goodwill of the natives, one Brian Fitzpatrick, a servant of Godfrey, killed a Coosa Indian in the late summer of 1671, after Gray, Owen, and Mathews had visited a Coosa village the preceding spring.

The murder by Fitzpatrick generated a "hot contest" between Yeamans and West, almost certainly over the wisdom of provoking the Indians into fights when the colony remained desperately weak; retaliation came from the Coosas in the form of attacks on the settlers' crops, followed by an inevitable declaration of war, in turn, by the Carolinians on September 27. Godfrey and Gray received command of what passed for the provincial forces and they, in conjunction with the Grand Council, promptly commenced orchestrating the transport of captives to the Caribbean as slaves. The degree to which Yeamans and his "party" acted in concert remains unknown, but the rapid chronology of murder, war, and enslavement suggests a high degree of familiarity with the pattern on their part.[132]

In the meantime, though, other factors had intruded on the management and prospects, just as they seemed to ripen, of the colony at Ashley River. Significantly, the Calendar of State Papers, Colonial Series contains no entries from the proprietors between January 2, 1672 till the end of April (one entry referring to a meeting scheduled for the very end of April regarding "Captain Kingdon's affairs"[133]) then just one—"Concessions of the Lords Proprietors of Carolina to 'certain persons in Ireland,'" dated August 31—for that entire summer.[134] Although Shaftesbury wrote several letters about the Bahamas in the autumn of 1672, he created just one document related to Carolina for an entire year. His next communication with his "darling" is a note, dated August 13, 1673, to his client, Stephen Bull.[135] Moreover, the proprietary entry books go blank until April 10, 1677. The Lords convened in 1671 and met on March 29, 1672 to consider a buy out of Sir William Berkeley's share but we have no record of another meeting until November 13, 1674.[136]

The primary reason for this breakdown in communication, of course, was the outbreak of another war between England and the Dutch Republic—the subject of Shaftesbury's famous *Delenda est Carthago* speech—which broke out in March 1672 after a long run-up. Shaftesbury, as Chancellor of the Exchequer and a member of the Treasury Commission, as in 1664–67, had to turn full attention to funding the war effort and preparing the fleet for combat as he had in 1665. Involved constantly in committee work, he assumed the vast and varied duties of Lord Chancellor of England in November 1672.

Matters grew worse the following year—undoubtedly, in Shaftesbury's view, one of the most fateful in his troubled lifetime. In 1673, the duke of York made his conversion to Roman Catholicism known and his royal brother, Charles II, entered into his secret Treaty of Dover with France. Shaftesbury regarded both of these events as precursors to the establishment of popery, tyranny, and slavery in England and, consequently, spent the last ten years of his life scheming with increasing desperation to save the kingdom from the clutches of Rome. Involving himself more deeply in this self-appointed task inevitably meant pushing Carolina off to one side.[137]

The "Cavalier" Parliament reconvened at Westminster in February 1673. In the midst of the session, the House of Commons passed a Test Act designed to bar from office anyone who did not take communion in the Church of England and declare against transubstantiation. Shaftesbury became the leading defender of this bill in the debate in the Lords. When the heir to the throne, York, declined to appear at services at Easter and then gave up his offices, the battle lines between "the little earl" and James began to be drawn. In the first instance, this struggle resulted in Shaftesbury's dismissal from office on November 9, 1673 in favor of Sir Thomas Osborne, earl of Danby, who became his other great rival. Shaftesbury remained, however, president of the Council of Trade and Plantations.[138]

The Third Anglo-Dutch War, in addition to distracting Shaftesbury prior to his departure from the woolsack, also necessarily again inhibited communication, migration, and trade between London and the colonies as its predecessor had in the mid-1660s. "Most of the boatmen on the Thames," a biographer of Charles II has noted, "were seized to fill the gaps in [Prince] Rupert's crews, while a hundred lighters were hired to transport the soldiers" to the Netherlands in the summer of 1673.[139] This insatiable demand for ships and seamen for service in the Channel and the North meant that maritime resources were devoted to the navy until peace was concluded in February 1674. The war also prevented the prospective New York migrants from removing to Carolina since the Dutch had retaken that province at the outset of hostilities.

News from Ashley River came in dribbles via Barbados from whence Sir Peter Colleton wrote secretary Locke that "Our friends in Carolina sing the same song they did from the beginning, a very healthy, pleasant, and fertile country, but great want of victuals, clothes, and tools." Crucially, Colleton remained convinced that the Lords should still listen to these appeals or else they would risk losing the investment they had already made. His partners just had to wait for the peace, according to Sir Peter, when a number of prominent Barbadians would move to the mainland. Then, he insisted, Carolina would take its place as the greatest of the English colonies.[140]

The war limped to an end in the spring of 1674. On December 26, the colonists reported their situation. Although their corn stocks remained satisfactory, an August storm had wiped much of them, along with their tobacco. With that in mind, the Carolinians requested a remission of interest on their proprietary debt, along with a supply of nails, livestock, and clothes as well as a minister and a surgeon. With regard to their expenditures, they offered to pay their future obligations in pipestaves. Moreover, settlement, undoubtedly due to the war, had apparently lagged: from May 1673, only one small family and two single men had arrived. This left, in addition to Shaftesbury's agent, Andrew Percival, only 170 men in Carolina while the single men departed "as fast as they can." This continuing population shortage meant that they could not establish towns. Thus, Locke noted laconically, they "desir women."[141]

The coming of peace meant a restoration of proprietary attention to these problems and the postwar responses of the Lords proved critical for the historiography of South Carolina as well as the early history of the colony. Vexed by continuing colonial requests for supply with no apparent plan to repay the monies already disbursed, compounded by allegations of ill-usage by officialdom, by the engrossment of riverside lands by settlers, by the pursuit of ranching to produce beef for the West Indian market rather than the cultivation of staple crops, the proprietors, under Shaftesbury's direction, reached a number of decisions. First, they determined that Yeamans bore primary responsibility for the shambolic state of affairs at Ashley River and replaced Sir John (who had died the previous August anyway) as governor with his rival, West. With Yeamans gone and peace seemingly at hand, Shaftesbury and his partners could agree to provide an immediate infusion of £700 with a promise of a further annual investment of £700 for the next seven years.[142]

They then issued a warning with this good news: the long-term viability of Ashley River remained very much in doubt. To improve its prospects, Shaftesbury directed the settlers to de-emphasize stopgap measures, such as the raising of livestock, and concentrate on producing commodities for trade with the metropolis. The cultivation of "wynes, oyles, and silkes" would secure incomes for colonial estates and enable the repayment of the proprietary investment.

The older colony had disappointed Shaftesbury and his partners because they regarded the settlement pattern that had developed in Carolina as unpromising "for the condition of the people and way of planting at Ashley River will be a hindrance to towns and the coming of rich men thither." Even so, the proprietary "design" for Carolina colonization remained the same: the Lords sought "the best improvements for this climate from all parts of the world, and experience in the right management of them." At least initially, these recommendations met with approval in the colony and the settlers made an effort to meet them. West wrote that the Carolinians would pursue any commodity that the Lords would suggest and recommended pipe staves, cedar, and tobacco as especially promising. He also sent "4 barrels of Tobaco for tast" and to test the market along with a sample of the best cedar in the province. The new governor thought, again, that staves would serve as the easiest means for the colonists to pay off their debts to the proprietors but he had concerns about the current price, set by the proprietors at three farthings. Indeed, he had "70000 pipe staves in his hands which will rot without shiping."[143]

Yet, to underscore his unhappiness with the colony, Shaftesbury announced plans to start his own plantation, St. Giles Edisto, which would exist independently of Charles Town. He appointed Andrew Percival, possibly the relation of a member of his household, Mary Percival, as steward and provided instructions to cooperate with West, to recruit leet-men from among the impoverished at Ashley River, provide stores (at a price) to his neighbors, experiment with livestock so that it could be provided inexpensively to weighty newcomers, create a commerce with the Spanish and with other English colonies and engage in the partial monopoly that the proprietors established over the Indian trade.[144]

A sign of good faith on the part of the settlers would have helped. Shaftesbury proposed that if the settlers agreed to pay the outstanding salary owed by the Lords to West and to clear their other debts, then the proprietors might consider forgiving their own outstanding debt. The governor, moreover, could take possession of the proprietary plantation, which he already managed, and could take his future salary from income generated by that property.[145]

These policies could have been a reflection of the malevolent political and social preeminence of Yeamans and the Barbadians and the corresponding impotence of the proprietors.[146] An alternative scenario, though, exists. Sir Peter Colleton, cleaning up a governmental mess on Barbados while his partners were sacking Yeamans, vigorously defended his good friend's conduct as governor. Colleton identified Sir John's chief fault as a reluctance to commit pen to paper.[147] Then, in light of both the customary early modern commingling of private and public interests and the realities generated by the third Anglo-Dutch War, we can certainly view the encouragement by Yeamans of trade between Ashley River and Barbados as not only beneficial but vital to the former's development. Significantly, despite his complaints about Barbados interests, Shaftesbury never sought a reduction in trade with the island; he only sought to discourage a primary reliance on grazing. In any event, concerns about "Barbadian" domination of the colony disappear from the record, along with Sir John Yeamans, after his death in 1674.[148]

By this time, though, matters in England had again interfered with communication between the proprietors and their province. Following the end of the war and his removal from the government, Shaftesbury made the dissolution of the Cavalier Parliament and Danby's ministry his primary objective, culminating in the publication of *A Letter from a Person of Quality to His Friend in the Country* in 1675. Upon its publication on November 8, 1675, the House of Lords directed the public hangman to burn the document. Coincidentally or not, four days later, Locke hastily departed England for what proved to be an extended trip to France leaving the proprietors without a secretary to handle their routine business and correspondence.[149]

Following Locke's sudden withdrawal, Shaftesbury continued his attacks on Danby and the duke of York. These activities culminated in his proclamation in parliament that the Cavalier Parliament had been automatically dissolved through an illegal prorogation by the king. The response of the House of Lords, orchestrated by Danby, ordered the "little earl" to the bar of the house to ask its pardon. Shaftesbury declined to do so and was committed to the Tower of London on February 16, 1677.[150] Although Shaftesbury and the Ashley River settlers had had their disagreements, his incarceration meant that the proprietor best disposed to the colony and the most active in encouraging it had lost his ability to help and influence it at a stroke. In the ensuing vacuum, the earl's colonial agents seized the helm of his "darling."[151]

Chapter 4 ～

The Rise of the Goose Creek Men

W e have already seen that West Indians were not preeminent amongst the Goose Creek men. Even less evidence exists to support the characterization of the "Barbadian" party (in whatever incarnation) as "Anglican." In the first place, Carolina—uniquely in the annals of English colonization in North America—came into being without a recorded clerical presence or even any religious overtones. We find no John Winthrop, John Cotton, Thomas Hooker, Roger Williams, Fr. John White, S.J., or William Penn at Ashley River and no John Donne gave a sermon at Paul's Cross to godspeed settlers; indeed, we find no clergyman recorded at all in the colony prior to 1695.[152] Ashley's lack of enthusiasm for the established church and the corresponding official countenancing of toleration undoubtedly translated into proprietary hesitation (or even deliberate omission) to deal with their province's religious affairs.

Whether by design or neglect, an enfeebled (at best) established church enabled Dissent to flourish, to the consternation of the Church of England clergy who ventured there, even after the establishment of the Society for the Propagation of the Gospel in Foreign Parts in 1702. It also meant that no clerical infrastructure existed to minister to communicants of the established church for at least the first decade of the colony's existence. Certainly, no instance exists of any colonist taking any interest in the Church of England's situation prior to 1702.

Notwithstanding the fog generated by the scant contents of the early record of Carolina, the nature of the correspondence itself reveals the tension that underpinned Anglo-American colonization: clients of colonizers began laying out the nature of government and society in the "New World" while keeping one eye on their connections with the metropolis. For Ashley River, where the attempt to transplant English norms and values to American soil was again famously formal, the situation of settlers creating a colony while keeping their faraway patrons informed of developments constituted the ligaments of imperial development.

Yet, the autonomy exercised by colonial clients did not inevitably, or even necessarily, lead to friction with patrons: the proprietors, for instance, expected their agents to use their own discretion in setting up a government within the framework set up by the Fundamental Constitutions and to maintain the colony economically by whatever legal means available. Of course, the Carolinians took advantage of distance to further themselves—indeed, the Lords expected their servants to profit from managing proprietary affairs—and to afford rather less attention to repaying the proprietary investment in the colony, but this did not mean that the interests of colonizers and colonists constantly conflicted, nor did it again mean that the "Old World" values proved inherently unsuitable for the American environment. In the end, governmental interests became subsumed by the provincial struggle to control provincial politics.

Politics then translated into colonial development, but not in the manner we have been told. The customary view of early South Carolina's development—and indeed that of Anglo-American colonies, generally— states that the colonists who joined Mathews' faction did not share Ashley's vision of a colony that provided for a hereditary aristocracy with entailed estates: this model, though placed the very same "Old World"-style restrictions that had prevented these younger sons of Barbadian planters and English gentry from advancing themselves at home and obliged them to seek better opportunities in Carolina where land was relatively easy to obtain. Hence, then, the consistent and successful opposition to the Fundamental Constitutions.[153]

Unfortunately, no evidence whatsoever exists to suggest that any settler ever objected to the Constitutions on philosophical grounds as an obstruction to American advancement or ever regarded them as in any way unsuitable as a blueprint for a colonial society. Instead, as we shall see again and again later, objections, usually disingenuous, came from within that framework, generally adopting the view that "unalterable" Constitutions had been "improperly" altered: the greatest dispute over ratification in 1682 revolved around the issue of which version of the Constitutions was in effect; nobody expressed any reservations about the document itself.

By extension, the record gives no reason to surmise that the Carolinians had problems with a system of hereditary aristocracy in the abstract. Indeed, such a claim would have to overcome a strong presumption to the contrary: the leading orders of early modern English society, and aspirants to membership in those orders, such as colonial planters, regarded aristocracy as the pinnacle of independent sociopolitical status and, correspondingly, shared Ashley's view that aristocracy provided the essential counterweight to monarchy on one side and democracy on the other.[154] America, with its perceived abundance of land, provided *more* opportunities to achieve aristocratic status, provided anyone in authority could have been bothered to bestow it; happily, the proprietors remained willing to do so down to the end of their administration.[155]

The emergence of these Goose Creek men certainly generated disagreement but the endemic political strife of proprietary Carolina centered on control of the local government and on issues of relations with Indians rather than on the Lords who would have preferred that their colonists sort things out themselves peaceably.[156] In the most important sense, patronage constituted a central element in this transatlantic relationship just as it did in the metropolis. This is not to say, of course, that clients could and did pursue their own agendas—even at the expense of their patrons—since they did so on both sides of the Atlantic. Rather, it meant that, notwithstanding the greater distance from their patrons, clients in Carolina still had regard for the duty they owed their masters. Disobedience or rampant disregard of instructions resulted in dismissal. Yet, in both England and in Carolina, the exiled could and did return to favor all the time for various reasons. Correspondingly, cooperation generally existed between colonizers and colonists. Thus, the Carolinians generally accepted the proprietary regime, at least until 1716.

The career of Shaftesbury himself presents an excellent illustration of how this system operated. His financial talents and connections with his father-in-law, Southampton, made him invaluable to the newly restored monarch in 1660 and his star rose. When he opposed ties with France and targeted the duke of York as an enemy of the kingdom, Charles II dismissed him. While some of his associates "kissed the king's hand" and returned to favor, Shaftesbury preferred to play his own game after 1673. He achieved a temporary success when the concerns, sometimes slipping into hysteria, created by the "Exclusion Crisis" and the "Popish Plot" carried him back to the Privy Council. However, when the furor over the "popish threat" receded, it took the "little earl" with it.[157]

In Carolina, people played similar games in miniature. Thus, we find prominent settlers of the proprietary period, moving in and out of power, employing office to further their own positions at the expense of their enemies, and appealing to the people for support in pursuit of their personal and political interests. Sometimes, they ran afoul of superior authority and suffered rebuke as Shaftesbury and other English political figures of the day did.

This situation required that they, on the one hand, serve their patrons as loyal clients. In addition to managing Shaftesbury's Ashley River plantation and interacting with Indians, Mathews, for instance, represented the interests of Sir Peter Colleton in the colony. Just as the points of contact furthered interests at the individual level, so the proprietors could and did collectively reach common ground with their colonists. For instance, the settlers agreed to the proprietary plan to pay their arrears to the Lords in exchange for West's delinquent salary and any new debts the Carolinians had drawn on the proprietors. This agreement, however, only shifted the salary issue away from the Lords to the governor, who did not wish to be paid in goods. The proprietors then proposed that the colonists tender to West whatever exportable commodities they could produce as payment. Then, if he refused to accept payment in kind, he could sell the produce for money.[158]

With respect to the distribution of land, the proprietary headright system "achieved outstanding success" through the liberal grants it offered. Significantly, even critics of the proprietary administration have acknowledged, "the headright system seems to have been administered efficiently and honestly."[159] The geographical and personnel problems that hamstrung the proprietary intentions to lay out 12,000-acre seignories, baronies, and colonies were not matters of dispute: they could not be avoided since surveyors, no matter how competent, could not change the landscape. Even Shaftesbury's decision to undertake his new St. Giles Edisto plantation does not necessarily constitute evidence of a deep-seated discontent with the progress of Ashley River. This move (which proved to be a non-starter, in any event) did not signal a breakdown in the relationship between colonizers and colonists: the earl, as noted above, not only maintained his Ashley River plantation, he expressed his willingness, even as he tried to found his independent enterprise, to continue working with and supporting the older colony.

The Lords did express their concerns repeatedly about the pattern of settlement. Yet, these warnings stemmed from their fear of the consequences of the remoteness of plantations rather than any frustration with the Carolinians. As of December 25, 1679, for instance, the proprietors revised their orders concerning land grants to limit the prospect of a "land thinly peopled," by reducing the headright grant from 100 acres to 70 for every free migrant with an additional 70 acres granted for every male servant and 50 acres for every female servant or male servant between 12 and 16 years of age. Servants finishing their term were eligible to receive 60 acres. Moreover, the governor was to take care in making grants of valuable riverside land.[160]

In the end, notwithstanding numerous warnings, the faraway Lords could do little to compel their colonists to settle together both to create towns and to provide a better defense as they themselves well knew. Settlers required land, especially along the rivers that constituted the motorways of Ashley River, to maintain and advance themselves and they naturally lay claim to whatever they could. The continuing paucity of European migrants meant that Carolinians could hardly help but spread themselves across the country thinly. The average individual land grant of 300 acres put quite a distance between neighbors. At the same time, the early modern pursuit of land-based independence unwittingly hampered the establishment of communities and rendered the colony vulnerable to attack, as the Lords warned.[161]

Even as the proprietary regime functioned, though, Carolina officials sought to feather their own nests and the Indian trade, the most lucrative economic avenue available to the inhabitants of Ashley River, naturally became the target of scheming and the basis of fierce contention among rivals in the colony. This traffic came to include Indian slaves, many of whom were sold to the West Indies or New England. The proprietors prohibited this commerce in 1677 as a threat to frontier peace, but the "dealers in Indians," obviously regarding it as profitable, repeatedly flaunted this prohibition. Yet, no one has connected the character of that important commerce in the 1670s and 1680s with political and social consequences for the province. The Goose Creek men did everything in their power to preserve their position even to the extent of putting the province in jeopardy and running afoul of their distant proprietary patrons.[162]

In any event, we know very little about the backgrounds of the inhabitants of South Carolina prior to their arrival in the colony. The cases of the Goose Creek men, though, do demonstrate how the system was supposed to operate and how it failed in this particular colony.

Maurice Mathews arrived at Ashley River, as we have seen, with the "first fleet" in 1670 as a client of Shaftesbury and Sir Peter Colleton. This leader of the Goose Creek men for over twenty years remained a key figure in the colony until 1693 when the fallout from the Seth Sothell fiasco (discussed below) obliged him to return to England (where he died) to plead his case personally to the proprietors. Yet, until 1681, when he was dismissed from his offices for enslaving Indians, he remained in proprietary favor, holding a variety of governmental appointments ranging from surveyor to member of the Grand Council. His ability and apparent loyalty earned him the respect and affection of Shaftesbury, especially after he ingratiated himself with neighboring Indians (who made him a cacique to his patron's delight) shortly after arriving in the colony. He also wrote a promotional pamphlet and offered his professional advice on land distribution and settlement to his patrons. On his final visit to London, he arranged for the engraving of a map, now in the British Library, that he had made of the province.[163]

At some point before 1675, though, Mathews became the ringleader of the Indian slave trade in violation of repeated proprietary injunctions, seeking the benefits generated by the traffic at the risk of peace with Carolina's neighbors. This behavior ultimately alienated him from the Lords (though not because he was "anti-proprietary"), but he also broke with Sir Peter Colleton for personal reasons that remain unknown. The deep-seated hatred

Mathews came to have for Sir Peter and his family, coupled with his desire to retain control of the Indian trade, rather than opposition to the proprietors generally, would explain the tenacity of his political stance.[164]

The behavior of his compatriots tracks that of Mathews. Andrew Percival, Shaftesbury's man at St. Giles Edisto, and possibly related to members of the earl's household, seems not to have been a fully fledged Goose Creek man. On the one hand, he traded with Indians and stood in the vanguard of the opposition to the Fundamental Constitutions. Apparently, though, he befriended the Scots who arrived at Charles Town in 1685 while Mathews and his confederates plotted their destruction (see later for a discussion). Sometime in 1682 or 1683, perhaps while Percival was visiting in England, a full-blown breach developed between him and the Shaftesbury family. After the first earl's death in January 1683, Samuel Wilson, Locke's successor as proprietary secretary, reminded the second earl of his father's plan to make Percival a landgrave until "his false and base dealing with him."[165] The nature of this "dealing" remains unclear: Percival's management may have continued to "injure" and/or he may have broken politically with Shaftesbury at a particularly sensitive time when the "little earl" was moving to extreme measures in his struggle with the government of Charles II. Or the earl may have concluded that Percival was cheating him in his plantation management.[166]

In any event, Percival became a creditor on the Shaftesbury estate in Carolina and held a mortgage on St. Giles Edisto. When Wilson moved to the colony with the second earl's commission to serve as deputy, Percival objected to its form thereby preventing Wilson from handling the Shaftesbury interest and leaving it in legal limbo. Unless the second earl could clear these obstacles, Wilson warned, "Mr Percival wil suddenly make sale of all things here as he please he being now sole Lord & Master without Complication." In 1685, Percival acquired the entire plantation, including servants and slaves, from Shaftesbury's widow.[167]

Percival subsequently assumed a leading role in Seth Sothell's controversial takeover of the government in 1690 and became an opponent of payment of quitrents.[168] By this time, the Lords had lost patience with Shaftesbury's former servant. "God hath blest you with a very good Estate in Carolina," they observed, "but the courses that some men in Carolina take, will certainly put it in a great hazard to be lost, for we cannot with a good conscience as things stand, advise any man to come amongst you for we value our honor before any thing we have in Carolina."[169]

James Moore, who became Mathews's primary lieutenant and eventual successor, arrived in the colony before February 1675.[170] Along with his chief, Moore "contemptuously disobeyed orders" by enslaving Indians in 1683, for which offense the proprietors "thought proper to put them out of their office as deputies." Ten years later, Moore, along with Percival and Quarry, led the opposition to the payment of quitrents. To proprietary satisfaction, however, he came to terms, paying his arrears in 1696 and leading to the "hope [that] the rest will follow his example."[171]

Moore became provincial Secretary in 1699. While in this office, he informed Edward Randolph, the anti-proprietary agent of the Lords of Trade, of a plan to investigate upcountry mines advising "that if empowered by his majesty, and he could receive encouragement for himself and friends he would take with him 50 white men, and 100 Cherokee Indians, to work with them if he could be secured against the lords proprietors claim."[172] Yet, subsequently, Moore served as Chief Justice (1700–01), acting Governor (1701–02) and Attorney General (1703) of the province.[173]

Robert Quarry, who came to Charles Town from Ireland in 1684 as part of a proprietary effort to curb piracy (for which see later), served as a deputy and held a variety of important offices: secretary, clerk of the Crown, receiver, escheator, and, briefly, governor.[174] Following the example of Mathews, he continually, though, disappointed his patrons, ignoring instructions, failing to communicate with them, involving himself with pirates, and harassing other settlers. Like Mathews and Percival, Quarry participated in the Sothell *coup* and avoided paying his rents.[175]

The Irishman also used the Palatine's Court as the venue for a petition against Bernard Schenkingh as sheriff of Berkeley County "as a person notoriously evil and infamous, who was ejected from the Grand Council for drunkenness and scandalous behavior, and fined by the Sheriff's Court." The Lords, for their part, noted this fine, supposedly appropriated for the "fortifications of Carolina" was "imposed out of malice" and remitted it adding that the council had no authority to "apply our money to any use."[176]

Quarry, in the meantime, had carried off the provincial records after he was barred from serving as clerk of the Sheriff's Court, although he submitted them afterward. Although "unwilling" to remove him, the Lords noted Quarry's lack of cooperation in delivering their instructions to the governor giving him power to deal with the secretary as he saw fit. The proprietors finally removed Quarry from all of his places on September 16, 1686.[177]

Mathews garnered a key recruit, one who ultimately succeeded Moore as leader of the Goose Creek men in the early eighteenth century, in Sir Nathaniel Johnson. On the face of things, Sir Nathaniel, arguably the most prominent person in the colony between his arrival in 1689 and his retirement from public life due to serious illness in 1710, qualified eminently as a member of the "weightier sort" of planter around whom the proprietors had envisioned their province would develop by building estates, importing servants, and, thereby, attracting other settlers. In addition to offering an apparent societal bellwether for Carolina, Johnson's career provides us with another classic example of an early modern "man on the make" and illustrates how such people at this time pursued advancement.[178]

Just a year after his arrival in the colony, Sir Nathaniel's plantation, "Silkhope," had 24,000 mulberry trees planted on it in an attempt to turn silk production into an income stream for the estate. The former merchant had joined the quest for income-producing commodities that, in June 1690, remained open although some planters had successfully turned to rice—a commodity that appeared to John Stewart, a relic of the Scottish settlement that fell victim to the Goose Creek men in 1686, to be ideal for the swampy Lowcountry, especially when planters, like Sir Nathaniel, followed his recommendations.[179]

A closer look at this career, though, reveals that while Sir Nathaniel had all the appearances of a model settler for Carolina, his politics remained checkered. Moreover, in the course of moving from Baltic Sea merchant to baronet, to governor of the Leeward Islands, to Carolina planter, his behavior raised eyebrows on a number of occasions. Johnson never succeeded in shaking off the suspicion, occasionally aired publicly, that, beneath a plausible veneer, his actions betrayed more sinister motives. Even at a time when people readily accepted that the political waters, on both sides of the Atlantic, were filled with mariners continually shifting their sails to catch what they perceived to be the prevailing winds, he achieved a certain notoriety.

Sir Nathaniel began his career in Newcastle trading with Russia, Sweden, Pomerania, and Hanseatic merchants. Sometime in the late 1670s, he ingratiated himself with the government, was knighted, and served in the Oxford Parliament as member for his hometown (but certainly not as a friend of Shaftesbury).[180] He seems to have first attracted public attention when he appeared as interpreter for the defendant, Count Conigsmark, at one of the most sensational murder trials of seventeenth-century England.

Conigsmark was charged with hiring the three men who had shot the Whig bankroll Thomas Thynne to death in St. James Park in July 1682. This murder had taken place in the hothouse political atmosphere of that summer and inevitably became a *cause celebre*. Whig pamphleteers proclaimed that the murder, like every other setback their cause endured, had been politically motivated, especially since the duke of Monmouth—Charles II's oldest and favorite illegitimate son and Protestant aspirant to succeed to the throne at the expense of his uncle, the duke of York—had left Thynne's coach just minutes before. At Conigsmark's trial, Sir Nathaniel Johnson suddenly appeared as interpreter for the count (the Baltic trader spoke Swedish, High German, and Pomeranian while the count spoke no English) but acted, according to the prosecutor, "more like an advocate" for Conigsmark. In the end, to the fury of the Whigs, the count was acquitted and they blamed Sir Nathaniel, purportedly acting on behalf of the government, for manipulating this perceived miscarriage of justice.[181]

In September 1686, James II appointed Johnson governor of the Leeward Islands.[182] After the king fled to exile in France a little over two years later, Sir Nathaniel found himself in the same quandary over where his loyalties lay as many of his contemporaries did. He behaved, though, rather curiously at this time. He declared to an unnamed official correspondent that "I am no Roman Catholic, but I think the Church of England teaches me the doctrine of non-resistance." He placed his islands in readiness against a possible French attack, but he also wrote King James after William of Orange's invasion of England "saying that I might be more useful to him in England than [on Antigua]." Having received no response to that suggestion since the king had run away instead of resisting William's army, Sir Nathaniel wrote his now-exiled sovereign via the governor-general of the French Antilles on nearby Martinique. By now, though, England and France were at war, and Parliament had declared William and Mary the monarchs of England: Johnson's attempts to contact the exiled James amounted to treason, notwithstanding his purported belief in non-resistance.[183]

A month later, Sir Nathaniel proclaimed William and Mary as the new sovereigns, pursuant to the order of the Lords of Trade and Plantation, but he also sought permission to withdraw from his office as he could not swear the oath of allegiance. He observed that his views "cannot profit me" and that before he went to the Leeward Islands "my circumstances were very strait and pinching, and are now considerably worse through misfortune and losses." In the meantime, while the government contemplated his replacement, he would do his duty but asked that it pay the arrears in his salary. It seems he did send to Barbados for reinforcements when the French attacked the English part of St. Christopher. However, he departed Antigua for his Carolina plantation on July 25, 1689 without waiting for his successor, appointing his deputy to serve in his stead.[184]

Retiring from public life as a nonjuror, while suspicious, was not, in itself, remarkable for this time. But, as it happens, we have an alternate view of Sir Nathaniel's conduct. According to this later account, Johnson, while governor of the Leewards, had written both to the French governor of St. Christopher as well as the French commander at Martinique. Unfortunately for Sir Nathaniel, his opponents on Nevis had learned of this correspondence and intercepted the reply. Johnson's letters apparently revealed "a plot to betray all the Ilands Into the french hands." Confronted by his irate planters, he claimed that, if they agreed to supply him with 1,000 soldiers, he would demonstrate his loyalty to the English state and its religion by retaking St. Christopher. The Leeward Islanders, though, dismissed these protestations, reminding Sir Nathaniel that the ousted James had sold England's American empire and his Irish kingdom to Louis XIV in return for French support in regaining his British thrones. Thus, they regarded his communication with Martinique as treasonable on its face. The planters then declined Johnson's suggestion to attack St. Christopher on the grounds that their military obligations only extended to the defense of their own islands, a response the governor had reportedly anticipated. However, in a move he did not expect, they then pressed him to swear the oath to William and Mary: he declined to do so and departed for his Carolina plantation in some haste, "the people there being ready to tear him in pieces."[185]

Whether he departed Antigua because of his refusal to break his oath to King James or because his plot to deliver the English West Indies over to the French to finance a Jacobite restoration had been exposed, Sir Nathaniel's presence in Carolina immediately made him—a baronet with substantial landholdings in the colony—the proverbial big fish in a small pond.[186] Still his professed sympathies for the disgraced James rendered him a dark character to many people, especially to the Dissenters and Whigs.[187]

Sir Nathaniel made a nice foil for Mathews. Both seemed to entertain a certain flexibility in their politics, both had attached themselves to the now-discredited government of James II, and, last but not least, both loathed the Colleton family. They apparently knew of each other and of their common anti-Colleton sentiments prior to 1689. According to the indefatigable pen of John Stewart, Johnson, also in England at the time, had learned of a challenge that Sir Peter Colleton had made to Mathews to fight at the Carolina Coffee-House. Without telling Mathews, Sir Nathaniel appeared on his behalf to duel the proprietor. Johnson allegedly shut Sir Peter up in an upstairs room and issued his own challenge in response to some words Colleton had spoken. Eventually, Sir Peter recanted and tempers subsided. Mathews subsequently told Stewart that Johnson hated Sir Peter Colleton "from his sowll."[188]

It seems that Mathews, as befit a "creature of Hobbes," did not rely wholly on political affinity or Christmas punch to bring Sir Nathaniel into his camp: blackmail provided an even better tool, according to Stewart. One day, with Mathews present, Stewart tried to convince Sir Nathaniel of the perfidy of the "Welsh prince," arguing that struggle over Governor Colleton's maintenance had been "a Trick and Iniquity in Mathies." The Stuarts Town veteran then moved on to the Carolina career of Captain Thomas Spragg (discussed later), of which Mathews claimed to have no knowledge. After this exchange, Mathews, How, and other Goose Creek planters entertained Sir Nathaniel lavishly over Christmas 1689 in order to secure his interest as a nobleman in the parliament summoned to address the war that had broken out with France.[189]

Then, at another gathering, an "imprudent" Mathews apparently held forth on "Papists here and a great man at Count Conigsmark's tryall" as well as on "bravado discourses at Antigo" before the Orangist invasion of England. Stewart wondered why no one had challenged "Mine Heer Mauritius" on these extraordinary remarks. Subsequently, he learned the answer. Visiting Silkhope, he found Mathews there reading letters from England, from which he deduced that the Goose Creek leader "had the ascendant of Sr Nathaniel and Knew all his secrets and how the crisis of state stood with him." Indeed, since Mathews had provided Stewart with the story of Johnson's exchange with Martinique in the first place, the Scot concluded that the correspondence had to have been treacherous. Sir Nathaniel's "weak" explanations and excuses further confirmed this suspicion. In order to avoid exposure and prosecution, then, Johnson apparently became beholden to the Goose Creek leader.[190]

Ironically, the proprietors opened the door for Mathews and his associates as Shaftesbury clearly intended for the Indian trade to play an important role in the development of the Edisto plantation as well as Ashley River. He had received reports on the frontier scene from his agents, Dr. Henry Woodward and Mathews, and they, through their "discoveries," had forged the connections that, Shaftesbury envisioned, would help Percival to coordinate intercultural relations and make them more profitable. Therefore, Shaftesbury instructed Woodward, on the promise of one-fifth of the profits of the Indian trade, to befriend the Edisto people in order to establish, in particular, trading relations to acquire supplies for the colony and pelts. He also directed the doctor to pursue a friendship with the more powerful Westos.[191]

The subsequent careers of these three Shaftesbury men—Mathews, Woodward, and Percival—that emerged out of the proposed Edisto colony had the most significant consequences for Carolina. Much of this behavior revolved around Indian relations, particularly with the Westo people, initially. Upon his arrival in the province, Percival reported that he could not set up the intended autonomous plantation at St. Giles Edisto and had, therefore, established himself on the Ashley River within the jurisdiction of Charles Town. At the same time, he told the proprietors that he had written the governor and council "to permit him a free hand with the Westoes."[192]

It remains unclear what Percival meant by a "free hand" but by the autumn of 1674 "strange Indians" had visited St. Giles. These visitors proved to be the "ferocious," "man-eating" Westos whose fearsome presence had encouraged friendly intercourse between other Indians and the first fleet back in 1670. Now, apparently apprehending another attack by the Cussitaws, Chickasaws, and Cherokees, Westo representatives came to Shaftesbury's plantation where they met with Percival and Woodward to discuss establishing relations with the Carolinians. On October 10, the doctor accompanied them on a trip to their town on the Savannah River, returning on November 5, with Westo friendship. This new amity also brought the Carolinians within the busy Westo trade network; Woodward anticipated the return of his new friends "in March with deare skins, furrs and younge slaves." Such a prospect would certainly help the situation of Charles Town and its inhabitants—and so it proved.[193]

A healthy Indian trade would also have helped resolve the festering issues of reimbursing the investment that the proprietors had made in the colony as well as of provincial responsibility for maintaining governmental officials. Proprietary expectations of reimbursement remained unmet in 1675 and the Lords, unsurprisingly, had become loath to pour good money after bad while their colonists seemed continually unable or unwilling to wean themselves. Still, though, Shaftesbury refused to give up and hoped that, together with Sir Peter Colleton, he could persuade his partners to continue to keep Carolina afloat.

The Goose Creek men struck their first recorded blow in 1677, coincidentally or otherwise, while Shaftesbury languished in the Tower. As we have seen, the Lords appointed agents to manage their colonial affairs, including the Indian trade. These men derived a share of the profits from these activities and conducted private trade in customary fashion. From the colony's beginnings, Woodward, especially, was deeply involved in Indian affairs, serving as interpreter with various peoples, reporting on the inland country, and, of course, engaging in trade on behalf of Shaftesbury and Sir Peter Colleton.[194] He then made his journey to the Westos whose hostile attitude, prior to that time, had, continually kept the colony on edge.[195]

Meanwhile, both Mathews, already a cacique in at least one village by 1671, and Percival, had become heavily involved in Indian affairs on behalf of Shaftesbury, the colony, and themselves by 1676.[196] When the Westos first "alarmed" the Carolinians in 1673, Mathews's connections made him a logical candidate to lead an expedition, ultimately cancelled, against these Indians.[197] The colony's Grand Council then concluded that Carolina's security required an alliance with the Esaw people who would provide a better understanding of the surrounding countryside, which would, in turn, facilitate a successful attack against the Westos. It selected Mathews to lead a delegation to the Esaws to pursue this initiative and, by the summer of 1674, he appears to have assumed responsibility for South Carolina's relations with all of its indigenous neighbors.[198] The Grand Council assigned him to deal with several suspected conspiracies at this time, authorizing him to seize, interrogate, and "destroy" Indians as he saw fit.[199]

Woodward had formed profitable connections as a consequence of his diplomatic triumph with the Westos while Percival also received a portion of the proceeds of the trade conducted at St. Giles Edisto.[200] On April 10, 1677, in order to build on this new network, the Lords commissioned the pair along with a Captain John Fisher to act as their agents in the Indian trade.[201] This new and formal Westo–Woodward connection would have alarmed other neighboring Indians, who commonly identified the Westos as "man-eaters," and their partner, Mathews.[202]

The stakes were relatively immense, especially in the circumstances of a fledgling colony. Percival oversaw St. Giles Edisto drawing a very nice average annual income of £200 sterling. Even if Mathews, who ran Shaftesbury's plantation at Ashley River, for which we have no accounts, made just half of that sum from trading with his friends the Esaws and other peoples, he would have been doing very well. Woodward collected over £100 sterling for his services in 1676, and his friends the Westos were, it is clear, by no means friends of the indigenous friends of Mathews. No direct evidence exists, predictably, to prove that the surveyor conspired to destroy Woodward's operation and connections. But circumstantial evidence, as well as evidence of subsequent bad acts, bad faith, and poor reputation of Mathews and his friends, strongly suggests that the Goose Creek men hatched such a plan.

Thus, in 1677 and again in 1680, war broke out, apparently with the encouragement—if not at the behest—of unidentified Indian traders, between Carolina and its allied Indians against the Westos, the result of which could not have been better for Mathews: his rival Woodward fell into disgrace and lost his most important source of trade as his partners were routed. Mathews and his associates thus assumed unrivalled preeminence in the Indian trade. Their group used their profits from the Indian slave trade, which received a boost from the Westo War and their economic position to become the leading political force in the colony at least from 1677. This faction then employed the sort of behavior exhibited here—intimidation, plot, and dissimulation—to see off subsequent threats.[203]

The first of these conflicts began when the Grand Council met on July 14, 1677 with Mathews and his associates Godfrey and Moore in their places. Having, it claimed, failed to receive "satisfaction" from the Westos, whom it also accused of making unfriendly inquiries about the provincial defenses and for the alleged murder of two Englishmen, the council ordered the interception of any Westos approaching the colony and appointed Mathews and another of his supporters, John Boone, to make neighboring Indians aware of its directive. If the Westos wished to compound for peace, they could meet a special commission at Percival's house.[204]

Curiously, the Grand Council issued this injunction just two months and four days (the duration of a reasonable voyage from London to Charles Town) after the proprietors created their limited monopoly over the Indian trade. The Lords, following Woodward's visit to the country of the Westos and Cussatoes, and the corresponding outbreak of peace, had declared that only traders who had received a license from Shaftesbury and at least one other proprietor could engage in trade south of Port Royal for the next seven years. The proprietors claimed they had undertaken this policy for the security of their province so that remote Indians could learn of its weaknesses and they noted that, during the seven-year limitation, anyone could still trade with nations to the north of Port Royal.[205] Woodward, it bears repeating, had Shaftesbury's license and was to receive one-fifth of the profits from the Indian trade.[206]

Nobody seems to have complained about the creation of this limited monopoly. Evidence of a falling out between Woodward and the Goose Creek men, though, does exist. On April 12, 1680, the Grand Council heard evidence of the doctor's alleged treachery. One "Ariano, an Aged and a Considerable person" of the Westos appeared and reported that Woodward had told his people that the Carolinians "were bad" and that they should kill Goose Creek men James Moore and John Boone when, as provincial representatives, they came to negotiate. Ariano also told the council that Woodward had told the Indians that Moore and Boone had spied on them in order to bring about their destruction. Moreover, Woodward allegedly told the Westos that if they accepted an invitation to go to Charles Town the English would seize them and sell them into slavery abroad as well as destroy their town. Less than two months later after receiving this testimony, the council—having determined that the Westos aimed to continue hostilites—ordered the release of enslaved Indians and a cessation of trade with the Westos.[207]

After ordering Woodward's appearance to answer these charges, the council recorded that it heard unspecified evidence against its most experienced Indian diplomat for several weeks. It then found that Woodward had plotted to encourage the Westos to destroy some unnamed Carolinians and to enslave certain neighboring Indians to the "great" detriment of the settlement and its security. It consequently barred him from contact with the Westos on pain of a £1,000 bond.[208]

Quite possibly the minutes of the Grand Council relate the truth of what transpired: that Woodward, who from all previous appearances, had served the colony and its proprietors faithfully for almost 15 years as interpreter, trader, and diplomat, had, upon receiving his commission to handle the proprietary trade with the Westos, encouraged his new friends to attack Ashley River, kill his fellow colonists, and enslave other Indians. Unfortunately, the journal of the Grand Council does not disclose the basis upon which it made its findings nor does any other evidence exist to support the government's views on the causes of this war.

Instead, as Shaftesbury tellingly observed to Percival in June 1682, "All the trade since Dr Woodward left it and Westoes were driven away belong wholly to you and me."[209] In addition, Mathews made a number of anti-Westo observations in his 1680 promotional letter.[210] Furthermore, Thomas Newe, a newcomer to Ashley River in 1682, found the colony in an uproar since "3 or 4" of its prominent inhabitants had traded guns and ammunition to some Indians who had used them to fight others, who had supplied a considerable portion of pelts in the province's trade. This ongoing war had disrupted a profitable commerce, retarded the settlement of Carolina, and had required the colony to send out (and absorb the cost of) an army.[211]

Thus, this war stemmed from an intercultural alliance opposed to Woodward and the Westos and it used the pretext of Westo attacks on and enslavement of other Indian neighbors to destroy that nation. With Mathews, Moore, Godfrey, and Boone involved in the government at this time, it was feasible for the Grand Council to generate "evidence" to support their contentions. Under this indictment, it was Mathews who used his position to engage in Indian slavery (of the Westos) and then accused Woodward of acting in the same illegal way. Significantly, Woodward never came to the attention of the proprietors for enslaving Indians outside of the context of the complaints against the Westos while Mathews came to be identified as the "Ringleader" of the significant Indian slave trade in the province. Thus, the winners of the war neither attacked nor overthrew the proprietary monopoly—they, indeed, benefited from it—but they gained practical control of the Indian trade.

Not only was Woodward discredited in the aftermath of the war, but Shaftesbury placed his trusted agents, Mathews and Percival, in charge of the peace, ironically in order to maintain harmony between Carolina and its indigenous neighbors. The proprietors instructed Percival to treat with the defeated Indians "upon honourable termes" before delivering the treaty article on trade, along with proprietary instructions, to Mathews. Significantly, Shaftesbury directed his men to keep Woodward—and everybody else—in the dark.[212] The proprietors also created a commission under the aegis of the Grand Council, headed by Mathews and Percival, to oversee Indian affairs, to regulate the Indian trade, to crack down on the enslavement of Indians, and to entertain and make recommendations concerning native grievances.[213]

Unfortunately, this appointment, as the Lords belatedly realized, put the foxes—who acted with "much greater regard to their Private Profits [than] Benefit to [the] Publick"—in charge of the proverbial hen house. While their instructions were making their way across the Atlantic, the commissioners had resumed hostilities against the Westos, much to the annoyance of the Lords, whom they had neglected to inform. Commerce and peace with neighboring peoples, the proprietors insisted, remained their chief diplomatic objective and amity with the apparently still-powerful Westos remained a centerpiece of that policy. Instead, those intentions had been blown.[214]

Two weeks later, on March 7, 1681, the proprietors offered further observations on the Westo War. Noting that the Carolinians had again attacked the Westos without proprietary knowledge, the Lords pondered whether the assault served the security of the colony or "simply to serve the ends of individual traders." If the latter proved to be the case, the proprietors took a dim view especially since the war risked security of the province for the pursuit of pecuniary gain. For its part, the Grand Council claimed to have based its continuing battles with Woodward and the Westos on one letter the doctor had allegedly written stating that if the Carolinians cut off trade with the Westos, the Indians would cut the throats of the colonists, and on another purportedly written by the governor of St. Augustine alleging that Woodward had encouraged an Indian attack on the Spanish colony and threatening reprisals. To reach a satisfactory conclusion as to the causes of the war, the proprietors requested affidavits from the Indian traders, along with certified copies of the letters.

The Lords explained that they had pursued trade with the Westos, especially of guns and ammunition, in order to secure the dependency of those people upon Carolina and thereby intimidate other Indians. Such a situation would have enabled the colony to protect friendly nations and "terrify" those who remained affiliated with St. Augustine. Instead, with the Westos "deemed ruined," a replacement had to be found in order to maintain a system of alliance. As far as Woodward was concerned, the proprietors left him to the law of the province for the time being.[215] Significantly, though, he received a proprietary pardon on May 23, 1682.[216]

Having won the Westo Wars, Mathews and his associates promptly contrived a relationship with their friends, the Savannahs, themselves former allies of the Westos, to provide guns, powder, shot, and other European commodities in exchange for Indian slaves captured, in conjunction with their friends in the Carolina government, in a series of wars. At the same time, the Mathews group contrived its own peace initiative with the Westos. The first phase involved an invitation to the nation's headmen under truce to negotiate a treaty with Governor West, who apparently remained uninformed of this plot, then seizing and killing them "in cold blood" and driving the rest of their people away. Then, in order to maintain the supply of slaves, the traders and the Savannahs (whose commerce in pelts had proven less lucrative than expected) attacked the Waniah people "upon pretence" that they had attacked a boatload of escaping Westos. The traders then "contrived" a "false alarme" in the province to defend their Savannah friends from vengeful Westos, even though no Westos seemed to have been near the Savannah towns and the "Indian dealers have written us there are not above fifty Westoes left alive & those Devided." Notwithstanding, this show of force gave the Mathews gang the chance to intimidate the Savannahs into an alliance with them.

Mulling over the proffered justifications and pretexts for colonial behavior, the proprietors questioned why their province had gone into an uproar and undertaken considerable expense to defend the relatively numerous and powerful Savannahs from the defeated and weak Westos. They further questioned the wisdom of enslaving the peace emissaries from the Westos and Waniahs. As the Lords wryly observed, peace with those peoples left open the question of where the Savannahs could obtain more slaves. Thus convinced that the slave trade had provoked these wars, the proprietors warned the colony of the consequences to settlement of perpetuating the vicious war–enslavement cycle.[217]

At this point, though, the Lords could hardly restore the *status quo ante bellum*: the Westos had largely vanished and the Goose Creek men had achieved preeminence in the colony. The faction now remained determined to keep their grip on the Indian trade. This determination stunted several plans to bring sizeable numbers of European migrants, while many settlers departed because of the unsettled character of Carolina's government.

Chapter 5 ∼

Plots

In the meantime, Shaftesbury having spent just over one year in the Tower, returned to his place in the House of Lords on February 27, 1678. During his imprisonment he had necessarily devoted his energies to gaining his liberty, which impeded any effort to oversee Carolina affairs. Then, in August and September, the government received information from Israel Tonge and Titus Oates of a Jesuit plan to kill the king and seize control of the government, sparks set ablaze by the murder (still unsolved) of the investigating magistrate, Sir Edmund Bury Godfrey, on October 12.

Shaftesbury played a leading role in fanning this fire, which came to be known as the "Popish Plot," supporting news accounts, supplying "informers" (who, like Oates and Tonge themselves, invariably proved to be perjurers), and calling for the summoning of parliament in order to investigate matters more thoroughly and to exclude the Catholic duke of York from the succession. These efforts, in the last phase of his career, which increasingly preoccupied him, culminated in the desperate, almost farcical attempts to coordinate assassination and rebellion and took precedence over Ashley River. In 1681 and 1682, though, Shaftesbury's mind briefly refocused on the colony as one possible cure for the perceived threat from Rome and so "peopling" efforts resumed. These new migrants, however, ran afoul of the Goose Creek men who, ironically, adopted the same ruthless and cynical philosophy toward their enemies as the "little earl" did toward his.

Systematic migration from Western Europe to Ashley River resumed after 1680. While Locke toured France after his speedy departure from England in late 1675, he made contact with members of the Protestant community in that country. Under pressure from an increasingly hostile government, Huguenots had begun to trickle into England, Ireland, the United Provinces, and the Palatinate in search of more hospitable climates. Although no direct confirmation exists, it seems likely that the conversations in which Locke turned to Carolina as a prospective habitation for these migrants, which the former proprietary secretary relayed to his friends.[218] From the proprietary perspective, French emigration would not only have increased the number of settlers, but through their "industry" and particular "skill in planting vineyards and olive trees and the making of silk" they would contribute to the wealth of the kingdom and of their lordships (for which, they hoped, the Crown might be willing to contribute a subsidy to the voyage). In any event, again, the proprietors reached an agreement with Rene Petit and Jacob Guerard to transport some 80 Huguenot families to the province. Petit and Guerard each received manors of 4,000 acres for their trouble.[219]

The arrival at Ashley River, in 1680, of the Petit-Guerard settlers and the family of Daniel Axtell, London merchant and son of a regicide, served as a precursor to a more concentrated movement of people to the colony.[220] Shaftesbury's deep-seated fears over "popery and slavery" became intertwined with renewed promotion of Carolina after Charles II suddenly dissolved the Oxford Parliament on March 28, 1681. The earl and his Whig associates, including his fellow proprietors, Sir Peter Colleton and the Quaker John Archdale, along with the proprietary secretaries Locke and Wilson, and others—the lawyers Aaron Smith and Robert West, the minister and controversialist Robert Ferguson, and the Huguenot merchants John Dubois and Thomas Papillon—had, with great fanfare, targeted this parliament as the climax of their campaign to compel Charles II to bar his brother from the succession. Indeed, the Crown later alleged that Shaftesbury and his circle, under cover of conducting Carolina affairs, had plotted at Oxford to seize the government by force. According to this charge, which was never proven, Captain Henry Wilkinson came to the university town ostensibly to accept a commission as deputy governor of the colony that provided a pretext for him to take a place in Shaftesbury's guard at the parliament. This unit was supposed to seize the king and force him to change the succession when the occasion prevented itself.[221]

Instead, the monarch surprised the members by sending them home after just five days. This summary action made it clear to Shaftesbury and his party that the likelihood of future parliaments—and, therefore, access to legal methods to deny James the throne—was now slim, especially, as they suspected, Charles had solved his short-term financial problems through subsidies supplied by his cousin, Louis XIV. Consequently, they turned to alternative remedies for preserving themselves and the realm (as they saw the situation), including withdrawal to Carolina. Unfortunately, the nature of Shaftesbury's antigovernment activities means we cannot even be entirely certain of "Little Sincerity's" attitude toward the province at this time.

In any event, a promotional apparatus sprang up in London, Dublin, Belfast, and the Netherlands over the next several years advertising the benevolent climate, fertile soil, constitutional government, security of property, and liberty of religious conscience in the colony. Pamphleteers directed interested parties to the new Carolina Coffee-House that had, in accordance with the fashion of the times, manifested itself in Birchin Lane in the heart of London, a stone's throw, perhaps not coincidentally, from the Huguenot Threadneedle Street Church. This establishment now served as the base of Carolina operations where people could get information and express their interest in migrating there.

Meanwhile, the dissolution at Oxford had cooled the enthusiasm for "exclusion" and put Shaftesbury on the defensive. At the same time, his use of paid informants against York and Danby in the "plot" began to backfire spectacularly: the hapless Edward Fitzharris became trapped in his lies and was executed for treason while others, who had gone uncompensated, flocked to the government eager to give evidence against their former bene-factor. Taking no chances, on May 4, 1681, Shaftesbury received admission to the Company of Skinners, which meant that any governmental attempt to attack him through the courts would have to come in Middlesex where the local officials and juries were friendly Whigs.[222]

Fitzharris went to the block on July 1. The following day, the Privy Council (including his fellow proprietor, Craven) ordered the arrest of Shaftesbury who was committed to the Tower for the second time in his career. Out of circulation, he once again had to concentrate on regaining his liberty. Indeed, in September, he reportedly offered, via the earl of Arlington, to withdraw to Carolina if the king would grant him a pardon. According to the earl of Longford, Shaftesbury also asked for £3,000 to offset the trans-portation costs. Charles declined this offer, observing that "his lordship knew the law very well, and by that he should stand or fall." It is interesting to ponder the possible effects for Carolina had Charles permitted Shaftesbury to go there. The king, however, did not believe the earl would actually depart into exile but, instead, would proclaim that the government had extorted the conditions of his release.[223]

In the meantime, the secretary of state, Sir Leoline Jenkins, received regular reports on the movements of Wilson. According to this evidence, the proprietary secretary was incredibly busy at this time, although not with Carolina; indeed it seems the province by design occupied a decidedly secondary place in his mind to liberating his patron and, by extension, the kingdom in the latter part of 1681.[224]

The government had sufficient information to commit Wilson to the Tower to join his master on October 10, 1681 and their joint application for bail two weeks later under a writ of *habeas corpus* was refused. However, the grand jury—handpicked by the Whig sheriffs of London—duly returned an *ignoramus* on November 24; Shaftesbury and his loyal secretary were bailed four days later.[225]

Action on the Carolina front, regardless of Wilson's apparent attitude, then heated up and migration and sedition moved hand in glove after Shaftesbury's bail was discharged in February 1682. That spring, a number of disaffected English persons made the move to Carolina; their leaders included Joseph Morton, appointed governor of the colony on May 10, Thomas Smith, Daniel and Rebecca Axtell, and Benjamin and Joseph Blake (son-in-law of the Axtells), brother and nephew of the admiral of the parliamentary navy during the Commonwealth.[226] They brought with them "five hundred people to Carolina in a month." In addition, a group of Scots, many of them "disaffected," planned a colony for the Port Royal area. They formed a company and entered into negotiations with the proprietors. At the same time, Huguenot migration continued. These migrants, like the Lords, envisioned a province whose tolerant religious and constitutional climate would attract additional migrants and bring prosperity and security to all settlers.[227] To build on this sentiment, Ferguson and Wilson each published Carolina promotional tracts noted previously.[228]

In addition, the Whig sheet, the *True Protestant Mercury*, gave Carolina prominent coverage while it monitored "popish" activity. Number 125 of this gazette included a description of the "Constituted Government, by reason of the great number of persons, who do continually resort to that hopeful Plantation" as a supplement to Wilson's description it had published the week before. The next issue included an item dated March 21, 1682 which reported that the proprietors—Shaftesbury, Craven, the earl of Bath (guardian of Sir George Carteret's infant heir), Sir Peter Colleton, John Archdale (who had acquired Baron Berkeley's share), and a Mr. Vivian (acting for the second duke of Albemarle) had purportedly met at the Carolina Coffee-House "where there was a great resort of people of all sorts, who came to receive satisfaction in several particulars, and do find all things so well answer their expectations, that they intend very speedily, with their Wives and Families, to Transport themselves thither." The item announced that the Lords, "to the accommodation of such," would be meeting each subsequent Tuesday.[229]

No record, though, exists to indicate that these subsequent meetings ever took place. Presuming the March 21 gathering actually did occur, it must have been an uncomfortable if not incongruous assemblage. Shaftesbury, of course, was a Whig chief dedicated, with the support of Colleton, to excluding the duke of York from the succession. Across the table would have sat Craven, equally dedicated to the preservation of the Stuart dynasty and the accession of James. As a member of the Privy Council, he had signed, as we have seen, the warrant committing Shaftesbury to the Tower in July 1681, and he had commanded the troops deployed by the king to control London and the road to Oxford during the short-lived parliament in March. The earl of Bath, a newcomer to the proprietorship and a staunch friend of Shaftesbury's hated rival, Danby, completed the Tory balance.

Furthermore, the council (with Craven in attendance) had just forbidden a Whig feast (at which Shaftesbury was supposed to have figured prominently) as "seditious, and tending to raise distinctions and confederacies amongst his majesties subjects" that had been scheduled for the very same night as the advertised gathering of the proprietors.[230] Curiously, this is the only public announcement of a proprietary board meeting that we have (and no minutes or other record of it exists) and, it seems, there had not been a meeting of the Lords since July 1, 1681—the day before the Council—again with Craven in attendance—committed Shaftesbury to the Tower.[231]

Still, all of this activity attracted interest, at least north of the border. On July 31, 1682, the proprietors, now including the merchant Seth Sothell who had purchased the Clarendon share, entered into Articles of Agreement with the Ayrshire gentlemen Sir John Cochrane of Ochiltree and Sir George Campbell of Cessnock, the agents of a newly formed Scottish Carolina Company. This document gave the Scots an unoccupied county of their choice divided into 32 squares of 12,000 acres apiece. In return, the Scots agreed to acquire at least four more squares annually beginning September 29, 1683 at a penny per acre quit rent starting three years after settlement commenced payable to the proprietors' receiver in Carolina.[232]

To encourage this Scottish settlement, the proprietors returned to the Fundamental Constitutions, revised them twice, and then submitted them to their colonists for ratification for the first time.[233] "Thinkeing after thirteen years Consideration it was convenient to fix ym," and since the "Scotch & some other Considerable men yt had a mind to become settlers in Carolina," the proprietors took the opportunity to revise the Constitutions and present them to the freeholders of Carolina for their approval in 1682. Twenty years after the formation of the proprietorship, five of its original members had died and three of the original shares (those of the Berkeleys and Clarendon) had passed into the hands of other individuals either by inheritance or by purchase. Some of the changes made in the two 1682 editions reflected a desire to give precedence in the proprietary hierarchy to those who had been Lords on March 1, 1670 (as in the new Section 59) over the newcomers.[234]

Other alterations reflected the desires of the Scots. Initially, these Presbyterians would certainly have objected to the language of Section 96 in the 1670 version, which had established the Church of England in Carolina describing it as "being the only true and orthodox, and the national religion of all the king's dominions." The January 1682 version dropped the obnoxious reference to "orthodoxy" and merely identified the established church as "being the Religion of the Government of England."[235] Revisions made in August 1682 went further: the Church of England remained the only religion in Carolina eligible for direct public subsidy, but such contributions could only be obtained by voluntary subscription. At the same time, other churches, excepting "the Church of Rome," gained the power to tax their membership to pay the salaries of their ministers, a clause obviously aimed to appeal to the proposed Presbyterian community.[236]

The opportunity also presented itself to reform the Fundamental Constitutions still in abeyance. The Scots "hinted to us" the potential for abuse in a system in which members of the Grand Council were appointed for life (Section 31) and other officials appointed by the proprietors, such as judges and sheriffs, had responsibility for choosing juries. Thus, the Lords changed the Constitutions to give the provincial parliament the authority to punish misbehaving members of the Grand Council and other officials and removed the temptation to pack juries by providing for their selection by drawing lots. They also empowered their governor and deputies to ratify the new version that would go into effect with the consent of the Grand Council and two consecutive parliaments.[237] Most importantly, they amended Section 51 to give the parliament the sole power to approve or reject legislation (the introduction of which remained the sole province of the Grand Council) without the need for further approval by the Palatine's Court.[238]

The proprietors also streamlined the process of presenting issues of concern to the government. Previously, Section 66 of the Fundamental Constitutions had directed grand juries and assize judges to refer cases, laws, or issues, as they deemed appropriate, to the proprietors' courts that, in turn, would refer them to the Grand Council. The January 1682 Constitutions added a clause to this section stating that if the Grand Council failed to act on these findings for six months the parliament could take them up on their own accord. The August version also clarified the procedure for legislation and replaced Section 51 with a new Section 81. Under this provision, the Grand Council retained the sole responsibility for preparing bills that, after three readings and passage by a majority, were to be sent to the parliament for its approval. The new Section 81 also provided detailed guidance for handling personal complaints against landgraves and cassiques.[239]

Some of those involved in this colonizing enterprise and who entered into these articles also came to involve themselves in the plots against the government that began to hatch at this time. Consequently, the intentions of the Scots have been shrouded in controversy almost since the ink dried on the paper over three centuries ago. The government, after Shaftesbury's death, came to believe that the venture served as a pretext for Shaftesbury to invite "the heads of the disaffected party" in Scotland to go to England "under pretence of purchasing lands in Carolina, but, in truth, to concert with them the best means of carrying on the design [for a general insurrection] in both kingdoms."[240] This finding was fervently denied by supporters of the opposition, notably the Presbyterian hagiographer, Robert Wodrow, who provided some details of the agreement between the Scottish subscribers, as well as some of their names, in his account.[241]

Even today, disagreement rages on the nature of these proceedings. Richard Ashcraft's discussion of antigovernment activities in the 1680s claims that some "Scotsmen—George Campbell, John Cochrane, and William Carstares—began to drift into London on the pretense of consulting about their colonial interests in the Carolinas" in the summer of 1682. Later, in January 1683 after Shaftesbury's death, the council of six plotters—John Hampden, Jr., Algernon Sidney, Lord Howard of Escrick, the duke of Monmouth, Lord William Russell, and the earl of Essex—sent Aaron Smith to Scotland to coordinate plans "under the guise, formerly employed by Shaftesbury, of inviting the Scots to London for a meeting about their economic interests in America." Archibald Campbell, ninth earl of Argyll, had escaped from Edinburgh Castle, where he had been committed for treason, and gone into hiding in London at the beginning of 1681. Argyll sought to assume the leadership of Scottish discontent and, apparently, entered into communication with Shaftesbury at some point about coordinating a rising. Yet, other writers have maintained that the Stuarts Town project constituted more than a cover for the "Rye-House Plot"—the reported plan to murder Charles II and his brother in July 1983 as they returned from the Newmarket races—and more than a project for nonconformists to flee persecution and that it demonstrated genuine Scottish interest in overseas trade and colonization.[242]

It seems, though, that Wodrow actually was nearest to the truth (inasmuch as the precise movements of traitors/rebels can ever be learned), when he grudgingly conceded "whatever Meetings might fall in afterwards under the Covert, yet such a Design was at first really projected."[243] The evidence prior to the end of 1682 indicates a sincere Scottish interest in Carolina dating from 1670s: they formed their vehicle for settlement, sent agents to the colony to inspect prospective locations, negotiated with the proprietors for land grants and suitable revisions to the Fundamental Constitutions. They did so both because they viewed America as an opportunity for investment and because of the difficulties nonconformists were experiencing with the Scottish ecclesiastical and councilor authorities in the period after the murder of the Archbishop of St. Andrews, James Sharp, and the encounter with government forces at Bothwell Bridge, near Glasgow (May–June 1679). These objectives naturally brought the principals of the Edinburgh venture into contact with Shaftesbury, who had expressed sympathy for the problems of these Scots and whose offer of colonial religious toleration had relative appeal for them.[244]

By 1682, in fact, the Scottish undertakers had been searching for an appropriate American location for a colony for some time. Undoubtedly, these were men keen to advance themselves and their country, as Shaftesbury and the original proprietors had been.[245] The most active members of the group appear to have included Sir John Cochrane, Sir George Campbell, Sir George's father, Sir Hugh Campbell, and their Ayrshire associate John Crawford of Crawfordland, the Edinburgh merchants Sir Robert Baird (who acted as cashkeeper), George Mosman, George Clark, and Charles Charters, the prominent attorney Sir George Lockhart, George Scott of Pitlochie, Henry Erskine, third Baron Cardross, and Walter Gibson, a Glasgow merchant. Mosman, Baird, Patrick Johnston, and Charters appeared before the Scottish Privy Council in February 1681 with an "overture for the improvement and trade of the kingdom" through the encouragement of manufacturing, especially of linen. At the same time, they submitted a memorial addressing the notion of Scottish colonization in America.[246]

It seems anachronistic, though, to separate "economic" from "religious" reasons for colonization. Certainly, people like Sir John Cochrane and Sir George Campbell and their associates did not. Some of them had plotted and suffered for "true religion." As the pages of Wodrow relate, the government fined and imprisoned them on a regular basis for allowing conventicles, harboring Bothwell rebels, and avoiding the services of the established church. Indeed, the Crown had begun sending their "disaffected" brethren to Carolina (Gibson was heavily involved in this convict traffic) and other colonies.[247] The Edinburgh authorities fined Mosman (£300 for himself and £150 for his wife), Clark (800 merks for himself and £300 for his wife), and Johnston (£100 for himself and £150 for his wife) for not attending church in 1683 although the council set these verdicts aside.[248]

In the summer of 1682, however, just as the proprietors and the Scottish agents were reaching agreement on the Port Royal colony, other events intervened. At least some of the Scottish undertakers back in Edinburgh remained unaware that colonization had become subsumed by treason; Carolina became a subterfuge. The venture collapsed in the face of arrests, exile, and lawsuits although a partial salvage did occur when the colony led by Lord Cardross, finally sailed for Port Royal in July 1684.[249]

The first glance at the evidence of colonization activity between July 31, 1682 and the discovery of the Rye-House Plot one year later, wrapped as it is in the swirl of plot, disappointment, and fear of the block, generates considerable skepticism.[250] Most of what has come to light about the activities of these plotters during this year comes from the testimony of informers.

Here is what can be known with relative certainty from the summer of 1682, before turning to more dubious testimony. Notwithstanding the self-serving character of much of the later evidence, we have documentation that shows that, at least prior to the second visit of Sir John Cochrane and friends to London in January 1683, the Scottish venture to Carolina was undoubtedly legitimate.

In April, Scottish plans to buy land in New York for £15,000 from an unnamed sympathizer fell through, even though under the terms negotiated the Scots could have established Presbyterianism and enjoyed a "joynt interest" in legislation and government. With the New York deal having collapsed, Carolina, its "constitution" being better suited to their minds, became the preferred site for colonization.[251]

The proprietors had encouraged this change of mind by altering the Fundamental Constitutions and providing a county for settlement with no obligation if the Scots failed to take it up. In July, then, the Company had agreed to the Articles with the Lords while William Dunlop, an Edinburgh associate of Gibson, declared his intention to migrate, possibly with some 50 or 60 servants.[252] On July 31, 1682, Cochrane and Sir George Campbell of Cessnock entered into their agreement with the proprietors.

On August 15, the government approved the Cochrane–Cessnock venture, notwithstanding its subsequent belief that it was a pretext, although the Lord Advocate observed that the "Carolina project encourages much our fanaticks, thinking they ar now secur of a retreat."[253] The duke of Albany (to use York's Scottish title) noted that he "was not a competent judg of Sir J. Cocherans pretensions" and referred the matter to the Council. But, he acknowledged that he had told Sir John that "I was glad he and others of this perswation though of going there, because they would carry with them disaffected people."[254]

Having cleared this vital hurdle, the Scots company, on September 15, officially designated Cochrane and Cessnock as their agents, ratified the July 31 agreement with the Lords, prepared to send Crawford of Crawfordland to Ashley River to find the best location for their plantation, and agreed to pay £10 for each of the 100 acres they acquired. This memorandum of understanding indicates that the Scots believed that they were to exercise considerable autonomy in governing their colony: the proprietors granted each of them the power to appoint a landgrave and two cassiques in accordance with their holdings and directed their Charles Town officials to commission the justices of the peace and sheriffs nominated by the Scots.[255]

Cooperation between themselves and the English was vital to the success of the Scottish colony, the undertakers realized. To that end, Cochrane sent a letter of introduction for Crawford to Governor Morton—himself a recent arrival at Charles Town and probably a like-minded individual in terms of religion and politics—that included a copy of the Articles of Agreement with the proprietors. Cochrane asked Morton to supply men and boats to help the Scottish commissioners investigate the country, noting the importance to the colony of the reports that would be made and hoping to reciprocate when the occasion presented itself. Indeed, the Scots expected such favorable accounts of Carolina from their agents and the provincial government that they planned to send over "suche a considerable number of Gentlemen and ministers And such a strength of people well provided of all things necessary as will exceedingly raise the reputation of that province." This influx would bring benefit to those who had already planted in Carolina since it would serve, on the one hand, as security against the Spaniards and, on the other, would improve trade with the Indians. The success of all this, though, they understood, "depends upon this tryall" and the encouragement it received from Morton and Axtell.[256]

The day after the undertakers and their agents decided on their strategy, Cochrane, now back in Edinburgh, wrote the earl of Aberdeen, Lord Chancellor of Scotland, acquainting him with the agreement he and Sir George Campbell had reached with the proprietors for establishing their Carolina plantation. The king had approved the plan and the 72 undertakers (Sir John enclosed a list) had prepared a ship to sail from Greenock on October 1 with four pilots and two gentlemen to secure the best available land. Sir John invited Aberdeen to join the venture that promised to improve "the honor and advantage of this nation."[257]

A letter to the Carolina Company, dated September 27, 1682, purportedly signed by Shaftesbury and Sir Peter Colleton, confirmed the Articles of Agreement. Two days later (presumably while the September 27 letter made its way to Scotland), the Company met and approved the Crawford voyage. In England, *The True Protestant Mercury* advertised the printing of Joel Gascoyne's new map of Carolina in the beginning of October. Two weeks later the Whig sheet reported glowingly on the "hopeful and flourishing condition" of Carolina with particular hopes for vineyards along with olive and mulberry trees for silk production receiving their perennial due.[258]

On November 21, the proprietors advised their colonists that they had agreed to further changes in the Fundamental Constitutions with the "Scots and other considerable persons who intend to be settlers in Carolina."[259] By this time, though, the wheels had already begun to come off. Shaftesbury's efforts to block James collapsed with the Tory seizure of the government of London in September 1682. The selection of pro-government sheriffs, following the riotous failure to swear in alternative Whig sheriffs on September 26, gave the Crown control over jury selection in Middlesex and opened the way finally to indict "Little Sincerity" for treason. Fearing arrest, Shaftesbury went into hiding, apparently the very same night (which makes the date of the letter to the Scots very curious).[260] Nevertheless, he continued plotting with Ferguson, Argyll, Robert West, and others until he became fed up with the waffling of his associates over what courses to take. He fled, under cover of a fire in Wapping on the night of November 19, to Holland where he died on January 21, 1683.[261]

When Crawford of Crawfordland returned to Scotland, then, he must have found matters in an uproar. The departure of Shaftesbury had left his associates, both plotters and colonizers, confused as to their next steps. Plotting, at least for a number of the Scots, took precedence and now we must turn to the embarrassing wealth of depositions collected from Rye-House informants who sought to save their own necks at the expense of their confederates in the summer and autumn of 1683. These inevitably shifted blame on to the shoulders of the deceased, such as Shaftesbury, the exiled, or the already condemned, and away from the deponent and others helping the government with its inquiries. Most of the informers identified Ferguson, "the Plotter" and Carolina promoter, as the brains behind the operation and Ferguson was conveniently across the North Sea in Holland at the time.

These revelations provided the basis for the arrest on treason charges of the Campbells, Crawford (who had returned from Carolina just in time to become implicated), Robert Baillie of Jerviswood, and Algernon Sidney by November 1683.[262] Yet, significantly, notwithstanding the potentially dubious character of the informations, none of these prisoners ever denied the contention that Carolina served as a pretext even though this defense would have offered them the best means of refuting the case against them.

Once the Crown moved against the plotters, a battery of witnesses in England and Scotland testified to the same story. The involvement of Thomas Walcot, Irish landowner, associate of Shaftesbury and former Cromwellian officer, in the activities of the "disaffected" must have especially raised alarm bells.[263] Witnesses generally agreed that Walcot had come to England from Ireland to plot treason at Shaftesbury's, behest in November 1682 under the pretext of becoming governor of Carolina, that Shaftesbury had used the colony as a cover for the coordination of plans with Scottish conspirators, and that, in January 1683, the republican Sidney (a prime governmental target) had sent Smith again to Scotland to bring back Cessnock and Cochrane to London under the pretense of discussing Carolina affairs but, in reality, to plan insurrection or, in the alternative, the assassination of the royal brothers.[264]

At their trial, Sir Hugh and Sir George Campbell confessed to meeting co-conspirators as other witnesses had described.[265] Yet again, significantly, neither they nor any of the defendants in Scotland or England ever denied the testimony that Carolina was a cover for the gathering of Scots in London in 1683 or provided evidence to the contrary: evidence that might have brought escape from execution.[266]

Against this testimony comes the account of Gilbert Burnet, bishop of Salisbury, of the trial of Lowrie of Blackwood, chamberlain to the marquis of

Douglas. According to Burnet, who claimed complete knowledge of "all the steps they made," the sentencing of Blakewood to death for treason on February 7, 1683 "put all the gentry in a great fright." This scare, he claimed, "revived among them a design, that [Sir George] Lockhard had set on foot ten years before, of carrying over a plantation to Carolina." Apparently, the duke of Albany, keen to have large numbers of disaffected people move to America, supported the plan.[267]

Moreover, the earl of Tarras, Commissary Alexander Munro, and James Murray of Philiphaugh all testified that Sir John Cochrane, Munro, and Baillie of Jerviswood had traveled to London under "pretence" of furthering the Carolina project. They met with the Cessnocks, William Carstares (William Dunlop's brother-in-law), and William Veitch with whom they talked of supplying money to Argyll in the Netherlands.[268]

Then there is a remarkably self-serving letter from Ochiltree written to the earl of Aberdeen after Sir John had already been cited by the Scottish Privy Council to appear to answer charges of treason. Cochrane in London had decided to catch Aberdeen up on his Carolina colonization plans in June 1683. Now, Ochiltree informed the chancellor that although the negotiations over the Fundamental Constitutions had not produced an entirely satisfactory result, the highly favorable descriptions of the country that he had received from Crawford and others boded well for the Scottish plantation.

Then, Cochrane proclaimed himself "amased" to hear that the government had laid an indictment for high treason against him for harboring Bothwell rebels. Sir John insisted that he had been abroad at the time of the uprising, that none of his "people" were rebels, and that he had never entertained any rebels. Indeed, he proclaimed that the duke of Albany himself had thanked him for his efforts in tracking down enemies to the state. These new accusations arose at a particularly bad time, he observed, since they might hamper colonization plans. He begged the chancellor to consult with those who would establish his innocence and restore the "good oppinion" of the royal brothers and invited Aberdeen to join the investors.[269]

Of course, the plans came to a halt anyway. Obviously, Shaftesbury's sudden departure interrupted negotiations. However, at the same time, the witness statements seem to agree that by the time the earl went to ground, Carolina had become a convenient cover for the movement of people—not to America, to be sure, but to engage in assassination and rebellion in Britain and Ireland. Sir George Campbell and Sir Patrick Hume fled to Holland while Cochrane and Sir Hugh Campbell were let off with a warning.

To add insult to injury, the Scottish Carolina Company fell into litigation. Happily for historians, but unhappily for Sir Robert Baird and the Edinburgh merchants, whose bemusement at this turn of affairs we can only imagine, this required the cashkeeper to produce his accounts in order to show, undoubtedly to his further annoyance, that his partners owed him money. Sir Robert had dutifully recorded the money he had received and paid out from September 1682, including £17 to Crawford, with a deficit of £56 8s 4d. Significantly, he ceased paying out money after October 11 although he collected some shares up to December 23. Patrick Crawford, a seaman on the nine-month voyage to Carolina to inspect the coast and run the rule over prospective locations for the Scottish plantation won a judgment for back wages after a lengthy suit that Baird, Charters, Mosman, and the other Edinburgh stay-at-homes had to pay.[270]

The collapse of the Scottish Carolina Company did not mean, though, that the idea of fleeing persecution by going to Carolina did not go away, especially when the government commenced another crackdown on the "godly" in Scotland after 1683. But although they talked and thought about removing, they invariably wound up remaining. The wife of the Reverend William Veitch, Argyll's escort on his escape to London, pondered such a move in language remarkably familiar to students of the earlier seventeenth-century migration to New England. Concerned that her God had abandoned Scotland and "His Church" in these "killing times," Mrs. Veitch received a suggestion from her husband that she might consider migrating to Carolina. This notion bred consternation in her mind over whether to stay in "these covenanted lands" or depart: after consulting scripture (notably Habbakuk iii, 17–18 and Matthew x, 23), she decided not to cross the Atlantic.[271]

In the same vein, the preacher Thomas Hog, having been "liberated" from the Bass prison around 1683, after his conviction for "holding private conventicles," was banished by the council who ordered him to depart the country within 48 hours unless he would post a bond of 5,000 merks not to preach. He went to Berwick and then London intending to take the first ship for Carolina, but was rounded up in the wake of the Rye-House Plot. While in his chamber, he resorted to prayer for guidance from which he was interrupted by a mysterious gentleman who engaged him in "a discourse about sufferings for a good God and good cause," gave him £5, and then left. This "interposition of Providence"—an angel, according to Hog—thus turned him away from America.[272]

At the same time, the government continued its assault on intransigents. Refusing to compound, they were offered the choice of transportation to the plantations (usually Carolina) or the block. While some accepted, others, concerned that compromising in any way with a "heretical" government would cast a shadow on their commitment to "true religion," had grave doubts. John Dick, one of these prisoners, regarded transportation, in the end, as an act of providence delivering him from his enemies.

However, Archibald Stewart, a prisoner of conscience in the Glasgow Tolbooth convinced of his salvation, refused to parlay with "Antichrist." Preferring martyrdom to migration to Carolina he was duly executed on March 19, 1685.[273]

John Erskine of Carnock, brother of Lord Cardross, carefully considered migrating at this trying time, as his diary reveals. He met with his brother and a Mr. Gordon, who had knowledge of Carolina "and much commended the country." With the plotters against the government in the Tolbooth or executed, other godly folk gone to serve in the army in Flanders, and the bishops in their pomp, he began to have "some thoughts of going to Carolina" in May 1684. Several considerations, though, particularly his studies and his family, presented themselves in opposition to an American move. At the end of the month, he considered the good character of the parties involved in the plantation project, the reportedly desirable landscape of the province, and especially, the respect accorded religion there. On June 2, he pondered the issue of removing again, seeking to ascertain divine will on the matter. Although this remained frustratingly impossible to ascertain, Erskine ultimately went to join Argyll in Holland.[274]

Changes of heart amongst the "godly" concerning Carolina, whether real or pretext, also made themselves apparent to the government of Ireland, which was concerned both about the movements of Dissenters (at this time, there was frequent communication between the north of Ireland and southwestern Scotland, the home of the Cessnocks and Sir John Cochrane).[275] The bishop of Derry informed the duke of Ormonde, Lord-Lieutenant, in January 1683 of unprecedented correspondence between "phanaticks" in his see and Britain that suggested "some great mischief is now brewing." Many spoke of migrating to Carolina to escape the clutches of the ecclesiastical authorities, but the bishop believed this response to persecution was only raised to convince the "elect" of the need "to fight for their own homes, and drive us from ours."[276] Ormonde received similar news from the bishop of Raphoe and from Newtonstewart during 1683.[277]

By August 4 of that year the scales had fallen from the eyes of the government. An indignant Albany wrote the duke of Queensberry that he was "of your mind that Carolina was only a pretense to carry on their damnable designs."[278] This interpretation passed into general belief by the fall, as all of the colonizing and plotting efforts of the Whigs had come to naught.[279]

Chapter 6 ～

Stuarts Town

Some people picked up the pieces and some did leave the "covenanted lands" for Carolina. On July 1, 1684, Cardross, Dunlop, and their associates took ship aboard the *Carolina Merchant* in the River Clyde along with 35 prisoners from Edinburgh and Glasgow for a total company of 140. Cardross assumed the rights of the Scottish Carolina Company under its Articles of Agreement with the proprietors and planned to set up his colony at Port Royal.[280] At the same time, a Mr Thomas Ferguson informed the proprietors "that himselfe and Divers familyes are Removeing from the north of Ireland to Carolina" and asked that land be set aside for their use. Notwithstanding the reluctance of many "godly" to migrate, the Cardross expedition, followed by Ferguson's colony, raised expectations among the proprietors that 10,000 Scots would make their way to Carolina.[281]

Unfortunately, these expectations ran into setbacks from the outset. Initially, it took three weeks for a "fair wind" to blow up so the company could weigh anchor.[282] While waiting to depart Greenock, the notorious master of the *Carolina Merchant*, James Gibson (brother of Walter, "a very evil man"), along with a "corrupt" Dunlop apparently contrived to deprive the imprisoned passengers of money and cloth that well-wishers had brought to them and provided them with minimal food "with a little beer" and no water. When the prisoners—Cameronians as opposed to the Cardross settlers, who were led by moderate presbyterians—objected to hearing sermons from Dunlop, who had compounded, in radical eyes, by accepting a license to preach from the bishops, and to singing psalms with him, Gibson drew his sword on them. When John Dick arrived in Carolina, Dunlop allegedly refused to honor the £30 bond he had paid to substitute for the share of his freight and took the prisoner as his servant and he died. While still in Greenock, Gibson kidnapped Elizabeth Linning when she came on board to visit the prisoners. Taken to Carolina, she was able to escape to

Governor Morton who provided her with an attorney and convened a court where Gibson confessed his behavior and she was released.[283]

In addition to engaging in kidnapping, the Gibsons and Dunlop allegedly paid scant heed to the need of the transportees, who suffered from "ill usage at sea, getting little meat or drink, and what they got being for most part rotten herrings and corrupt water." From these highly dubious beginnings, then, Stuarts Town took root but never served as the beacon for godly arrivals that its leaders had hoped.[284]

Then, even before Cardross arrived in the colony, a number of Carolinians had taken umbrage both with the proprietary proposals to change the Fundamental Constitutions as well as to the notion of a semi-autonomous county on their southern boundary, to the shock and dismay of the Lords. The proprietors quickly identified the enslavers of Indians as the masterminds behind this "Jealousy": the proposed reforms would have given the parliament authority over their trading activities while turning to jury selection by lot would have broken their control (as colonial officials) over the courts. Instead, then, of welcoming proprietary attempts to further secure the liberties and curbing the oppression of their settlers, the "great men in ye Government" convinced the people "that wee did intend thereby to inslave them."[285]

The opponents to the 1682 Constitutions, such as Percival, framed their arguments around the supposedly immutable character of the original version. They claimed that there could only be one set of "fundamentalls" and that they had sworn their allegiance to the July 1669 document to which the proprietors had affixed their seals.[286] To switch versions now without "the advice and consent of the freeholders" would, they claimed, set a precedent enabling the proprietors to change the nature of the constitution whenever they felt like doing so.[287]

The nature of the 1682 changes makes the substantive objections of these settlers unclear since the proprietors had only amended the original Constitutions to devolve more responsibility for government on the colonists. Indeed, none of the changes appears to contain language that leading South Carolinians could have found objectionable (perhaps least of all the clarification of the master–slave relationship that resulted in the new Section 109 noted earlier). Most of the alterations made in the March 1, 1670 version were procedural. The Lords refined the character of the proprietorship itself, clarified the creation and "dignities" of the aristocracy (including providing for the courts-leet), redrew the court system, established registries for recording land transactions, births, deaths, and marriages, and created organs of local government, such as constables and mayors. A broader change required parliament to enter into "a free and full debate" when any proprietor or deputy protested against any act. If "the major part of any of" the proprietors, the landgraves, the cassiques, and the commons voted against a bill, then parliament was to throw it out.[288]

Thus, the opposition reasoning stunned the proprietors and many settlers who regarded the July 1669 edition as an imperfect work-in-progress, one that had been superseded in any event by the temporary laws put into effect when the first settlers arrived at Ashley River. At that time, matters in England intervened before a final draft could be ready to go with the "first fleet." So a rough copy, notwithstanding the proprietary seals, was sent to give people on Barbados an idea of the proposed governmental frame. The Lords insisted that "not soe much as a Copy was kept by us and this was long before Any persone Landed in South Carolina to begin the Settlement there soe that we doe not, Nor ever did own the Constitutions dated the 21st of July 1669."[289] To the proprietors, the January 1682 edition (the August document remained a draft since Shaftesbury had departed in haste during its preparation), which "differ[ed] very little from those of the 1st of March 1669[70]," provided an even higher degree of protection for their settlers.[290]

Since the reservations expressed by opponents made no apparent sense, the proprietors strongly suspected that they served as a cover for the machinations of the Goose Creek men, for whom a settled government and a corresponding boost in migration posed a direct threat. These "dealers in Indians" certainly annoyed the Lords with their "bost they could with a bole of Punch" gain control of the government and then pass laws against selling arms to Indians—which they enforced against their enemies and ignored themselves.[291]

Mathews and his men made no scruples either in their logic or in their schemes to block what they regarded as interference with their plans for continued personal enrichment via the Indian trade. However, they did not oppose the concept of proprietary rule nor did they necessarily oppose the Fundamental Constitutions in principle. Even in 1691, they still insisted on adhering to the draft of July 1669, although the proprietors had never approved it. At the same time, the Indian slavers maintained the fiction of equating constitutional change with tyranny.[292]

These views carried the day notwithstanding the fear of supporters of constitutional government that discarding the "fundamentals" would mean the end of religious toleration, naturalization, land registers, and other colonial rights and privileges. Yet, their efforts to expose the pretensions of the Mathews cohort—again to the amazement and consternation of the Lords, who again feared for the future security and strength of their colony without a settled government—failed.[293]

A careful examination of the record supports the proprietary suspicions about the character of opposition to the Fundamental Constitutions. Moreover, the response of the Indian traders to the Cardross settlement provides additional support for the conclusion that these Goose Creek men generally opposed the twin concepts of settled government and "peopling" favored by their fellow colonists: the successful spread of settlement would have threatened the Indian partners of these traders and the establishment of constitutional government would have, correspondingly, threatened the control of the colony that Mathews and his associates exercised via the illegal Indian slave trade.

By 1684, the tumults of the Westo Wars and the distractions of English affairs had permitted the "dealers in Indians" to gain the ascendancy as the surviving Lords, particularly Craven, the sole remaining original proprietor, now assumed the reins in the aftermath of Shaftesbury's departure and Carolina's entanglement with disaffection. In the spring of that year, they commissioned two veteran officers from the army in Ireland, conceivably on the recommendation of the duke of Ormonde, to serve in their administration. Sir Richard Kyrle, who had commanded a company of foot in that kingdom, became governor.[294] Robert Quarry, an officer in the Irish infantry, arrived as a proprietary deputy and clerk of the court.[295]

Whether or not Kyrle and Quarry knew each other in Ireland remains unknown but the proprietors intended that they work together, with Quarry to serve as a deputy governor, to restore order and integrate the new Scottish settlement into the colony. Sir Richard received instructions on how to pursue the tall order of breaking the power of the Goose Creek men—who had, for instance, now assumed the power to choose members of the Grand Council whenever they felt the need to do so—as they continued to ignore repeated proprietary injunctions and warnings against enslaving Indians.

As a first step, the Lords ordered their new administration to deprive Mathews, their long-time servant and "Ringleader" of the slave trade, of all of his offices. Then, "some weake & evill minded men have been perswading the people that they would find wayes how to avoide paying us the penny per Aker rent," even though the rents did not fall due until 1689, the proprietors directed Kyrle to maintain their preferrred practice of granting land by indenture and quitrent, although, if grantees preferred to purchase their land, the Lords would agree to sell it for 12 pence per acre after seven years.[296]

They also recommended that Sir Richard strive, where previous governments had failed, to create more towns in the colony in order to promote security and trade and they instructed the new governor to annul an act that the parliament had passed to suspend prosecutions for foreign debt. As with the Indian slave trade, the opposition to quitrents, and the negligence with respect to town-building, the proprietors lamented, those into whose hands they had placed the care of Carolina had manifested little regard for proper government and justice. Now, by barring actions to recover foreign debt, they observed, the Carolinians "publish to the world that any man who takes his neighbor's goods has only to come to Carolina and he will protected by law." If the sheriffs or justices of the County Courts had anything to do with this bill, Kyrle was to dismiss them.

Furthermore, elections, crucial to control of the government, had remained a root problem. Contrary to instructions, they had been held on different days in Berkeley and Colleton counties in 1683. The proprietors told Kyrle he should dissolve the parliament elected in this way and "hold a new election for both counties on the same day, that persons may not have the opportunity to run from place to place, and awe the people, and hinder freedom of election." They also reminded him that grants of office made by governors remained temporary until upheld by the Lords.[297] Last but not least, Kyrle was to take care of the Scottish colony, which was to serve as the seat of the new Port Royal County.[298]

Unfortunately, the best-laid proprietary plans again fell apart, for Sir Richard died almost immediately after he arrived in South Carolina on the heels of the Cardross settlers. West had left the province for health reasons, so the Grand Council chose Quarry as interim governor (not unreasonably since the Lords had suggested to Kyrle that he appoint Quarry as his deputy). This officer, though, threw in with the Goose Creek men (since they constituted the most powerful faction in the colony at this time, it seems unlikely that Quarry would have acquired office without their acquiescence). Thus, Mathews and his friends easily retained their commanding political position. The inevitable delays in transatlantic affairs meant that the proprietors did not even acknowledge receipt of the demise of the governor until the following March. They did not know yet that West had departed for Boston and Quarry had assumed the governorship and they thought Morton, as the resident landgrave, had returned to office.[299]

Kyrle's death and the quick return to the status quo predictably created more election headaches. This time, Berkeley County, headquarters of the Goose Creek men, objected to the proposed selection of an equal number of members of parliament from each county; Berkeley demanded representation based upon population—naturally since Berkeley contained more inhabitants than Port Royal or, more significantly, Colleton County where many of the enemies of the Indian slavers lived. The Lords, again, could not understand the objections to the accepted way of doing things unless those objections stemmed from ulterior or base motives. They asked a series of rhetorical questions that set forth the benefits of the metropolitan system of selecting parliamentary representatives, concluding that the only reason for objecting to equal county representation must be, "as persons of very good creditt have written us from Carolina," that it attacked the position of the Mathews cohort.

The Goose Creek scheme of proportional representation, the proprietors further observed, placed the government of Carolina in the iron grip of the "dealers in Indians." They could then choose whomever they wished for parliament and the Grand Council, pass whatever laws (and ignore them) they pleased, and cater to the popular whim by advocating the nonpayment of quitrents. The Lords again warned that this sort of behavior "makes sober and considering men weary of living amongst you, And others cautions of comeing to you." To prevent this unhappy result, the proprietors first directed that each county should select four members of parliament. But, significantly, they continued with their original philosophy of delegating responsibility: the governor received the power to appoint proprietary deputies when sudden vacancies occurred in order to keep the government running. The Lords also maintained their willingness to sell, rather than rent, land if grantees wished while they continued to insist that grantees sign deeds. Officials who did not follow instructions (such as the Indian slavers Mathews, James Moore, and Arthur Middleton) were to be dismissed forthwith.[300]

Predictably, Mathews and Moore circumvented the rules for selection set forth in the Fundamental Constitutions and the Temporary Laws to rejoin the Grand Council in place of Andrew Percival and Bernard Schenkingh "although," as the Lords noted wryly, "Mr Percivall hath not been absent two yeares, & how Mr Skenging came to cease to be one of the Grand Councill we know not." The selection of Mathews and Moore also apparently came "by open voyce" and "by surprize, & when there was not yet ye full proportion of Members suffered to sit in ye house." Mathews and John Boone also contrived to become deputies even though this "illegal choice" was "an Incroachment upon ye peoples Libertyes of Choice."[301]

Thus, the Cardross settlers arrived in a deeply divided Carolina. Having disposed of Woodward and established themselves as the preeminent force in the colony, Mathews and his associates had moved to cement their position. Joseph Morton, Daniel Axtell, and other planters, many of them post-1680 arrivals and radical Protestants, opposed their machinations and supported ratification of the Fundamental Constitutions as well as the intended Scottish settlement on the colony's southern frontier.

The threat posed by Stuarts Town to their interests obliged the "dealers in Indians" to administer a *coup de grace* to the endeavor. Luckily for the Goose Creek men, the Scottish plans quickly degenerated from an unpromising start: their voyage from Glasgow had generated controversy and different reports on, particularly, fatalities. Upon arrival, Cardross and Dunlop reported to Sir Peter Colleton that the sickly air in Carolina "took away great many of our number and discoraged others" so that they deserted the colony. Then, a sister ship bearing settlers from Belfast sank within sight of Charles Town. This pair of disasters proved nearly fatal in themselves to the design, reducing its numbers to 51 and convincing another shipload of Scots to settle elsewhere. Still, the battered remnant persevered and established itself at the promising location of Port Royal.[302]

There, they laid out their colony in a healthy climate next to a fine harbor. Forty-one of the 220 "toun lots" were promptly granted out, while a number of English families expressed interest in moving south to the settlement. Also, "ther are severall families coming to us from Antego and other plantations," possibly Scots.[303]

Indigo looked a likely commodity and prospects for expansion glittered. Cardross asked permission to claim Santa Catarina, which the Spanish had abandoned upon news of the establishment of Stuarts Town. It also seemed possible to connect Port Royal to the mines of New Mexico. As for the neighboring Indians, they desired commerce and the Scots desired to oblige. Most significantly, the Yamassees, "the most considerable of them all," had left St. Augustine and attached themselves to Stuarts Town. Although still at a preliminary stage, the trade the Yamassees promised "may verie probablie be considerable and advantageous" if the proprietors would approve it.[304]

Unfortunately, the Goose Creek men had other ideas. The proprietors themselves noted, "the Lord Cardross and others [were] affronted and barbarously used the first day of their landing in Carolina by those very men that promoted the rejections of the amendments" to the Fundamental Constitutions. According to Dunlop, whose letters offer us the widest view on the colony during the period between 1684 and 1688, although West, Morton, Percival, Paul Grimball, and others had treated the Scots courteously and encouragingly "ther were some upon the place who wold be esteemed grate men there, who not only did what they could to discoradge us to setle here, but both used us uncivilie and dealt with severall of our number to deserte us, which some did."[305]

Then, Cardross had the effrontery to attempt to compete with the established interests on the Carolina frontier. His plans to exploit western mines and involve himself in the Indian trade, especially with the numerous and powerful allies of the Goose Creek men, the Yamassees, did "already provock the Inevey of severall particular persons, who, meinding their own privat Intrist mor than that of the lords proprietors or the good of the province" moved to "opres our designe and endeavour to render us contemptible in the eyes of the Indians about us."[306]

The ultimate result of this opposition, though, remained beneath the horizon in January 1685 as the Scots ensconced themselves at Port Royal and more Yamassees had joined them.[307] Caleb Westbrook, an English trader and spy, reported to Charles Town that over a thousand Yamassees and three "nations of Spanish Indians" had arrived, with more expected daily, including ten caciques. Westbrook noted defensive concerns for Carolina in this mass gathering, which he suspected the Spaniards of orchestrating. While he awaited instructions from his overseers, three Yamassee cassiques had led an attack on the Spanish allies, the Timacuas.[308]

This Westbrook may also have acted as an *agent provacateur* on behalf of Mathews and his associates hoping to draw the Scots into a frontier war with St. Augustine as well as with various Indian peoples. Such a result, conceivably, would have resulted in defeat for either Stuarts Town or the Spaniards, both rivals of the English traders, which would have completely cleared the way for the enslavers of Indians to continue their dubious activities. The Yamassees by this time constituted the leading trade partner of the Goose Creek men and, conceivably, could have been encouraged or provoked into an attack on the Scottish settlement. At least two other observers saw Westbrook in the company of the Stuarts Town leaders in their negotiations with Indians and one suggested that he had encouraged Cardross to support the attack on the Timacuas. Why a new frontier settlement containing just 51 inhabitants would have plunged into an immediate provocation of the Spanish and their friends—unless it had received some sort of encouragement from elsewhere (namely Charles Town through Westbrook)—remains entirely unclear.[309]

But other opportunities to eliminate this competition presented themselves. First, the Goose Creek men moved to render the Scots "contemptible" in the eyes of the proprietors as well as the Indians. This scheme bears a remarkable resemblance to the *coup* against Dr. Woodward and the Westos when the Carolina government (i.e., the Goose Creek men) collected "proof" of frontier treachery, which it then used against its enemies. Curiously, Woodward himself was involved, this time on the side of his old enemy, Maurice Mathews. In any event, the plan against the Scots started with the "arrest" by Westbrook and one Thomas Hambleton (aka John Hamilton), purportedly on the authority of Lord Cardross (although Cardross's involvement remains unproven), of Woodward and five other Englishmen for entering the "Scotch precincts" without license. After an immediate protest from Charles Town, the traders were speedily released.

They then promptly appeared, with "several Yamassee Indians," before Mathews and his associates in the Grand Council, Quarry, John Godfrey, John Moore, and Thomas Gibbes, to swear a series of affidavits alleging that Cardross sought to bar English traders from the area south of St. Helena upon pain of imprisonment, that the Scots regarded themselves as an independent settlement from Carolina, and that the Scots had sent Westbrook to attack the Timacuas and seize them as slaves thereby threatening to plunge the entire region into an Indian war. Significantly, the supposedly antiproprietary councilors duly relayed this testimony to the Lords.[310]

The Charles Town government then directed Westbrook to take a Scottish prisoner and make a fuller report on Stuarts Town without telling

Cardross. At the same time, the Carolinians ignored Scottish concerns about allegedly sinister activity on the part of the Spanish and certain notorious Indians. Finally, the Grand Council issued a warrant for Cardross's arrest when he failed to appear before its inquiry into the alleged arrest of the English traders.

For his part, the Scottish leader pleaded illness for preventing his appearance and assured the Grand Council of his continuing loyalty to Charles Town. It seems likely, given the relative strength of the colonies, along with the hostility of the English, that Cardross's plea of illness coupled with his declaration of fidelity and his petition to the proprietors for blank deputations indicates an attempt to flex (and acquire) political muscles against the Mathews group.[311]

Another front in the campaign against the Scots opened with what hagiographers have regarded as a kind of Carolina Grand Remonstrance: 12 members of the Commons House of Assembly publicly refused to subscribe to the new "fundamentalls," claiming the original July 1669 version was "unalterable." Morton, now back in the governor's chair, excluded these legislators from their chamber for their refusal. Protesting, for their part, their loyalty, the dismissed legislators and their supporters decried the governor.[312]

Then, on August 17, 1686, "3 Spanish halfe Gallies with 155 men" sacked Stuarts Town. From Port Royal, the invaders moved up the coast where "plundered Mr Grimballs & two of the Govrs [Mortons] plantations carried away from him 17 Negroes & whyt servants & destroyed another plantation of Mr Axtells." The Spanish then departed in the advance of a hurricane and the march of 200 Carolinians.[313]

Dunlop now pondered the question of starting over. With the woods already reclaiming the cleared ground and livestock running wild, time was of the essence if the Scots hoped to limit their losses. To encourage rebuilding, he lobbied Charles Town to undertake a revenge attack against Florida and, along with Cardross, persuaded the Huguenots to consider moving south to Stuarts Town. He also advocated the expediency of "purchasing Negroes at Barbadoes soe these are the only profitable Servants & with the leist Charge are maintained; both in clothing & Victualls [which] whyte Servts doe abundantly consume."[314]

The end of November saw rising optimism: a reprisal force was ready to march on St. Augustine, Dunlop had laid in a substantial herd of cattle at Charles Town, and he remained confident that the French would lend their strength to the rebuilt Stuarts Town.[315] However, in December, the Spanish returned to finish the job, not only destroying the remnants of the first invasion, but also the enthusiasm of the Huguenots for Port Royal.[316]

The Spanish attacks may constitute the highlight, albeit temporary, of the career of Maurice Mathews. Again in parallel with his Westo triumph,

Mathews lit the touch paper of war and then sat back and watched the confla-
gration ruin his enemies. Cardross and his settlers, the plantations of Morton,
Axtell, and Grimball, and those Yamassees (also attacked by the Spanish) who
had had the temerity to trade with Stuarts Town bore the brunt. To complete
the victory, the invasion would have rebounded onto the invaders, long-
standing competitors in the Indian trade of the Goose Creek men: the
outraged Carolinians quickly mobilized to attack St. Augustine and it is
perhaps significant that such an assault would have violated the peace then
existing between England and Spain; had it taken place, could have resulted
in the execution for treason for the anti-Mathews governor, Morton.[317]

Only the coincidental arrival of a new governor, James Colleton, and his
declaration of martial law prevented the reprisal from going forward. In the
aftermath of the whole Stuarts Town debacle, the Lords directed Sir Peter
Colleton to inquire into the whole affair. What Sir Peter discovered
convinced him "of ye insollent behavior of soom in Carolina" toward Lord
Cardross and his followers. Most particularly, he dismissed the claims
advanced by the Goose Creek men that the Scots had plotted frontier war.
Instead, he found, undoubtedly to his shock, that his former client Mathews
lay at the bottom of the whole affair. Sir Peter learned that Mathews had
encouraged "the Yamassee Indians to Rob plunder of the Spanish Ch[urch]es
who had brought away great quantityes of church plate rich copes and altar
vestments" and "to mack the trouble appeare by other hands if any complaint
shall be made thereof by the spayniards." Sir Peter's former client had then
"caused the information to be given the Spanish Ambassador" and "privitely
endeavoured to insinuate to the Roman Catholicks feare that the Indians
were sent on to Rob and Spoyll the Spanish Churches by [Lord Cardross]
owt of your hatred to the Roman Catholick Religion." Hence, the "revenge"
attacks on the Scots and the Yamassees who, Mathews suggested to the
Spanish, had carried out the attacks on the churches.[318]

The discovery of this treasonable double-dealing resulted in an eclipse of
Goose Creek power just at the moment when it might have held sway before
all. Instead, Colleton, with the support of Landgrave Thomas Smith,
Grimball, John Stewart, and other enemies of Mathews, now held the upper
hand. According to Smith, Mathews now began to ponder breaking away
from the authority of Charles Town. The landgrave informed Dunlop, then
preparing to return to Britain, that "severall discontented gent: in this country to bee on ye wing for Catte Island [northeast of Charles Town] where
they hopes may live without interruption by men of Sense which they
abhorr." There, they had formed a government in which "M[aurice]
M[athews] is to Governor Councillor Judge of all County &c." "Although,"
Smith observed, "some of us on shore laugh in our sleeves att ye Government

they have fancied & appointed for yt Island," these pretensions had to be exposed for the preservation of the colony.

On Cat Island, Mathews may have also concluded that he needed new patrons in the metropolis for protection. By a fortunate coincidence, *HMS Drake* then arrived in Charles Town with a captain, Thomas Spragg, apparently willing to align himself with the Goose Creek men. Spragg's behavior remains something of a mystery but Dunlop's friend John Stewart later vehemently complained "how that piratical Roage," apparently abetted by James Moore, "had damaged the planters in 2000l. value" thereby "ruining many familes" while leaving "a staine and Blott that yow in Gooscreek will nevr be able to wipe of [f]." His "other illegall villanies"—including the seizure of another ship's master and "receaves of Negros Runing from their Masters"—"deserv'd hanging if he could [have] been gott." Instead, to Stewart's indignation, "at that tyme when he wes in his height of pryde and illegall extravagancy lik a pirat rather than a King's Captan yet the Grandees and pillars of the province forsooth caresses cajols and banquets him as if he had been a good man and high admirall of England." Consorting with Captain Spragg, the sworn enemy of Sir Peter Colleton, gave Mathews access to Spragg's own patrons, Samuel Pepys, Admiralty Secretary, and Pepys's superiors, the Lord Admiral Lord Dartmouth, and James II himself.[319]

For his part, Spragg found occasion to send a "packquet" of documents to Pepys under cover of a warning about the activities of his "Enymy" Sir Peter Colleton, opponent of the government of James II and proprietary friend of Smith, Axtell, Morton, and the other foes of the Goose Creek men. Although the "pacquet" itself remains lost, this letter suggests a government interest in and, possibly a relationship with, through Spragg, Mathews and the other "Catt Islanders."[320]

The Goose Creek leader apparently tried to use these connections when Dunlop made plans to join Cardross who had moved to London to consider his next step in conjunction with the proprietors. Carolina's "men of sense" gave the Scot a copy of the colony's charter with which to argue against the Cat Island scheme before the Lords. Since the metropolitan friends of these "discontented gentlemen" had retired from public life or died, the prospects for curbing the pretensions of Mathews and the others looked favorable. Smith, though, warned Dunlop of a plan "discoursed at Goose Creek" and involving Spragg, to maroon him in the Bahamas or leave him aboard another vessel—although, in the end, Spragg's irons missed their target.[321]

Thus, the Stuarts Town experiment subsided. Dunlop ultimately rejoined Cardross—using alternative transport to *HMS Drake*—when it became apparent that few of his cohorts were willing to try again. But all turned out reasonably well for the survivors: the popish king, James VII (James II in

England), fled his thrones in December 1688 and the forces of the "godly" defeated his supporters when they tried to rally. This meant that William of Orange had to accept Presbyterianism as the Church of Scotland as part of the deal that brought him to the Scottish throne. After 1689, with "true religion" established, Carstares, Cessnock, and other Dutch exiles assumed positions of prominence in the government while William Dunlop became principal of the University of Glasgow.[322]

Regrets from some Carolinians at their departure and exhortations for their return did not lure Cardross and Dunlop back to Charles Town. These entreaties (which also indicate that "Goose Creek" complicity in the Spanish attack had come to be fairly common knowledge by April 1690) fell on deaf ears: circumstances in Scotland had changed and, perhaps, Dunlop and Cardross had no desire to again put themselves at the mercy of Mathews and his friends.[323]

Surely, though, the failure of their enterprise and the cessation of Scottish interest because of the treachery at Goose Creek had profound consequences for South Carolina. In the first place, the proprietary expectations of 10,000 migrants from Scotland—whether or exaggerated or not—did not materialize. Had a fraction of these numbers appeared—had the Goose Creek men not "affronted Lord Cardross" and discouraged Morton and Axtell in the mid-1680s, not rejected the Fundamental Constitutions and placed the government of the colony in an uproar, the number of white inhabitants of South Carolina would undoubtedly have increased, perhaps markedly.[324] Instead, prospective migrants to Carolina changed their minds "which is the reason," the proprietors noted, "why so few have come to you but the French."[325] Those whites who did arrive—and survive—lived in a place they termed "more like a Negro country" by the first quarter of the eighteenth century, even though some of this demographic development came from a preference for slave labor (the proportion of which had become increasingly African by 1710) and the achievement of rice cultivation that had also come to manifest itself by 1690.[326]

Stewart's letters to his friend Dunlop give us a relatively clear window into developments in the colony at this time and this correspondent tells us that the arrival of James Colleton as governor in November 1687—even though it halted the revenge attack on St. Augustine—signaled the beginning of a period of further tumult. The Goose Creek men viewed Colleton's presence as another fundamental threat and they spared no pains to destroy him and his supporters. The resulting furor nearly tore the colony apart at the seams.

Chapter 7 ~

Treachery

Unaware of the Spanish attack on their colony, the proprietors actually named Colleton as governor to deal with the festering problem of piracy.[327] Like the Indian slave trade, trafficking with pirates offered a lucrative, disruptive, and illegal way to American advancement; both royal authorities and the proprietors had a difficult time keeping it in check. Pirates roaming the Caribbean found Charles Town a convenient and safe haven in the seventeenth century and continued to linger on the scene until the local government finally took vigorous action to suppress them in 1718.[328]

With a close connection between their province and pirates a matter of public record, the Lords periodically urged their colonists to separate themselves from seagoing predators, instructing Kyrle in 1684 to pass legislation barring pirates and providing penalties against them and their Carolina confederates.[329] Although the act was passed on November 23, 1685, in reality, of course, proprietary efforts to halt piracy remained dependent upon local cooperation. As long as Quarry, Boone, and other prominent Carolinians (accusations also fell against Morton, but the grounds for these remain murky—they could have been smoke blown from Goose Creek) turned a blind eye or provided active encouragement to their activities, corsairs continued to use the colony as a base for their predations. Alerted that their colonists continued to harbor these threats to commerce, the proprietors dispatched Colleton from Barbados to put teeth into the antipirate campaign, ordering him to arrest Morton and Quarry on charges of encouraging pirates and privateers and to remove the latter from all of his offices. In the end, though, the new law merely served as a blind for the operations of the latter, perhaps the biggest friend to pirates in the colony, who assumed charge of the government after Kyrle's death.[330]

Indeed, the proprietors feared that piracy had become so well entrenched in Carolina that they initially believed that Spanish had attacked Stuarts

Town and the coastal plantations out of anger at the Carolinians for harboring pirates.[331] Of course, this invasion had really come at the instigation of Mathews, about which both the proprietors and Colleton remained unaware until the results of the inquiry made the following year surfaced. The governor, armed with his commission to drive freebooters from the province, happened to arrive with no knowledge of the destruction wrought by the colony's neighbors and found the settlers in the midst of their preparations of their revenge on St. Augustine. The immediate need to cool tempers pushed the piracy issue to the back; the governor's first order of business became stopping the intended illegal assault on Florida, to try and sort out what had happened (and why) and to devise an appropriate (and legal) response to the Spanish attack—so he declared martial law.[332]

While Colleton remained in the dark, Mathews knew very well what had happened and why. Although apparently not unduly troubled by conscience, this "Jesuit for Designe politick but his secrets are open to all fawning and flattering when he intends deepest to kill or stab"—as John Stewart later described him—had considerable reason to regard the presence of this particular governor and his declaration with alarm.

In the first place, martial law prevented Mathews from grasping complete control over the frontier trade. His allies, the Yamassees, ranged far inland for the slaves that brought wealth and power to the Goose Creek men, while the Spanish had eliminated the Stuarts Town competition. That left St. Augustine itself and Carolina had been poised to drive away those competitors. Instead, though, everything had come to a screeching halt, at least temporarily.

Then, the arrival of the new governor posed a special obstacle to Mathews's schemes since by this time the once-cordial relationship between this "dealer in Indians" and the Colleton family had degenerated into bitter enmity. Around 1690, Mathews revealed to Stewart on at least two occasions his hatred of the Colletons and their friends.[333]

Although no direct proof exists, especially since Mathews himself created very few documents, the commission of Sir Peter Colleton's brother as governor probably meant even more to the Goose Creek leader than an effort to eliminate correspondence with pirates and to stop the Indian slave trade: it meant a showdown with his former patrons. This was a high-stakes challenge that Mathews could, by no means, afford to lose. If the Colletons prevailed, not only would his slave trading empire have come to an end, but his plot with the Spanish would come to light: a conviction for engaging in such a conspiracy would have meant the block. This reality goes a long way to explaining the intensity bordering on ferocity with which the Goose Creek men fought James Colleton and his supporters between 1687 and 1694, including the plot, noted above, to kidnap and maroon William Dunlop so that he could not report in person to the proprietors.

Happily for Mathews, he still had plenty of resources at his disposal. In addition to his "second," James Moore, Quarry, Percival, John Boone, Job How, John Coming, "Mad" Ralph Izard, Robert Daniel, Robert Stevens, and John Beresford all appeared among the "Goosquill enemys" of Stewart, Morton, Grimball, and other planters at this time.[334] Also, to help make up the numbers necessary to manage the Carolina parliament, Mathews and his associates recruited the support of the Huguenots who, as we have seen, had begun to migrate in relatively large numbers to the colony after 1684. Stuarts Town had required special handling: the Scots lived at the edge of Charles Town's authority, had powerful connections themselves, had goals that directly conflicted with the Indian slave traders, and knew the ins and outs of the early modern British political world. On the other hand, the French, as the leading student of this aspect of Carolina settlement has noted, who were politically naïve both in the ways of English-style politics and in the peculiarities of the Carolina scene, found themselves lost when they arrived. Moreover, the Huguenots, unlike the Scots, had no eye on the Indian trade. Thus, they not only posed no threat to Mathews, but they could be readily manipulated.

Axtell, the Blakes, and Morton would have expected these refugees from the *dragonnades* of Louis XIV to join them as a matter of course, especially since the Whig Sir Peter Colleton had arranged their recruitment from the proprietary end. Religious exile, though, had not made these *nouveaux arrivistes* enemies of "absolute" monarchy. Ironically, the Huguenots feared the disorder proffered by republicanism more than the tyranny of late seventeenth-century kingship. The Goose Creek men—friends of Pepys, the earl of Dartmouth, and, by extension, James II—would not have required much to enlist the French settlers in a struggle to prevent sympathizers to regicide and other outrageous notions from gaining ascendancy in the colony. Certainly, the Huguenots later did what the Goose Creek men told them to do in the matters of Seth Sothell and the 1704 Test Act.[335]

The submission of the French to leadership from Goose Creek enraged the opponents of the "dealers in Indians." Kindled by general English xenophobia and particular fears of French things after war broke out between the two countries in 1689, the supporters of migration, in a further irony, turned on the largest contingent of settlers in the colony: they passed a series of laws that prevented French nationals from owning property, from voting, and even from marrying outside the Church of England.[336] For Mathews and his associates, sacrificing their Huguenot allies to these passions, if necessary, posed no hardship (especially since they do not seem to have suffered overly from pangs of conscience in the first place): at worst, the French would depart the colony in the face of the hostility; at best, they would remain staunch allies.[337]

After almost twenty years in the colony, Mathews also knew what buttons to press to bring other Carolinians over to his colors. Like many early modern English gentry, the colonists were jealous of their perceived liberties and suspicious of the actions and motives of central authority. After the arrival of Colleton, Mathews and his friends used these feelings to advantage by emphasizing the "threats" to liberty posed by martial law, the efforts to have the Fundamental Constitutions ratified, and the payment of quitrents to the Lords that were scheduled to start falling due in 1689. Certainly, the proprietors favored ratification and quitrent collection. But, Mathews and his associates regarded these questions as important at the local level. If the Carolinians approved any version of the Constitutions and began paying their quitrents, the enemies of the "geese of Utopia" could gain the upper hand in the political struggle, perhaps permanently. Thus, although both of these questions necessarily involved proprietary authority, the real target of the Goose Creek men remained their local opposition: the tireless Stewart, Landgrave Smith, secretary Grimball, and Bernard Schenkingh.[338]

The "dealers in Indians" targeted these opponents rather than the proprietors because any characterization of the Constitutions as "oppressive" or the rents as "onerous" made no sense upon careful examination, as the Lords tried to make clear time and time again. Nor, did Smith and company constitute a "proprietary party." Indeed, under the first application of direct proprietary pressure on the political scene, in 1695, the "resistance" to paying quitrents quickly collapsed. The hyperbole and disingenuousness spread from Goose Creek, though, was sufficient to raise constant confusion and doubt, which, in the end, kept the colony off-balance—and this was sufficient both to maintain control over the Indian trade and to shield Mathews from prosecution. First, then, the Goose Creek men led objections to paying quitrents in specie on the reasonable grounds that the colony lacked hard currency. Then, after the proprietors readily amended their requirements to permit payment in commodities, the anti-rent party balked again, raising complaints about the form of the indentures that bound the grantee to pay.

Why did the Goose Creek faction oppose Constitutions and quitrents if they did not oppose the proprietors? In the first place, the establishment of constitutional government, it bears repeating, would have given the Carolina government greater authority to regulate the Indian trade and eliminate Indian slavery, the basis of Goose Creek power and wealth. As for the payment of quitrents, the Lords had earmarked that income, as everybody concerned knew, for paying the salaries of their officials. Since, by 1687, Colleton, Grimball, and other Goose Creek opponents held the top offices, a refusal to pay rents would have deprived them of their compensation: they would have had to serve without a salary or resign their positions. The results? More governmental confusion and paralysis at worst or, better, the return to power of Mathews, Moore, Quarry, and friends who did not need to concern themselves so much with the perquisites of office but who always craved political control over their rivals.

An opportunity to deal a blow to Governor Colleton and regain the initiative soon presented itself. Once the fever to attack the Spanish subsided, Colleton restored normal governmental service by calling a parliament in February 1689. Any meeting of this institution, though, provided meat and drink for the Goose Creek men as Mathews could use his sizeable faction and political savvy to orchestrate matters and the power of government for his own ends, as in the case of the Westo War. Now, noting that Colleton "was extremely in the good opinion of the people when he first assumed the Government" and their "power gone unless they could destroy that good opinion," Mathews and company "offered to pass an Act for an excise on imported liquors for his benefit, and in order to pass it made him turn out many [proprietary] deputies and disoblige others." Colleton's own naivete and cupidity played the governor into their hands. After he agreed to this plan to fund his salary, the Goose Creek men turned around and told "their friends in Parliament to hinder the bill, and then cried out against the avarice of the Governor, who would enslave and ruin the people. Then having damaged his good name they contemned and opposed him." The parliament ended on poor terms.[339]

In the meantime, the "Glorious Revolution" had swept Mathews's metropolitan patrons—James II, Dartmouth, and Pepys—from power. This turn of events, though, probably did not pose any particular philosophical difficulties for a man described as "on[e] of Hobses creatures yea I may say [a] linsy Wolsy atheist," even though it restored luster to Sir Peter Colleton's star.[340] Moreover, it produced an unexpected benefit in the form of Sir Nathaniel Johnson.

Unsurprisingly, given his deep animosity toward the Colletons, when Johnson arrived in Carolina in August 1689 he declined to make the customary approaches to Sir Peter's brother, the governor. Instead, Sir Nathaniel, according to John Stewart, wrote making his apologies that he had the gout, "a disease," the Scot claimed, "I never knew him to have nor evr proved him subject to since." At the same time, Mathews and his friends hastened to pay their respects to the baronet, the Goose Creek leader constantly inveighing against the Colletons, the Fundamental Constitutions, and Stewart—while, at the same time, working to ingratiate himself in the newcomer's mind, which the latter, as Johnson's advisor on rice and silk cultivation, tried, perhaps quixotically, to prevent.

Fearing that Stewart might undo his labors, Mathews insisted, first, that the Goose Creek planter Job How ("Knowing the situation of that designe better") should run out Sir Nathaniel's land, rather than the colony's surveyor, Stephen Bull. Then, audaciously, Mathews called on Colleton in the guise of a mediator, although "he that had not seen the Governor for a year and many months befor that had buffown'd and Lampoun'd his Honor with all the Venom and Satyre that ill Names and malice could dictat." Mathews then impudently sought to reconcile the governor to Johnson.[341]

Disregarding the adage "once burnt, twice shy," Colleton summoned another parliament in February 1690. He did have good reason to do so though: England remained at war with France and the enemy had captured the English half of St. Christopher and threatened Nevis, Antigua, and Montserrat. This disaster set off alarm bells and accompanying parliamentary writs in Charles Town. The Goose Creek men, with Sir Nathaniel now "espousing Mathie's interest," were ready to take advantage.

As Stewart put it, these "vipers in our own bowels gnawing the comonwealth in pices and fractions" aimed at nothing more than to "undermind our Goshen exposing the province designedly to ruine and calamity by a french conquest." Unfortunately, Mathews convinced the "Ignorant dull illeterate mole-ey'd Members" that word of "a popish faction" scheming to betray Carolina to the French was nothing more than a "Jealousie" on the part of his opponents. In the meantime, then, after their Christmas holiday had ended, Sir Nathaniel and Mathews, along with How and other friends had adjourned to Goose Creek to plot strategy.[342]

Their alleged plan began unfolding on February 14, 1690 when How, "prolocutor or dictator" in that parliament and a former London link-boy, rose in council claiming to have evidence that Colleton had betrayed his responsibilities to the proprietors and to the colony by governing in accordance with private instructions from the Lords, purportedly contained in a letter dated March 3, 1687, instead of pursuant to the charter and the July 1669 version of the Fundamental Constitutions, the version that the Goose Creek men maintained had remained in force and which the proprietors again rejected as an imperfect copy.[343] These instructions, How, Mathews, and associates later claimed, put the colonists into consternation as they altered the "unalterable" July 1669 Constitutions, the same argument they had raised successfully eight years before. Of course, the proprietors who had signed the March letter had been "misinformed." By implication, though, How blamed Sir Peter Colleton for the mistake and, more significantly, for the dubious attempt to tinker with the framework of government.[344]

As it happens, an examination of the letter in question reveals that the Lords never disavowed the Fundamental Constitutions. Rather, they only rejected the belief that the July 1669 version (which the colonists never ratified and which the proprietors had held in abeyance pending the arrival of more settlers anyway, as noted earlier) carried any weight, reiterating the observation they had made before in the debate over the August 1682 version. The original document, the Lords insisted, had been a "rough draught" sent on to provide guidance for the first settlers. Indeed, so far from arbitrarily imposing or withdrawing constitutions, the same letter reasserted the "people's" right to recommend "alterations" to the document's provisions so long as they were "for the Peoples good and better government of the place." The running problem from the proprietary perspective, though, remained those who "have made the greatest stir in this matter." Had they simply "satisfied their Ambition there would have been no opposition to them."[345]

The disingenuousness must have been palpable and, with Johnson and Mathews, two suspected traitors, at the center of the action, the atmosphere fraught. Percival himself had brought a signed and sealed copy of the Fundamental Constitutions when he left England in 1674.[346] Indeed, on October 3, 1674, the Grand Council, with Mathews in his place, had resolved that "the printed copy of the Fundamental Constitutions lately sent" by the Lords with Percival should be read in parliament.[347]

The Goose Creek men naturally chose to disregard the proprietary explanation, blithely claiming instead that, since the Lords had cast aside the Fundamental Constitutions without the approbation of the freemen (thereby violating their charter), the government had no validity after March 3, 1687.[348] Thus, everything Colleton had done for the previous three years "wer bot mushroum ordinances and Illegall Laws, yea disloyall traiterous and treacherous both to the K. and Lords." The meeting of the parliament itself violated the charter. With no legal standing to convene, How argued, the body must dissolve itself immediately and it did so, without the leave of the governor or deputies—and without making any sort of provision for the defense of the colony in time of war. For lending his weight to this argument, Sir Nathaniel Johnson received the complements and thanks of 20 members led by Mathews. It had been apparent, according to Stewart, to anyone who had observed the operation how Mathews had directed it by gaining the ascendency "of the great man with the Govr. of Martinico's Lrs"—another reference, of course, to Johnson's alleged treachery on Antigua.[349]

This cynical legislative policy left the colony desperately exposed, according to Stewart. With no money for powder, and the parliament departed, the governor, at the behest of the Scot, Landgrave Smith, and a reported 110 petitioners, but over the strenuous objections of Mathews, Johnson, Percival, and "all the geese," again declared martial law, in the absence of any other recourse, to secure the colony. Stewart wrote a tract (now missing) that advocated the legality of martial law under the charter and the Fundamental Constitutions while, for their part, Sir Nathaniel and Mathews interfered with the collection of signatures for the petition and worked diligently to hamper Colleton's efforts to ready Carolina for an invasion.

For instance, someone allegedly alarmed the neighboring Indians who were led to believe that the militia preparations against French invaders and the provincial ban on selling powder (also in anticipation of an attack) were part of a plot to destroy them. An enquiry revealed Mathews as the spreader of this rumor: upon exposure of his behavior, the "Welsh prince" subsided. Then, Moore secured the remarkably naïve governor's license to trade with the Cherokees, which raised an outcry as he took 60 men with him on this private venture at a time when Carolina was preparing for war.

These maneuvers prompted Stewart to compose a "naturall history" of the colony (now lost but briefly summarized in his surviving letters to Dunlop) which included his observations on the illegal demise of the February 1690 parliament and the Goose Creek plots in the preceding meeting of 1689, along with his comments on the likely prospects for the cultivation of silk and rice. The account, which was translated into French for the edification of the Huguenots, also compared the provincial charter with the Fundamental Constitutions and exposed the inadequacies of the Militia Act passed by the parliament before it dissolved itself, in order to "undeceave the people."

Stewart stressed, especially for the benefit of the French, that How's attack on the foundation of government threatened anarchy: the claim that the Fundamental Constitutions had no standing translated into an end to liberty of conscience and naturalization of aliens as well as to the other rights and privileges of (white) inhabitants. Notwithstanding the hostility from Goose Creek, he registered short-term success both in terms of the number of signatories on the martial law petition and by converting a number of his opponents to the Colleton position, including Quarry, Izard, and Moore. This effort earned the Scot the enmity of Mathews as well as the thanks of the Colletons as matters between the parties neared fever pitch with the governor, Smith, Grimball, and Stewart allegedly all targeted by a mob. The latter took to carrying a sword, which he drew on How.[350]

With the Indian slavers in disarray and Mathews hinting at assassination plots, Stewart advised a series of finishing strokes. He planned to send word of the seeming plot to betray Carolina to the French on to the proprietors and the Privy Council. At the same time, when the governor returned to Charles Town, Stewart told Dunlop, he would advise him to seize the papers of Mathews and Johnson to determine their involvement.

In the end, the French did not attack Carolina nor apparently did Colleton seize anyone's papers. Still, Stewart claimed to remember that Johnson had written a letter that hinted at Sir Nathaniel's desire to see James II return to power.[351] Armed with his deep suspicion that Mathews was behind the plot to bring the French into Carolina, the Scot confronted the baronet over his Jacobite sympathies (knowing that he would then inform Mathews) and proclaimed his determination to see the Goose Creek leader "clap't in Irons and banish't the Country, or wors." These threats obliged Mathews to go to ground again in June 1690.[352]

But, just as it seemed as if Mathews's number was up, fortune smiled yet again on the former surveyor and deputy. As accusations of his treasonable behavior accompanied Dunlop to England and martial law took hold in Carolina, and while his followers began to abandon their leader, the proprietor Seth Sothell arrived in Charles Town. Sothell's appearance gave Mathews a golden chance to rally his party and strike back against his enemies that he seized with both hands. It also made a further mockery of the proprietary visions of orderly settlement anchored by the "weightier sort."[353]

A proprietor through his purchase of the Clarendon share, Sothell seems to have been a respected London merchant and by June 13, 1680 was styled "Admiral" of Carolina.[354] He sailed for Albemarle to serve as governor there but was captured en route by Algerian pirates providing us with an example of the continuing hazards of an Atlantic voyage in the late seventeenth century.[355] After he finally arrived in Albemarle following his ransom, Sothell quickly managed to alienate the leaders of that colony who forced him to depart in the summer of 1690. Yet, notwithstanding—or perhaps because of—his prior difficulties, Sothell received the support of Mathews, Percival, Quarry, and their friends who saw his claims, through his proprietary status, to the governorship at Charles Town as a heaven-sent means of dispatching James Colleton and their other enemies. Conveniently forgetting their previous opposition to the Fundamental Constitutions, the Goose Creek men now argued that, under the terms of that document, a resident proprietor automatically assumed the governorship. Sothell duly assumed power.[356]

The Mathews contingent hailed the arrival of their new proprietary friend by submitting the unctuous and self-serving petition noted earlier. This document, remarkable even by the high standards for disingenuousness that prevailed in proprietary Carolina, provides the Goose Creek version of the history of the colony to 1690 and was probably composed by Mathews himself. As we have already seen, its authors had their blinkers securely fastened enabling them to misread, deliberately or otherwise, the proprietary intentions for the Fundamental Constitutions. Moreover, by now, the authors had mastered the art of attributing to their enemies the very behavior they engaged in themselves. Yet, even more remarkably, this document—at face value—has served as the basis of understanding the political character of early Carolina since the 1850s when William J. Rivers included it in the collection of documents he appended to his history of the proprietary period. It requires, therefore, further scrutiny.[357]

The petitioners adhered to their belief that the July 1669 version of the Fundamental Constitutions remained "the unalterable forme & rule of Government for ever," notwithstanding various "misinformed" efforts to ratify other constitutions that "the people" had opposed in 1673, 1677, 1682, and 1685. Consequently, the "disavowal" by the Lords of the original left the colony without any constitution and, consequently, government could only be based on the charter.[358] Now, "the people" had moved again to protect themselves, this time from Colleton whose own "disavowal" of the original Constitutions had left the colony teetering on the brink of anarchy with no authority to provide for its defense against the marauding French. The "tyrannical" governor underscored his capriciousness by dissolving parliament, and then, at the behest of "some few people," mostly the "ignorant," illegally proclaimed martial law over the "peaceable" objections of the legislature. Thus, *pace* Stewart, Colleton and his cronies bore the responsibility for leaving the colony dangerously exposed to its enemies. This "illegal, tirannical and oppressive way of Government" spurred "many" inhabitants "to leave the Cuntry." More fundamentally, the fault for the province's shortcomings lay, the petitioners claimed, with "those principally entrusted by the Lords Proprietors" whose attempts (tacitly encouraged by Sir Peter Colleton) to impose the various Fundamental Constitutions had disturbed "the good Inhabitants of this Countrey." Consequently, "many thousands of people have been detered from cominge hither to the disconsolation of those that are here, & ye disprofit of the Lords Proprietors and many alsoe left the Cuntrey, being not willinge to live constantly after soe uncertaine and unquiet a rate."[359]

These same individuals had also spread calumny upon the "Indian Deallers" leading to "severe reflections upon them" in proprietary letters. Sothell's petitioners regarded this as especially unfair since "both before and since those Letters, great endeavors have bin used to monopolize the whole Indian Trade, but wee forbare to mention it here" since it would reflect "upon som of the Lords Proprietors," except to note that James Colleton had unwisely sought to circumvent his own order prohibiting trade with the Yamassees.

The petitioners then observed that, after the Spanish invasions of 1686, the colony had been prevented from responding appropriately thanks to the arrival of the new governor. Instead of punishing St. Augustine, he had treated with Spanish ambassadors without even consulting the council. To the predictable dismay of the petitioners, these negotiations had violated English honor by ignoring "all the bloody insolencys the Spaniards had committed against this Colloney" and opened official commercial relations between the colonies, while ignoring the festering issue of slaves escaping to the Spanish town.[360]

The mishandling of the response to the threatened French invasion was another symptom, according to the petitioners, of Carolina's deeper malaise. Colleton and his allies had succeeded in turning out their opponents with the latter unable to respond to the claims (such as the alleged enslavement of Indians) made against them while the Lords remained ignorant of what was going on in their colony.[361]

A breakdown at the point of contact between the proprietors and their colonists had occurred, according to the petitioners, with most Carolinians having little or no interaction with the Lords. Moreover, because "four or five persons here" had blocked access to the proprietary board, many inhabitants with different opinions with respect to the Constitutions, land transactions, and the Indian trade had been discouraged from writing to the proprietors. This cabal had thus succeeded in "misrepresenting" the colony's views to its overseers.[362]

This communication blockage had led to all sorts of problems. For instance, the proprietors had confused the terms of their land grants by leaving out the value of quitrents in the form of indentures and by reserving a right of reentry. Originally, the land grants (and the Fundamental Constitutions) had set rents at one penny per acre or the equivalent in kind with no mention of a right of reentry. These oversights, the petitioners informed Sothell, had caused "many hundreds of people" to leave Carolina while "many thousands have forbore comeing hither." Indeed, they added, the original terms of indentures had induced migrants to come to the colony in the mistaken belief that "thousands would soon follow them." Unless the Lords returned to the old land grant system, the petitioners, warned, settlement would continue to lag. Fortunately, Sothell's arrival on the scene promised the happy opportunity to reconcile proprietors and colonists, not coincidentally by immediately removing the enemies of the Goose Creek men from the government and restoring proper channels of communication between governors and governed to the greater prosperity of the colony.[363]

Of course, it remains unclear whose version of this history—the petitioners to Sothell or John Stewart—bears the closer resemblance to the truth. For instance, Stewart and his associates may have been pandering to the "proprietary interest" while the Goose Creek men were leading the battle to preserve the liberties of (white) Carolinians. On the other hand, it seems far more likely that the petition presented to Sothell reads as nothing if not unctuous self-justification and as another manifestation of the Goose Creek practice of engaging in dubious behavior and then charging their enemies with the exact same behavior—all while presenting themselves as defenders of liberties and the colony's (and even the proprietors') interests.

For it seems that Mathews and his associates manufactured this whole crisis. For instance, the Lords, in a letter dated March 12, 1685, submitted 38 new articles of the Constitutions and voided all previous instructions and temporary laws. They also purportedly "ordered that ye third fundamentall Constitutions should be subscribed."[364] No letter of this date has been found but a letter from the proprietors of September 9, 1685 indicates clearly that, contrary to the beliefs of the petitioners to Sothell, the Temporary Laws and Instructions of 1672 remained in full force and effect as far as the proprietors were concerned.[365] Then, there are the remarkably similar suspicions concerning Jacobitism and treason that had been raised in the Leeward Islands concerning Sir Nathaniel Johnson, about which many Carolinians knew. And, finally, the history between Stewart and Mathews as related by the former to William Dunlop yields a relative bounty of information about "the Welsh prince"; the Scot had no reason to dissemble or explain himself privately to his compatriot.

Actually, Sothell and his new friends did not wait for the next parliament "to preserve the whole Colloney in peace and prosperity." Armed with the memorial expressing the purported sentiments of the population, the new governor declared that his predecessor had acted illegally in declaring martial law. This conclusion provided the justification for Sothell and his supporters to deprive their opponents of their offices and remove them from the Grand Council. They packed Colleton off to Barbados, assaulted and jailed secretary Grimball, and seized the provincial records. Sothell, with three cronies acting as deputies, completed the *coup* by calling parliament and passing a law that banished Colleton and barred him and his supporters from holding office in Carolina ever again.[366]

Sothell's maneuvers inevitably generated outrage and more letters to the colony's overseers, this time from the enemies of the Goose Creek men. Incredulous, the proprietors remarked that Grimball's "imprisonment (if the account given to us be true) is illegal, arbitrary and tyrannical, and so contemptuous of our authority that we can hardly believe it." They ordered the restoration of the secretary, as well as Schenkingh to his office as sheriff of Berkeley County. Sothell had replaced Schenkingh with Quarry, even though the Lords had "put [Quarry] out of office for receiving pirates, and for other misconduct."[367] The Lords also disallowed the law disabling Colleton as it was passed in improper form, not ratified by three deputies "and in itself being illegal and repugnant."[368] Finally, they removed the "deputies" installed by the *coup* and revoked the governor's power to appoint proprietary deputies to vacancies as hazardous, in light of Sothell's behavior, to the province's health; they gave the power of reappointment to the other deputies by majority ballot.[369]

The proprietors further declared that, although, pursuant to the Fundamental Constitutions, as resident proprietor, Sothell had a claim to the governorship, no single Lord could assume the government without the approval of his partners. Moreover, since the other proprietors had never given Sothell the authority to act on behalf of themselves or the proprietorship—except pursuant to the obnoxious Constitutions of January 1682, "those being the onely constitutions agreed or signed to by all the eight proprietors"—he had no authority to appoint magistrates or officers without the approval of their deputies. Any Lord who pretended to act with such authority committed high treason while anyone who accepted offices from such a purported governor committed a "high misdemeanour."

Confronted with this *melee*, the Lords declared yet another inquiry: while Sothell had declared to his partners his willingness to submit to their instructions, their deputies had reported otherwise. The colonists in Albemarle had also raised grievances that required an examination into Sothell's conduct there.

The proprietors, for their part, expressed their intention on the one hand to treat Sothell fairly, but, on the other, they remained committed to preserving their colonists from governmental oppression and unjust dealing. In the same vein, they reiterated their insistence that their sole policy remained to encourage migration to Carolina by promising a liberal form of government. In America, migrants would then rent their lands, but neither for proprietary profit nor to permit officials to amass large fees and "grow rich by the ruin of ye people."[370]

As they had in the case with the Scots, the Goose Creek men adopted here the tactic of accusing their enemies of engaging in the same illegal behavior in which they themselves had engaged: Governor Colleton had declared martial law to preserve the colony from the likely possibility of a French attack when the parliament, at the behest of two suspected traitors, had left it defenseless. However, the Goose Creek men assured Sothell that they, in fact, had been the preservers of the colonists' liberties even as they tried to provide for their defense. In their view, Colleton "did sett up martiall law on purpose to Ingrose the Indian trade to himself," a concept that the Indian slavers regarded as wholly unacceptable, as the Scots had found out to their cost.[371]

In any event, the resulting uproar from these banishings and beatings obliged the Lords to step in again and unravel the tangle. On May 13, 1691, they appointed a remarkably balanced panel, consisting of James Colleton, Thomas Smith, Stephen Bull, Ralph Izard, and John Farr, to investigate the behavior of Sothell and his associates. At the same time, the accused, together with Quarry and Percival, sent "a paper" defending themselves and their conduct, along with two representatives, Percival and Mathews, to England to provide a fuller account to the proprietors in person. Notwithstanding these efforts, the proprietors again unequivocally disavowed the July 1669 Constitutions.[372]

After hearing the evidence, the Lords suspended Sothell on November 8, 1691 and recalled him to London to explain himself (although after his suspension, he remained in the colony for a time and "pretended a right to the Government to the great Disturbance of the quiet of our Province"). To replace their disgraced partner, they rushed Colonel Philip Ludwell, a Virginian who had been in Albemarle cleaning up the mess Sothell had left there, to Charles Town and, at the same time, ordered the restoration of secretary Grimball, their deputies, and other officeholders to their places. In the meantime, Mathews and Percival informed the Lords that the Carolinians preferred to be governed under the charter directly. Thus, the proprietors officially abandoned the Fundamental Constitutions, although they (and their colonists) continued to follow them in the breach as they were entitled to do pursuant to the powers originally granted to them under the charter.[373]

The record of this time in the province's history indicates that even though the rival factions were ready to shred each other to bits, the conduits of deference and condescension between the colony and its proprietors remained open. Obviously, the interests of the Lords and those of their colonists did not always jibe. When their deputies on the scene, though, could not handle a matter, the Lords did work to redress grievances. Throughout the seventeenth century, whenever problems arose, Carolinians looked to the proprietors to sort out their difficulties and the proprietors generally made the effort to provide considered responses. Moreover, unlike the upheavals that occurred in New England, New York, and Maryland in the wake of the "Glorious Revolution," all of which entailed some sort of connection with events in the metropolis, the Sothell affair remained a colonial affair and, significantly, entailed no calls for a fundamental change in the government.[374]

Still seeking to encourage the building of towns, along with migration and commerce, and with the Fundamental Constitutions now in limbo, the proprietors gave Ludwell two sets of instructions, one private and one public. The public instructions reconstituted the proprietorship and its offices. In light of the Sothell debacle, the Lords directed that deputies and governors could only be removed on order of the Palatine (the senior proprietor on March 1, 1670, the earl of Craven, and after his death, the senior in terms of years of service) and three additional proprietors. Every Lord had the right to choose a deputy to sit on the council with temporary vacancies to be filled by ballot of the other deputies. When a proprietor died, a successor's right had to be confirmed by the Palatine and three other proprietors. Governors were to appoint a chief judge, if the Lords had not, and create courts with clerks and marshals with the governor and deputies serving as the court of appeal.

Ludwell, in particular, was to call an assembly with 20 members, chosen by the various counties, to meet with the deputies, landgraves, and cassiques as a bicameral legislature that now replaced the Grand Council. All bills had to go to the proprietors for approval. The governor and three deputies could prorogue the Assembly and suspend any officer except other deputies and the receiver, while all laws lapsed after two years unless confirmed by the Lords.

With regard to the Indian slave trade, the proprietors ordered Ludwell "to suffer no Indians within 400 miles of Charles Town to be sent out of Carolina." The governor, as commander-in-chief, was (again) to crack down on pirates, enforce the Navigation Acts, create additional rules (apparently left to his discretion) for the government with the acquiescence of three other deputies as necessary, and keep peace with the Spanish.[375]

Ludwell's private instructions noted Sothell's defiance of the Fundamental Constitutions and the contemptuous refusal of constitutional government, and so the Lords, starting afresh, based their new directives on their charter as their colonists requested. Nevertheless, the governor was not to call a meeting of the assembly until the Carolinians consented to the body's power, under the Constitutions, to propose laws. In addition, admitting "that the Goose Creek men are resolved to opose all wee shall order right or wrong," the proprietors directed Ludwell to keep the faction out of government "untill they shall change that principle."

The Lords also wanted the governor to report on provincial grievances and to investigate further the charges made against both James Colleton and Sothell, including the legality of commissions awarded by these governors, their cooperation (or lack thereof) with instructions, and the propriety of the declarations of martial law; in cases involving extortion, he was to make restitution. If Ludwell found too many people involved in the dubious Sothell takeover, the Lords instructed, "you will try the ringleaders only." At the same time, the proprietors urged him to investigate reports of pearls, to sell land to those grantees who disliked paying rents, and to encourage (again) the establishment of new towns.[376]

Yet, the Lords could not and would not control provincial elections and the new Commons House of Assembly created by the post-Sothell reforms provided a natural forum for the complaints of the Goose Creek men. These "representatives of the people" sent 13 grievances to Ludwell and the deputies in September 1692 and added a fourteenth a year later. Some of these objections included problems with the indemnity. But they also included, unsurprisingly, complaints over the proprietary form of conveying land, and a corresponding lack of agreement on a receiver.

Also, unsurprisingly, the power of the governor to declare martial law, purportedly contrary to the charter, and the refusal of the deputies to act without informing the proprietors caused consternation.[377] On April 7, 1693, the proprietors offered reassurance. They reminded their colonists of their directive that acts be passed "with the advice and consent of our Deputies, Landgraves and Casiques, and delegates of the freemen or major part of them" as "should be thought necessary for the better government of our Province" and then ratified by the governor and "three or more of our Deputies" before they could become law. After ratification, laws "should continue in force for two years, and no longer, unless" ratified by the Palatine and three or more other proprietors. This process was not to be followed with respect "to all matters relating to the Courts of Judicature," fees, officials, or procedure as "practiced during the Governments of Landgrave James Colleton and Landgrave Joseph Morton." These "being matters which will admit of delay without exposing the safty of the inhabitants of our Province to any foreign enemy, or attempt of the Indians"; laws on these matters were not to go into effect until approved by the Palatine and three other Lords.[378]

The proprietors also disallowed an act that gave sheriffs the power to select jurors by lot. This practice, they claimed, would give sheriffs complete control over jury selection and might allow "notorious favorers of Pyrates" or other "enormous crimes," to control verdicts. Instead, the Lords suggested an act based upon Section 67 of the Fundamental Constitutions whereby a child would draw names of prospective jurors out of a bag.[379]

Finally, the proprietors disallowed an election that gave the franchise to "all persons" who swore they had incomes of at least ten pounds. They agreed that freeholders should comprise the electorate, but the act made no mention of the time that electors had to actually reside in their county: "it is so loose that by this Act all the Pyrates that were in the Shipp that had been plundering in the Red Sea had been qualified to vote for Representatives in Carolina, which being of dangerous consequence to the Inhabitants."[380]

The Goose Creek men, in the meantime, kept up their quitrent complaints. The first settlers, they observed to Ludwell, "laboured under a Continental watch and Guard to defend [the colony] and themselves from the attempts of the Spanyards" and consequently suffered deprivation "even to the dispair of their lives." Then, they began to flourish "by which means the fame of this place, beyond the Seas, encouraged many People in Europe and other Parts to come hither and settle, and they did readily and willingly take the Conveyance for lands that was then granted." Settlers, both old and new, were happy and "doubted not but all difficulties were over." However, "those Halcyon days did not continue long, their Lordships were Pleased in [1682] to alter the first Grant and order a new conveyance for Lands to the great dislike of the People," leading to many settlers moving away, others exhausting their resources while they awaited proprietary redress of their grievances, unsettled land titles, and a general lack of enthusiasm for improving plantations generating a corresponding poverty for the province.

Then, since Charles Town continued to attract pirates (since Quarry and others had helped them)—who "attempt the plundering and burning" of the place—the capital required fortifications, "but cannot be done without very great charge to the inhabitants." Forgiveness of the arrears would help here, as well; the loss of "the only place of trade and strength in the whole Province" would "necessarily unsettle & ruine this now thriving

Colony, & will oblige us to provide for the certaine payment of their rents hereafter, & make the collection thereof very easy."[381]

It is unclear, however, what these petitioners found objectionable in the 1682 changes in the form of land grant. The new language provided for a limited right of reentry for the proprietors so that they could collect rents that had fallen six months in arrears. Furthermore, this limited right was reserved for nonpayment of rent only after 90 days. Neither of these clauses authorized, permitted, or mandated the proprietors to retake possession of land. All this form provided was a means for the proprietors to ensure the collection of their rents (again, at only one penny per acre) and the payment of their officials. Undoubtedly, the complaining colonists sought to have this legal mechanism scrapped so they could avoid the payment of even this nominal rent and the corresponding subsidy of their officeholding enemies.[382]

To help Ludwell, the proprietors, at least temporarily, took a more active role in the government of the colony by reserving the power to ratify laws dealing with juries, elections, court proceedings, and the assembly to themselves. Not coincidentally, these institutions had historically provided the platform for Goose Creek machinations and the Lords correspondingly recognized that their oversight would help prevent the enactment of "unreasonable laws"—and the blame for such falling on the head of their governor.[383]

Revamping the government really provided a new vehicle for remedying a number of serious issues—the payment of rents, the form of land grants, relations with the Spanish, regulation of the Indian trade, and, most centrally, the problem of fierce factional enmity—that still required attention. Indeed, the convulsions created by Sothell had exacerbated political mistrust. The tricky task of papering over these divisions, which, of course, involved resolving the other problems, fell to Ludwell. Yet, the instructions he received from his employers demonstrate not only that the proprietors cared about their colony; they continued to devise solutions for its problems that should have provided reasonable satisfaction to their colonists.

With respect to the quitrent dispute, the Lords observed that they had first ordered their receiver to collect rents in scarce hard currency. This instruction had provided the pretext for the objections from Goose Creek that complained of the hardship in paying in rare specie rather than in commodities. But, once they became aware of the hardship of paying in money for their tenants, the proprietors swiftly abandoned their demands that rents be paid in silver, and returned to accepting rents in commodities.[384] Indeed, the Lords had agreed to instead accept quitrents, since "there is little [English] money in Carolina," in Spanish money, cotton, silk or indigo as early as October 6, 1690, just as the Sothell affair was heating up.[385] With this reason for nonpayment removed, by 1693, Moore, who had been "one of the principal opposers of the payment of rents," had come to terms and the Lords expected Percival, Quarry, and other recalcitrant planters to follow his lead.[386] More fundamentally, the shift in quitrent policy shows that the proprietors listened to the grievances of their colonists and worked to find an agreeable redress.

In the case of indentures for land grants, though, the Lords had to be firmer. Without taking the elementary precaution of inserting language in the rental agreement that bound the tenant to pay rent and retaining the landlord's right to reenter the land in the event of nonpayment, the proprietors would have ended up, for all practical purposes, giving away land. Eliminating the indenture form, moreover, would have left the Lords with no legal leg upon which to stand when pursuing delinquent tenants. The Goose Creek argument unsurprisingly attracted popular support in Carolina but acceptance of the plan would also have left the salaries of officials unpaid and left settlement patterns in even greater disarray, thereby risking even greater crises than those that actually occurred.

As early as 1686, the proprietors declared that they found objections to the form of indenture to be extraordinary. The Lords resolved to stick to indentures, announcing that those who did not care to pay them rent could leave the colony. Undoubtedly, they noted, those who objected had little, if any, familiarity with conveyance practices in England where every landowner paid a rent of some sort; they regarded it as inconceivable that any "reasonable or just man" with "honest Intentions" would take up a rental and then refuse to sign a document obliging the payment of that rent. Ultimately, the proprietors warned that if people persisted in refusing to sign indentures, they would stop granting headrights.[387]

The Lords also insisted, contrary to rumor, that they had never thought of switching the form of land grant. Such "cunning Insinuations" might have led "some weak and ill principled men" to "believe them" thereby creating another fault on the lines of communication between the proprietors and their settlers; everyone concerned should act to prevent such "misunderstandings" in order to encourage "a good correspondence." This would, in turn, promote migration to the colony and prosperity for its planters.[388]

Consequently, the Lords expressed satisfaction with Ludwell's report that even their leading enemies did not contest their title to the land in Carolina and their right to dispose of it as they pleased.[389] Prospects for a favorable settlement of the quitrent issue now looked bright since secretary Grimball had informed them that Moore, the leader of the anti-rent movement, had agreed to pay his arrears. This submission, the proprietors observed, should lead to the collapse of the resistance of Percival and Quarry. If not, they instructed Ludwell to prosecute them and other holdouts. Rents, they reminded the governor, when collected should be used for official salaries, including his own, while money realized from land sales should go to England to pay proprietary expenses, including the rent owed to the Crown.[390]

Indian slavery remained, though, the underlying issue of contention. Having been unaware of Sothell's friendship with the Goose Creek men, the proprietors had presumed he would take steps to resolve the thorny questions of compensation for "Negros" taken by the Spanish and of quashing the Indian slave trade. They, therefore, had recommended to their rogue partner that he establish "a fair correspondence" between Charles Town and St. Augustine whereby the Spanish might pay the English for escapees. In the end, though, they suggested that the Carolinians had no recourse for African slaves taken to Florida by Indian raiders: this was *quid pro quo* for Indians taken as slaves by the Yamassee allies of Carolina slavers.

Even so, reports had continued to reach proprietary ears that Indians continued to be "sent away again under hand which cannot be done if our Officers did not connive at it or did use their utmost diligence to prevent it." Outraged about the continuation of this trade, but not about enslaving Africans, which posed no external threat to their colony, the proprietors laid into their colonists: "these poor people have done no harme nor Injury are harmless and honest ye most pat of them, and without whom you can never get in your Negros that run away." The Lords issued yet another injunction against "this pernicious Inhumane barbarous practice which wee are resolved to break through." If officials turned a blind eye or participated themselves, they were to be put out of their places and punished.[391]

Obviously, Sothell's political affiliation had precluded any effective policy against the Indian slave trade and its practitioners; he and his allies must have laughed up their sleeves at missives from the proprietors proscribing the "sending away" of Indians. However, his suspension presented another opportunity to bring the practice under some sort of control and for settling relations both between Carolina and its neighbors and among the province's factions.[392]

Political "jealousys," though, still hamstrung Carolina. No act of indemnity passed the assembly because the members disagreed who should be punished for the Sothell administration and how. Moreover, the Lords felt so uncomfortable approving an indemnity that they issued a general pardon in order to resolve all disputes. Yet, they instructed that same assembly to properly provide for the province's defense in order to avoid a repetition of the 1690 scenario. If it failed to do so, the Lords ordered Ludwell to dissolve the body so that the proprietors could demonstrate to the imperial government that the Carolinians had declined to take appropriate care of their province. The governor was not to convene another assembly "untill you are well assured they are in a better temper."[393]

The fallout from these "tempers" hit the unwitting Huguenots who complained to the proprietors about a law passed that designated them as aliens (since the Goose Creek men no longer needed their support). The Lords did not express much sympathy, noting that the assembly, controlled by the ostensible friends of the French, had created the "hardships." Since the Huguenots had seen fit to ally themselves with those who had successfully opposed the Fundamental Constitutions and their "wholesome provisions" for religious toleration and denization, the proprietors wondered, could they expect full redress from the risk this opposition now generated against their property? The proprietors tried to provide what reassurance they could by directing Ludwell and the council not to seek the forfeiture of any French estates. But they advised the aliens in future to watch out for "the Envy and Injurys of the people there" so that they would "not be misled by our and your Enemys, and such as would have Carolina in an unsettled condition for by ends of their owne."[394]

By April 1693, the rose of Ludwell's administration had lost its bloom. The governor had quarreled with the deputies over his salary and the collection of rents, worrying the Lords: "We do not see how the Government of Carolina can be carried on, if you put yourself out with all parties, and especially our friends." They encouraged him to reconcile with their deputies.[395] They also gave Ludwell supervision over Grimball in the matter of quitrents, since the receiver should have accepted Moore's offer to pay his arrears. In addition, the law of England for distraining rents should be followed in Carolina, they wrote, which would pay the governor's salary out of income in his own hands while allowing grantees to pay their rents in their own counties.[396] Ludwell himself, though, apparently had had enough. Even as these directions made their way across the Atlantic, he had left Charles Town and Thomas Smith, the senior landgrave in the colony, had become governor, in accordance with the supposedly moribund Fundamental Constitutions.

This change in government, though, seemed to signal the end of this extended period of particularly fierce factional strife, thanks to the sudden departures of a number of Goose Creek men, including Quarry, from the jurisdiction in fear of a possible lawsuit brought by James Colleton, accompanied by the even more critical journey of Mathews and Percival to present the Goose Creek argument in the Sothell case to the proprietors; they died without returning to Carolina.[397] The Lords happily noted Landgrave Smith's report "that some of ye Troublers of ye quiet of Carolina have left And that you are of opinion that if 3 more were gone the Countrey would be soon in a setled condition." The proprietors recommended that he now pursue, in accordance with English law, those who had made and "false and scandalous reports and seditious speeches and Insinuations" in order to better maintain public order.[398]

Moreover, on April 12, 1693, the proprietors had finally issued their general pardon for acts (except for treason, piracy, and non-payment of rent) committed prior to November 8, 1691 (the date of Ludwell's commission as governor).[399] This law, along with the withdrawals of Mathews, Percival and Quarry, seems to have eased the mutual fears of recrimination and, correspondingly, permitted Carolinians to take tentative steps toward reconciliation. In the end, no one was censured.[400] Before he died in November 1694, Landgrave Thomas Smith advised the proprietors of the "growing condition" of Carolina, "And the happy peace & perfect union he had by his proper conduct reduced them to." Secretary Grimball seconded this "very encouraging" view.[401]

Even so, Smith, a Dissenter and staunch foe of the Goose Creek men, had difficulties maintaining order during his brief term in office. James Moore and Sir Nathaniel Johnson remained on the scene and they and their remaining associates retained sufficient influence to make life difficult. Despite Moore's cooperation on quitrents, a number of Goose Creek men declined to pay. This attitude, in addition to the continuing provocation of the Indians and the ongoing problem of pirates, plagued Smith's government as it had his predecessors. Thus, notwithstanding his subsequent sanguine report, the landgrave seems to have retained doubts about his ability either to maintain authority over or to reconcile with his enemies. He informed the Lords on October 12, 1693 that the continuing political "ferment" generated by the Goose Creek men caused "many of ye people to remove into other parts of America."[402]

The death of the Goose Creek associate and Indian trader, Caleb Westbrook, apparently at the hands of a Savannah Indian may have raised additional concerns. It certainly worried the proprietors, who suspected it constituted retaliation for the murder of some Indians by English traders during Sothell's tenure. Fearing the prospect of yet another frontier war, especially after a Charles Town grand jury had thrown out an indictment obtained by Ludwell against those traders, they ordered Smith to investigate the matter thoroughly and to insure that he gave justice to the Indians (as well as the English) in order to avoid violent consequences.[403]

The Lords also moved quickly to head off any Goose Creek resurgence by agreeing with Smith's suggestion that they send over a proprietor, John Archdale, to act as governor expressing high hopes that the official proprietary presence in the colony would defuse the factions, attract migrants, bolster the colony's reputation for trade and planting, and so contribute to its prosperity.[404] Thus, the new proprietor-governor received additional instructions to deal with the usual issues: to oversee the taking of town lots in Charles Town and to obtain reversions on unimproved grants (as well as other grants), consider issuing a charter for the town, and to work on building more towns to encourage trade. His partners also directed him to reexamine, with the cooperation of the Grand Council, the Fundamental Constitutions and to implement those provisions he regarded as "more expedient for ye better establishment of our Government for ye good and wellfare of our people" after presenting his recommendations to the assembly and the other proprietors for their approval. He was also to drain marshes, fortify Charles Town, "take care that ye Indians be not abused and that all means may be used to civilize them," and, finally, bring order to the land-granting process, including the reservation of quitrents.[405]

Archdale registered a number of successes in his one-year tenure. Perhaps most significantly, the presence of a proprietor in the colony proved sufficient to lay the quitrent dispute to rest. Archdale even created a rent-roll that confirmed the settlers had paid their arrears.[406] Thus, with the "Goose Creek" presence reduced in scope, a rent-roll in place, staple crops in production and the government seemingly stabilized, it must have appeared to the proprietors in 1695 that at last the colony had arrived on a sound footing. They certainly felt optimistic enough to prepare another draft of the Fundamental Constitutions for ratification. And, after all, 25 years, even with all of the disruptions caused by the "dealers in Indians," still came reasonably close to Sir Francis Bacon's old timetable.

The Lords, however, cautioned their colonists that the sort of behavior they had exhibited had placed the colony's survival in jeopardy and could not continue. "Great numbers" of migrants would have arrived in the 1680s "had not newes come from Carolina that the alterations [to the Fundamental Constitutions] so much liked here were rejected in Carolina and the Lord Cardross and others affronted and barbarously used the first day of their landing in Carolina by those very men that promoted the rejections of the amendments." "[N]or," they added, "will people come there untill things are better settled, nor can wee with honour or a good conscience Invite men to come amongst you for wee will not deale disingenuously with any man upon any consideration whatsoever nor If wee would have the power to compell men to come and live and continue under a government they do not like or amongst persons the unquietness of whose tempers will allow of no peace of settlement." As a result, they warned, "men will dye in Carolina for some time faster then they are borne or grow up and if none come to you, your numbers will by degree be soe diminished that you will be easily cut off by the Indians or pyrates which we leave to be considered by you that you may know the consequence of hearkneing to men of unquiet and factious spirits."[407]

Chapter 8 ~

Tests

Certainly, anyone who might have bothered to take stock of South Carolina in 1695 would have detected an unmistakable whiff of transition as well as unhealthiness in the air. The arrival of Archdale and the departure of a sizeable contingent of Goose Creek men, including their ringleader, Mathews, certainly changed the political landscape of the colony and gave everyone a chance to catch their breath. On the other hand, the 1694 deaths of Goose Creek adversaries, Sir Peter Colleton and Landgrave Thomas Smith, removed respectively the most active of the proprietors and a Carolinian who possessed the rare qualities of integrity, honesty, and public spirit.[408]

Also, by 1695, the cultivation of rice, especially, as well as silk and other merchantable commodities had started to progress while the Indian trade continued to be lucrative. Charles Town, at least, had begun to emerge as a recognizable municipality. However, to regard the period from 1695 to 1700 as one of relative "peace and prosperity" for the proprietary period, as one leading study has, seems to overstate the case. Undoubtedly, the presence in the colony of an adept proprietor—first, Archdale, and then, Joseph Blake— helped hold together the Carolina political nation. Yet, cracks remained, and, when the occasion presented itself, the successors to the competitors of the 1680s and early 1690s quickly returned to the lists.[409]

Indeed, new arrivals, particularly William Rhett and Nicholas Trott, joined holdovers such as James Moore, Sir Nathaniel Johnson, and Job How in reheating differences, after Blake's death in 1701, to a frenzy that may even have surpassed the agitation of the Sothell takeover. These newcomers continued to view office and politics as the means to pursue private interest contemporaneously with the public interest. In the days before a civil service, it was normal—indeed, expected—for officeholders to mingle the private with the public. The manner in which one rose in politics came—quite consciously—from the connections one made with patrons and with other clients, as we have seen. In Carolina, Rhett and Trott followed this rule, as Mathews and others had before them, by coming into favor with the proprietors at some points and, at other times finding themselves on the outside. Ultimately, though, the new version of the old scene came to involve directly the Crown for the first time in the colony's history.

Unquestionably, however, the presence of a proprietor with duly constituted authority lubricated the points of contact and, correspondingly, reduced client tendencies toward independence. Thus, Archdale and the Commons House of Assembly reached an accord to pay the proprietary debt of some £1,700 owed as back salary to Governors Morton, Colleton, and Smith. They also agreed to build a fort for Charles Town and to take steps to insure the future collection of quitrents. In return, the Lords agreed to discharge the quitrent arrears.[410]

After a year in Carolina, Archdale decided to leave the proprietorship and return to England, handing over his dual role as proprietor-governor to Joseph Blake, a person esteemed both at the proprietary board and in the colony. Sensing the chance to build on Archdale's achievements, as well as on the enactment of the 1697 Naturalization Act that granted the Huguenots denizen status thereby securing their estates, and given to believe that their colonists shared this desire to have their liberties thus secured, the Lords instructed Blake to try once again to establish constitutional government, with the particular aim of preempting future quarrels over land grants and their form.[411] To that end, with the cooperation of colonists Robert Daniel and Edmund Bellinger, the proprietors prepared yet another incarnation of the Fundamental Constitutions for ratification by the assembly.[412]

The slimmed-down version of April 1698 contained only 41 sections (that of August 1682 had 125). Yet, although considerably reduced in scope, it retained the previous philosophy of the superiority of landownership ("since all Power and Dominion is most naturally founded in Property"). It also retained the categories of landgrave and cassique (Section 7) and required both members of parliament and voters to have a certain estate under Sections 8 and 9 (although the size of these estates remained unspecified). However, it tacitly recognized that the "peopling" process had not proceeded as hoped and consequently eliminated the elaborate court system set forth in previous entities, as well as the concept of "leet-men" (this concept seems to have failed to strike a chord with prospective migrants at a time when the population of England had, as we have seen, leveled). The specifics provided for the selection of jurymen in 1682 also disappeared.[413]

Under the new Section 1, power "to call and Dissolve Parliaments, to pardon all Offences, to make Elections of all Offices in the Proprietors' Disposal," to designate ports, to disburse monies from the public treasury, and to exercise a veto over bills passed by parliament remained in the

Proprietors' Court (formerly the Palatine's Court). But, again, the constitutions generally accorded proprietary status (except in pardoning offenders and creating ports) to deputies on the scene (as well as, of course, resident proprietors) and they acted as the Proprietors' Court in the absence of their principals from the colony (Section 2).[414]

On the other hand, the language of Section 7 appears to reflect an important change in proprietary intent. By 1698, especially with Sir Peter Colleton dead, the Lords no longer promoted migration as they had in the 1680s. Thus, the constitutions no longer served primarily as a means to lure "the weightier sort" to Carolina. Now, instead, the proprietors wanted to reinforce the connection between the provincial aristocracy and the government in order to improve the prosperity and government of the colony.

Consequently, only those people who had actually taken up their acres and had an unspecified number of slaves or tenants and who had a "real and personal Estate shall not be worth at least ____ pounds" could qualify as landgraves and cassiques (under Section 13) or, under Sections 8 and 9, serve as members of Parliament. As a further discouragement to absenteeism, Section 14 provided that any landgrave or cassique (or their descendants) who failed to take up their position in parliament within 40 years would lose their titles and privileges forever.[415] To broaden access to the Carolina aristocracy as well as to encourage orderly settlement, the Lords reduced the size of baronies from 12,000 acres to 4,000 acres for proprietors and landgraves and 2,000 for cassiques (Section 20).

The 1698 Constitutions also provided regulations for the selection (Sections 10–12, 15) and convening (Sections 16 and 17) of biennial parliaments. Under Section 11, again in accordance with a desire "for the preservation of the Balance of Power according to the proportion of the Property," the number of members from each county was to be determined according to the amount of taxes paid by each county.[416] Moreover, the inclusion of new Section 18 suggests that the Lords sought to ease the problem for their colonists of keeping laws in force in a transatlantic government. Under Section 83 of the August 1682 Constitutions, laws lapsed at the following parliament unless the Palatine and three other proprietors had ratified them. In the 1698 version, the Lords changed this provision so that all laws passed by the Parliament, by the governor and by three additional deputies remained in force until the Palatine and three other proprietors registered their opposition.[417] Finally, these Constitutions established the Church of England (Section 26) but maintained toleration for other denominations and "Professions" provided they registered themselves with the government (Sections 27–36, 38–39).

Notwithstanding these provisions, the 1698 attempt to enact constitutions went the way of previous efforts. The Lords observed "tis for ye Peoples sake wee desire they may pass not our owne, and when they can judge calmly & wisely they will be glad to lay hold of such an offer."[418] Yet, one month later, having received a remonstrance from the assembly, they expressed surprise that Blake had not pursued ratification more forcefully.[419]

The Commons House of Assembly, according to one reading of its journal, rejected what proved to be the last proposed set of Fundamental Constitutions because a majority "opposed the establishment of a provincial house of nobles."[420] It remains unclear, though, exactly why Carolinians in 1698 would have regarded such a concept with distaste. In the first place, a provincial nobility had already begun to form, even though the Fundamental Constitutions had never been formally approved: Joseph Morton, senior and Jr., Daniel Axtell, Bellinger, Joseph Blake, and Thomas Smith, senior and Jr., all resided in South Carolina as landgraves after 1680 while Sir Nathaniel Johnson was a resident cassique.[421] Moreover, philosophically, no evidence exists that any member of the Carolina body politic opposed the notion of a land-based aristocracy as the foundation of society and politics; if Axtell, the regicide's son, accepted an hereditary title, it is hard to see how any other planter in the colony would have turned one down.

This leaves faction again as the reason for opposition to ratification. Had the Constitutions been ratified, the foes of Goose Creek, who constituted a substantial majority of the nascent aristocracy would have controlled the upper house of parliament giving them a perennial advantage in the pursuit of legislative business. Since the proprietary board at this time remained cool toward the dealers in Indians—Colleton allies William Thornburgh and Thomas Amy controlled three of the seven surviving proprietary shares and with Shaftesbury's grandson, Anthony, Lord Ashley, constituted a hostile majority—for the immediate future, at least, all aristocratic creations would, in all likelihood, have been enemies. Further support for this suspicion comes from the reality that, at the same time the Lords presented the Constitutions for ratification, they also sent blank commissions for Goose Creek opponents Morton, Jr., and Daniel to create landgraves and cassiques. Also significantly, the proprietors relied on Daniel and another anti-Goose Creek figure, Bellinger, to assist them in the preparation of the latest incarnation of "fundamentals."[422]

Thus, to forestall the disaster of an aristocracy (and, therefore, a society) dominated by their opponents, the Goose Creek men had to defeat the Constitutions and, in doing so, cast opprobrium on the provincial aristocracy that underpinned them. They succeeded: the proprietors finally gave up on the idea of Fundamental Constitutions and returned to governing directly under their charter.[423]

The death of Blake on September 7, 1700 followed by that of the Palatine, the earl of Bath, on August 21, 1701 proved to be pivotal events. Blake's demise enabled Moore, Johnson, How, and new friends, such as the

Bermudan Trott and Daniel, who switched sides, to regain control of the government. As in the past, they used transatlantic connections to local effect. When the new Palatine, John, Lord Granville, took power with the proxies of two other members of the proprietary board in hand, the new generation of Goose Creek men quickly allied themselves with this powerful patron. As in 1690, their activities brought the colony to its knees.

So, what happened after September 1700? When Governor Blake died, either the younger Morton or Bellinger, as the landgraves resident in the province, should have automatically succeeded to his office pursuant to the Fundamental Constitutions, even though they remained unratified. However, councilors Moore and Daniel objected to both on the grounds that they were ineligible to hold proprietary office since they also held royal commissions as judges of vice-admiralty—even though they had held royal office since at least April 29, 1697 and no one had previously registered a complaint. Yet, the majority of the council accepted the argument rejecting the claims of Morton and Bellinger and appointed Moore instead.[424]

By the time he assumed the governorship of South Carolina, James Moore, veteran of the colony's political wars, lieutenant of "Hobses creature" Mathews, and preeminent Indian trader and planter in his own right, had lived in the colony for over 25 years. Purportedly, he sought, upon taking his new office, to pursue a policy of "conciliation" between "Anglicans" and Dissenters in the colony and to regulate the Indian trade. Thus, he declared to the Commons House that he would assent to any proposed regulation of the Indian trade, even one that stopped it or prevented him from engaging in it. His administration punished seven (unidentified) traders for violence they perpetrated against the Yamassees. By way of response, the legislators asked Moore to appoint Thomas Nairne, a trader from Colleton County, as agent for the colony's Indian affairs and they passed a bill that prevented the sale of goods to Indians on credit. The governor's failure to agree to these reforms "seems most likely" to have occurred because "there was an honest disagreement on the most suitable form of control."[425]

On the face of things, this interpretation seems plausible. However, it neglects to consider that Moore, now leader of the Goose Creek men, seems to have taken part in at least one prior "reform"—the commission created by the proprietors after the Westo War in 1677—that had masked an attempt to monopolize the Indian trade. It also fails to note that the Yamassees had served as the primary trading and political partners of the Goose Creek men since they had combined with Mathews and Moore to crush the Westos and Dr. Henry Woodward at that time.[426] Considering Moore's behavior in light of what we know about "Goose Creek" operations prior to 1700 gives rather more weight to the charges of his opponents that he was out to engross the Indian trade himself.[427]

Happily, for the Goose Creek veteran, just prior to his *coup*, an exceedingly helpful ally, Edward Randolph, happened onto the scene in 1699. Moore used this agent of the Board of Trade (and self-appointed enemy to proprietorships and those who served them) as a new means to advance himself. Through Randolph, he could secure royal backing for his plans to expand his Indian trading connections more deeply into the interior and to construct mines inland. The Moore–Randolph mutual admiration society also gave the Indian slaver another powerful friend against his local enemies, while, at first glance, it enlisted Moore in the increasingly vigorous effort to bring the English Empire more fully under central authority. This, to Randolph's mind, meant doing away with proprietary colonies.[428] To Moore's mind, though, the character of imperial authority did not matter so long as it smiled on his personal agenda.

The Board of Trade man duly reported that he had conversed with Moore, "a Gentleman of good Estate in this Countrey; he is Secretary of the Province and a Deputy to Sir John Colleton," and passed the details of the trader's plans on to the Board of Trade for its consideration. Moore told Randolph that if the Crown provided "good Encouragement" for the scheme, he, along with 50 white men, some Cherokee guides, and a "Negro Smith," would retrace a journey he had made with Mathews across the Appalachian Mountains in 1690 (the expedition that secured James Colleton's license to depart when Carolina feared a French attack). He claimed to have found seven types of mineral ore at that time and sent them with Mathews to England to have them checked when Moore's old partner had gone to compound with the proprietors after Sothell's tenure as governor in 1693. Two of these ores had proven "very go[o]d and one indifferent." Significantly, the Spanish had begun working mines within 20 miles of the site Moore had discovered and, apparently, intended to build up their presence in the area—a concept, the Carolinian added without apparent irony, opposed by the Indians on the belief that the Spaniards would then "make Slaves of them to work in those Mines." The Goose Creek man asked Randolph for help in securing his claim against the proprietors to any mines he found, noting the inability of the Lords to properly defend the territory from Spanish incursions.[429]

Randolph, of course, readily endorsed this plan as he shared his new friend's frustrations at the hands of the proprietors. First, he pointed out that the mining project would cost the Crown nothing if it failed, since the loss would fall on Moore and, if the Lords found out that he had gone behind their backs to the Board of Trade, he would lose his offices as well as his investment. The proprietors would also use their governor and council against this developer of imperial projects "and at least force him to leave the Country as has been formerly practiced upon men of good Estates in this

Province." If the project succeeded, on the other hand, he noted, it would be of "great import to the Crown."[430] Initially, Moore sat on his mining scheme, purportedly fearing that news of a mine in the interior of southeastern North America would encourage the French to increase their threatening presence adjacent to his own "weak" colony. In 1699, though, with England and France at last at peace (at least temporarily), the Indian dealer and Randolph agreed that it was now time to pursue this project.[431]

These proposals, unsurprisingly, confirmed Randolph's own view of Carolina and its overseers. Arriving in Charles Town in June 1699 as part of his official tour of the American colonies, he immediately noted that Blake held his office despite a prohibition made by the King in Council against proprietor-governors and in disregard of an Act of Parliament against frauds. As for the colony itself, Randolph scoffed at the results produced by the proprietorship: the Lords had kept much of the colony's land, especially the most fertile parts, for themselves, a practice, he further noted, that inevitably hampered settlement, resulted in a predominance of enslaved Africans in the population, and rendered the security of the handful of inhabitants problematic.

Proprietary neglect became acutely apparent, Randolph claimed with indignation rising, when the Spanish had attacked Carolina in 1686, and the Lords had not responded. Left to fend for themselves, the colonists had equipped five ships and armed 400 men to take St. Augustine. Then, the arrival of James Colleton intervened; the new proprietary appointee threatened the Carolinians with the noose "if they proceeded, whereupon they went on shoar very unwillingly" even though the Spaniards, upon hearing of the English threat, had abandoned their town and its castle. According to Randolph and the "credible information" he had received, Colleton passed up this chance to finally destroy the Spanish presence in Florida because it conflicted with his own plans to open trade with Florida.

Now, 14 years later, another foreign threat to Carolina, the French, had moved into the vicinity by building their fort at Mobile. It seemed doubtful to Randolph that the proprietors would help defend this vital imperial frontier since they had neglected to send even "one barrell of Powder or a pound of Lead to help them" during the recent war. Indeed, it seemed to Randolph that many settlers had concluded that they could not count on the Lords to defend them "and are resolved to forsake this Country." Thus, a number of the "chief men" asked Randolph if the Crown might send troops to protect them from the French and so preserve "this plentiful Country."

Randolph seconded this request since, notwithstanding apparent proprietary indifference, the struggling Carolinians had made "great improvements" in their colony. The planters had produced cotton, wool, ginger, and indigo, commodities that could increase customs revenue, and had turned to making naval stores and growing rice, which only required some "encouragement from England," possibly in the form of customs relief, to further improve the province's economy.[432]

Do these reports from Randolph, however, demonstrate that Moore was anti-proprietary? Was the Goose Creek man an imperial-minded expansionist? Do these documents even provide any sort of reliable picture of the character and history of South Carolina as of 1699? The answers to these questions, at best, still remain unclear. In the first place, Moore's attitude (as conveyed to Whitehall by Randolph) seems not to have extended to some principled objection to the proprietary government. He continued, for instance, to accept proprietary office, including, without apparent irony, that of receiver of rents.[433]

Quite possibly, Moore, as an honors graduate of the Maurice Mathews school of cynicism and obsequiousness, told the easily flattered and influential Randolph exactly what he wanted to hear. Sir Nathaniel Johnson, as we have seen, received the same treatment from the Goose Creek men when he arrived in the colony. If the proprietors found out about his conversations with Randolph, at worst, Moore might lose his offices until he temporized— this had happened before. At best, though, he retained his place and made connections in the metropolis that could be used at a future date. He, therefore, encouraged the belief the proprietors were to blame for the colony's shortcomings: this "gentleman of good Estate" simply confirmed what Randolph had known before he ever came to Carolina. Not surprisingly, Randolph's account of the travails of 1686 blamed James Colleton for failing to pursue the (treasonable) attack on Florida and omitted to mention, for instance, the convulsions of the Seth Sothell period, even though Sothell was a proprietor whose behavior would have provided ready ammunition for an anti-proprietary view of empire.

Unsurprisingly, on the other hand, Randolph dutifully recorded the alleged venality of Archdale, Blake, and their associates, all of whom, in 1699 either held or had held proprietary office. Coincidentally, all of these people were also opponents of Moore who again undoubtedly provided Randolph with his information. The proprietor-governors had allegedly allowed pirates to trade, collected "kickbacks" by unlawfully seizing and releasing ships, and even sold gunpowder to the Indians.[434] The other proprietors, apparently misinformed by "those that defraud and delude them," had chosen "very naughty men" as their deputies and officials to the great detriment "of this most thriving settlement in these parts of America." Moreover, the Lords had neglected to provide in any way for the colony's defense leaving the entire country from the Bahamas to beyond Pemaquid exposed to invasion.[435]

Yet, the language in Randloph's accounts is remarkably similar to those made in the 1690 "petition" to Seth Sothell composed by the Goose Creek men. In all of these documents, the proprietors had chosen the "wrong men," thanks to "misinformation," and listened only to those who "defraud and delude them" while they consistently ignored the views of the opponents of the "deluders," who, of course, only had the best interests of the country at heart.[436]

Thus, from the joint perspective of Moore and Randolph, James Colleton had thwarted the 1686 scheme against the Spanish rivals of Carolina's Indian slavers, but now, with the deathwatch on for Carlos II, war with France and pro-Bourbon interests in Spain had become likely. An attack on St. Augustine and Louisiana would provide the opportunity to get rid of these puny rivals once and for all. The French, newly established, were an unknown quantity but could not be allowed to threaten Carolina. However, what, at first blush, looked like imperial conflict (and may even have seemed so to Edward Randolph), to James Moore was more local political and economic conflict: encroachment from anyone—Scots, French, Spanish, English, Westos—on his trade routes without his acquiescence was unwelcome and had to be dealt with. Attacking the Spanish in Florida and the French in Louisiana for Moore did not strike a blow for the English Empire. It defended the interests of James Moore and his allies. At the same time, attacking Archdale, Blake, and proprietary appointees did not make Moore an opponent of the proprietorship; it certainly meant that he was willing to use the Crown and its resources for his own purposes.

The Goose Creek man's transparent affection for the sort of royal rule personified by Randolph becomes apparent from other evidence. Joseph Morton, Jr., writing ironically in his capacity as vice-admiralty judge, complained to the Board of Trade about the lack of compliance with the Navigation Acts in Carolina. Indeed, the Commons House of Assembly had just passed a law that enabled the Carolinians to limit both the prize fees of admiralty officials and the punishments levied on smugglers, while at the same time (in time-honored Goose Creek fashion) installing juries for vice-admiralty courts. Of course, these citizens tended to err on the side of leniency when considering fines for their accused friends and neighbors as that had been the point of creating these courts without juries in the first place. Then, Moore had usurped the governorship. Not coincidentally, in Morton's view, the new governor acted immediately to approve the act requiring juries for admiralty cases which had failed to pass during Blake's tenure. Significantly, the Board of Trade directed the proprietors to disallow it as contrary to the commissions of admiralty judges formulated by parliamentary statute.[437]

In any event, as governor, Moore adopted a more stringent attitude toward his opponents possibly in light of England's imperial interests and the threats posed from the south and west. Expecting an imminent declaration of war against France, the new governor asked the Commons House to provide funds for defense and to support an attack against Carolina's Spanish and French neighbors. However, the members apparently did not share the governor's imperial perspective and refused this request. Moore responded by dissolving the body and calling for new elections.[438]

The ensuing election held at Charles Town degenerated into a fracas, as Quarry subsequently informed the Board of Trade and as a battery of pamphleteers subsequently informed the London public. In the aftermath, the Commons House ordered an inquiry, but Moore promptly prorogued the assembly. However, when the members returned, the governor's opponents used the session to extend the investigation resulting in another prorogation. By this time, the long-awaited War of Spanish Succession/Queen Anne's War had broken out. Moore immediately put his plan for an attack on St. Augustine before the reconvened legislature. A preemptive strike on the Spanish, he argued, would prevent their reinforcement by the French. The Commons House demurred but "pressure" from the governor coupled by the news of the official declaration of war prodded them into financing the expedition in September 1702.[439]

By the time of this campaign, Moore had acquired a long experience with South Carolina's frontier, especially its warfare, and with the colony's Spanish neighbors. He had, correspondingly, developed substantial contacts with the Yamassees and other Indians who logically could have provided intelligence reports. Yet, Moore seems not to have thought through his plan for capturing St. Augustine—unless the objective really was, as his opponents charged *ex post facto*, a smash-and-grab operation conducted primarily to seize plunder and slaves. Indeed, one could argue that the assault on Florida constituted the climax of Moore's long campaign against the Spanish missions and their indigenous inhabitants.[440]

In any event, the South Carolina army quickly overran the Spanish town but lacked the means to reduce the stone Castillo de San Marcos into which the inhabitants fled. Moore invested the fort and sent his second-in-command, Daniel, to Jamaica for appropriate munitions. Unfortunately for the besiegers, a pair of Spanish men-of-war arrived from Havana first. After a two-month siege, the English hastily burned the town, stole what they could take, and withdrew.[441]

To say that the size and armament of the San Marcos bastion, built in 1679, was "unexpected" to Moore, who had fought in campaigns as far south as the Florida Keys, and, hence, the expedition's lack of appropriate preparation, as two leading studies of early Carolina have claimed, beggars belief.[442] Aside from Moore's lengthy involvement in frontier affairs and long-standing connections with Carolina's Indian neighbors, the governor's friend Randolph had sent the Board of Trade in 1699 "a Draught of the Town & Castle of St Augustine with a short description of it by a Gentleman who has often been there" observing "It's done exactly true, more for service then for show."[443]

Considering Moore's knowledge, either he hoped that the element of surprise would carry the castle or, with the prize in sight, he became overly ambitious.

This fiasco ignited another Carolina political dispute. The Commons House, still dominated by Moore's supporters, registered its "thanks" to the governor for his services in leading the expedition. However, the governor's opponents demanded an investigation. More than reputation and pride were at stake: the siege had generated a cost overrun of £4,000 sterling that Moore proposed paying off with paper bills of credit. In the meantime, he sought to proceed with a campaign against Pensacola. The opposition responded with demands for regulations of elections, the Indian trade, and naturalization (the Huguenots having again submitted meekly to authority). These differences of opinion soon spiraled into riot.[444]

Several narratives purporting to chronicle the behavior of the Indian slavers were created by individuals who were opposed to them and outraged by the turn of events in the colony at this time. Before turning to the pamphlets published by various interested parties, we should note that some people made complaints about Moore and his associates before they went public and they made their more immediate and private objections to a curious quarter: Robert Quarry, former Goose Creek man and friend of pirates. As we know, Quarry left Carolina following the collapse of the Sothell government; by 1703, he was ensconced in New York as a vice-admiralty judge. That Moore's enemies communicated their complaints privately to Quarry and that the former Goose Creek planter saw fit to relay these complaints to the Board of Trade suggests that we should take the published anti-Moore accounts as reasonably accurate chronicles of events. The new judge's letter to his superiors also indicates that his Carolina correspondents provided the basis of the language used in the subsequent published accounts. In other words, the people who objected to Moore's behavior had formulated their opinions before they went to press and they did not, therefore, compose their documents with one eye on public opinion: Quarry received his letters in June 1703 and the first anti-Moore pamphlets did not see the light of day until well over a year later.[445]

This poacher-turned-gamekeeper's contacts in his old colony reported "a very strange account of the great disorders which have happened" in Charles Town following "their unfortunate disappointment and miscarriage against St. Augustine." Quarry's informants told him that the massive costs of this expedition, some £8,000, had "fallen very heavy upon the Country" and left the Carolinians at a loss at how to pay them. He wrote the Board of Trade that his old running partner seemed bent on destroying the colony: he had tried to control an assembly election through force and the votes of unqualified persons, including Huguenots, "Negroes," members of the upper house of the parliament, and then launched his attack on St. Augustine, even though the colony lacked the requisite armed vessels or siege guns; hence, "the designe [was] contrary to all reason and sense." Without assistance from Queen Anne's government, he warned, this undertaking would bring ruin to Carolina.

Opponents of the war proposed to make provisions to pay the debt in exchange for redress of their grievances against the government, particularly in terms of the recent election. Moore, though, "refused these good offices," which provoked the withdrawal of the majority of the members, who entered their protest, followed by "a great Ryot for many days" involving attacks on some of the "Gentlemen of the best quality in the Country." To add insult to their injury, Moore declined to hear their complaints and denied them access to the courts to pursue those who had abused them.

In the meantime, the proprietors had appointed Sir Nathaniel Johnson— freed from his oath to James II by the exiled king's death—as governor, but, for reasons that remain unclear, he did not see fit to claim his office until the outbreak of this disturbance.[446] However, when the aggrieved colonists petitioned Sir Nathaniel for redress, "he tells them it is now too late, but he would take care for the future, no such actions should be allowed." The resulting perception of a lack of justice for these gentlemen, Quarry reported, created a resolution among them to go over the heads of the governor (and the proprietors) and petition the Board of Trade itself for relief.[447]

This choice of governor naturally overjoyed the Goose Creek–controlled Commons House. Their address of thanks identified Sir Nathaniel as "not only the most honourable and most capable to administer the Civil Government of any your Lordships hitherto placed over us" as well as "the only experienced military Commander Wee ever had," which was particularly vital since the war had begun with France, although this ignored the suspicions raised about Johnson back in 1690. Thus, the assembly proclaimed their eagerness, given appropriate proprietary and imperial support, to defend their province and try again to capture Florida, this time under Sir Nathaniel's leadership.[448]

No French invasion came, but the Charles Town government did attack— the Dissenting enemies of the Goose Creek men rather than the Spanish—by passing a Test Act that gave responsibility for overseeing religious affairs to a board of commissioners, predictably dominated by Sir Nathaniel and his associates while barring those who did not conform to the Church of England from office. They found the timing right for such legislation as it sat in accordance with the views of the new Palatine, Lord Granville. A "High Tory," he participated vigorously in efforts at this time to clamp down on the practice of heterodox English officials of indulging in "occasional conformity" to avoid the prescriptions of the metropolitan Test. Although he had no prior experience with Carolina politics, he naturally approved of the Goose Creek maneuver to hobble their Dissenting opponents.[449]

Enraged, the law's opponents advanced this argument in a series of public appeals designed to curry popular opinion in London and support in the House of Lords.[450] Even prior to the ratification of the Test, the Carolina Dissenters and their allies, alarmed at the drift matters had taken, had sent an agent, John Ash, with a petition asking the proprietors to redress a series of grievances brought on by the failed assault on St. Augustine.[451] After Granville declined to entertain these complaints, Ash began to compose a tract setting forth the abuses of the Moore administration. He died, though, before he could finish it and, on November 4, 1704, Johnson and his supporters passed their Test. Daniel Defoe, mouthpiece of the Dissenters in London, completed Ash's tract, which became one of the first rounds fired in a small barrage that aimed to have the obnoxious legislation overturned by higher authority.[452] Published in London, where "occasional conformity" remained a heated issue, between 1705 and 1707, these documents all tracked the recent history of Carolina to support their arguments. All of the anti-Establishment writers pointed a finger at Johnson and his allies as responsible for the legislation that, the pamphleteers argued, now endangered the province's—and by extension, England's—future.[453]

These pamphlets reminded the Lords and other readers that the Fundamental Constitutions had contained "wise Provisions" for religious toleration and other "Encouragements" for Dissenters to migrate to Carolina, which had increased trade and, correspondingly, customs revenue and profit. Their authors then denounced the base and irreligious behavior of Moore, Sir Nathaniel, Rhett, and their associates but, they noted, what could anyone expect from the defender of count Conigsmark (Johnson), two escapees from the Fleet Prison (Rhett and James Smith a/k/a Serurier), a "broken Haberdasher" (speaker of the Commons House, How), and an enslaver of Indians (Moore) who had collaborated in bankrupting the colony while pursuing pecuniary projects, illegally seized the government, managed irregular elections, assaulted "principal inhabitants," clergymen, and pregnant women in the street, and established a detestable "High Commission Court," all "to the utter Ruin of the Constitution of Church and State." Naturally, Moore's assembly had refused to ratify the Fundamental Constitutions so thay could "have the better Opportunity to prey upon the Country, by leaving it in a more unsettl'd State and Condition" which would then bring "fatal Discouragement of the further and better Settlement" of Carolina.[454]

Faced with this flurry from the printing presses, Granville and his own patron, the earl of Nottingham, chief opponent of "occasional conformity," managed to get an answer to the Dissenters' tracts into print. This account predictably claimed that the Palatine and the Carolina government had acted legally (and reminded readers that the Fundamental Constitutions had never been ratified) to preserve both church and state from the schemes of the Dissenters and blamed the enemies of the Goose Creek men for creating the tumult.[455]

In actuality, the plan for Establishment in Carolina had little to do with religion and, not coincidentally, the Church of England opposed the provincial Test.[456] In the first place, the established church had a minimal presence in the province in 1704 and a questionable one, prior to the appointment of the Reverend Samuel Marshall to St. Philip's in 1696, notwithstanding all we have been told about an "Anglican" party. Indeed, the timing of the legislation and its particular language, that made the Carolina clergy subject to the approval of the parishioners, New England–style, lends strong support to the belief that one of the Act's chief purposes was to keep the clergy that did exist, notably the Reverend Edward Marston, in check rather than to promote the Church of England.[457]

This cleric, like Sir Nathaniel, had been a nonjuror before swearing allegiance to Queen Anne upon the death of James II; coincidentally, both men also hailed originally from Newcastle.[458] On the face of things, this flirtation with Jacobitism, as well as a common geographical origin, might have promoted a bond between the minister and the governor. Yet, instead, they became fierce enemies as Marston, to Sir Nathaniel's outrage, joined the opposition to the Goose Creek men. From the perspective of Marston and his friends, such as the younger Thomas. Smith, Ash and Joesph Boone, the supporters of Establishment had behaved outrageously. For the circle of Johnson and Moore, Marston and the Dissenters constituted an immediate danger to order and a continuing threat to their political control.[459]

The Goose Creek men had to back down when the House of Lords disallowed the Test. Instead, Johnson and his supporters settled for new legislation that provided salaries for the Anglican clergy at provincial expense and set out parish boundaries, but was stripped of its predecessor's obnoxious provisions, such as the power of the commissioners to remove ministers and orthodoxy for officeholders. Although the more fervent opponents of Establishment objected, the revised situation pleased moderates and, perhaps most importantly, Huguenots, for whom the act made special provisions. The coming to power of a Tory ministry in 1710, which passed an Occasional Conformity Act the following year, solved the problem of metropolitan complaints about the alleged persecution of Carolina Dissenters.[460]

Perhaps more importantly for Sir Nathaniel's reputation, this settlement of the establishment issue had come after the long-feared attack by French and Spanish forces that came on August 27, 1706. Carried in five ships and landing at three locations, the invaders actually fared worse than Moore had at St. Augustine five years before, suffering 40 killed and leaving 230 prisoners when one of their ships was driven off, while the defenders lost only one man.

Johnson, by all accounts gained unanimous favor as he led the heroic defense of the province.[461]

What then were the effects of the pattern—for over 20 years—of riots, drubbings, dubious elections, planned kidnappings, alternative governments, plots with and ruinous attacks undertaken against the Indians and the Spanish, capped by these efforts to restrict access to political power? In terms of the proprietorship, Granville's political commitment to rigid conformity, proved costly. His refusal to entertain the Dissenters' petition made the first tear in the connection between the Lords and those colonists who had always supported constitutional government and orderly settlement. Now, these planters began to question the character of a proprietorship that would ally itself with the Goose Creek men and may, correspondingly, have come to question the future of the province. At the same time, the Palatine's willingness to put the best interests of the colony behind metropolitan political interests gave additional ammunition to opponents of proprietary colonies in the central government. In the meantime, once the joint French-Spanish threat subsided, the opponents of the dealers in Indians again took the offensive.

Chapter 9 ❧

Consternation

As it happens, their half-triumph in the battle over Establishment proved the beginning of the end of the Goose Creek men as a political force and, ultimately, they furthered their own demise. In the first place, although they had succeeded in placing the Church of England in Carolina on a public footing, the bitter battle over establishment had left the Dissenters and their friends awaiting their chance to take revenge. At the same time, the long-standing economic and political alliance between the "dealers in Indians" and the Yamassee Indians finally broke down in 1715. After almost 40 years of mutual benefit from the Indian slave trade, the Yamassees became fearful that their debts to their trading partners would result in their own enslavement and attacked the Carolina frontier. The colony barely survived this assault before the English drove the Indians to the protection of St. Augustine, a result that rendered the continuation of the Indian slave trade—the basis of Goose Creek identity and behavior since the 1670s—economically unfeasible.

The death of Granville, in 1707 proved particularly inopportune for his clients as it left them vulnerable to nonconformist efforts to get their own back. For the Dissenters remained active opponents of religious establishment and its sponsors as the Reverend Francis Le Jau, whose letters provide much of the evidence about the character of Carolina at this time, habitually observed. His hopes that "all those divisions will fall of themselves and the Spirit of Jesus reign here" failed to materialize. The prospects for forgetting bygones remained slim and, according to the cleric, religion only provided a mask for political activity designed to destroy the "best inhabitants" of the province.[462]

Thus, Le Jau noted that the "last Sedition arose from a Club of 170 men enter'd into an Associacon to stand by one another to ruine" Nicholas Trott, the provincial chief justice. This group "had a hearing and cou'd prove nothing against him" but commenced "upon another business in our 3d.

Assembly, met since I came which I am afraid will miserably end for the peace of this Country." The minister lamented again, "in the meantime no publick business is done"; but "what is most singular the women of the Town are turned Politicians also and have a Club where they meet weekly among themselves, but not without falling out among one another." These "singular women," who included "One of the regicides Widdows, Mrs Axtel, and Mrs Blake the true daughter of such a Mother are remarkably Zealous and diligent this way," insured, to the dismay of their opponents, that politics remained fraught with tension. When the collectors of the parish levy for St. Philip's Parish in Charles Town had the temerity to call at the house of Joseph Boone, still in London serving as agent for the Dissenters, they found Mrs. Boone with the second Landgrave Smith and his brother, "two of the Ringleaders of the Faction." They not only declined to pay their rates, but Mrs. Boone suggested that Trott, who had paid as an example, should have been hanged seven years before as he had "made all this disturbance."[463]

Such divisions continued into 1708. In March, Le Jau noted, "there is a Number of Civil Gentlemen thereabouts" Goose Creek.[464] Yet, "matters are not well settled in our Parishes, and the dissenters continuing to Proselyte People to themselves as they have done these 20 years past."[465] Strife among parishioners of the established church compounded this friction. The Reverend Richard Marsden had come to St. Philip's, Charles Town from Maryland in mysterious circumstances and replaced Marston when the congregation had put him out. Le Jau endeavored not to take sides in this dispute and continued his efforts to reconcile Sir Nathaniel Johnson's particular enemy to his people. However, he wished Marston had adopted a more respectful attitude to Sir Nathaniel, whom he regarded as the champion of the Church of England in Carolina.[466] As of November 1709, the fight continued, only, according to Le Jau, Marston had now (ominously) become an attorney, a means to further antagonize people.[467]

At the same time, some Carolinians continued to pursue the Goose Creek men through regulation of the Indian trade. Thomas Nairne, a Colleton County planter resident in Carolina since 1698, became involved in this commerce and joined Sir Nathaniel's enemies—Landgrave Smith and his brother, George, Ash, the widows of Axtell and Blake, and Joseph Boone—in renewing the fight for reform. Nairne and his friends apparently regarded the upheavals caused by Indian wars and the ensuing enslavement of the losers as a very dangerous and counterproductive policy by 1707. The French attack on Charles Town had been a wake-up call: if Carolina did not take steps to secure better relations with its Indian neighbors, the lucrative deerskin trade would dry up and the Indians would go over to the province's enemies. This alliance would, at best, halt the expansion of Carolina's trading interests and, at worst, put the colony at its greatest risk since the Spanish attacks in 1686. The would-be reformer, thus, began to think in imperial terms as James Moore had done several years previously.

Nairne, although a Scot, apparently satisfied the requirements of the 1704 Test since he sat in the Assembly as a member from Colleton County. Undoubtedly, though, he was a leader of the "country" party against Sir Nathaniel Johnson and his supporters. He failed to win reelection to the Assembly, possibly through Sir Nathaniel's connivance, in March 1706, but when the Test was repealed he returned to his place in the following December session where he composed the thanks submitted by the Commons House to Queen Anne for nullifying that legislation (to Johnson's annoyance). He also prepared bills to regulate elections and the Indian trade.

Unsurprisingly, the governor resisted this legislative program. When offered £200 per annum to replace the presents he customarily received from the province's Indian allies, Sir Nathaniel refused. Outraged, his opponents, led by Nairne, then sought to expose Johnson's involvement in the Indian slave trade contending, familiarly, that the dealers employed a practice of encouraging their allies to attack one another's villages in order to acquire slaves more quickly. The slave traders avoided punishment, Nairne charged, by having taking care to lavish presents upon the governor and his trading partner and son-in-law, Thomas Broughton.

One James Child had done precisely this: he told the Cherokees that the governor wanted them to attack another nation. They did, bringing in some 160 Indian slaves whom Child sold in Charles Town, half of them for the benefit of the governor. Although the Commons House freed the slaves, Sir Nathaniel declined to prosecute Child. The Nairne-led legislators then demanded stricter oversight of the trade. While their protests generated a prompt dissolution, the end of the session did not stop the "private whispers" that the governor continued privately to support the Indian slave trade.[468]

This festering situation erupted into yet another fracas when the assembly reconvened in June 1707. Nairne helped to draft a list of provincial grievances for the Crown's attention and pursued legislation that would give the Commons House the choice of receiver as well as control over the Indian trade. The colony still needed to pay off its war debts, but an impasse ensued while Nairne and his party attacked Chief Justice Trott. At the same time, the colony's paper money, first issued in the aftermath of the Moore attack on St. Augustine and again in 1707 continued to depreciate: £100 sterling equaled £150 Carolina currency in 1710, but £200 in 1714, and £400 in 1722.[469]

Sir Nathaniel and his supporters then claimed the power to appoint the receiver and the controller, which provoked another dispute. This argument was not settled until, over a month later, the governor finally approved assembly control over the Indian trade, and agreed to regulation of elections and the nomination of the officials. In exchange, a tax bill was passed, and

Johnson received a £400 "gift" for his pains along with an annual allocation of £100 to replace the gifts that the Indians had habitually brought the governor. Traders now had to take out licenses issued by commissioners appointed by the legislature; Nairne became the Indian agent for the colony and immediately undertook a diplomatic mission to Indians in the west.[470]

As we have seen, however, the Goose Creek men never conceded defeat readily and the opportunity for counterattack presented itself the following year when Nairne charged Broughton with enslaving some Cherokees as well as with the illegal seizure of deerskins that were allegedly public property. In response, Sir Nathaniel had the Indian agent arrested on charges, without apparent irony, of engaging in a Jacobite conspiracy. The governor then rejected a petition from Colleton County for Nairne's release and apparently suppressed exculpatory evidence. With his leading opponent in jail, Sir Nathaniel called a new assembly election that duly returned his supporters, with the exception of Colleton County. When, the new Commons House dutifully barred Nairne from the House and removed him from his position as Indian agent, the licensing system quickly broke down.[471]

Nairne never went to trial. Possibly, Johnson intended to let him rot in jail while supposedly awaiting instructions from the proprietors, although the Lords did not consider his instructions "relating to the presentation of Nairne for treasonable words" until April 1709 when the reformer was in England and then "defer'd the same till Mr Trott shall advise."[472] While imprisoned, though, the displaced Indian agent made use of his time by composing a memorial on the French threat to Carolina for the attention of the earl of Sunderland and preparing a map showing the English, French, and Indian settlements in southeastern North America in order to illustrate the province's imperial importance. He was also reelected to the Commons House only to be promptly expelled because of the treason indictment against him. The assembly also inquired into his affairs as agent, an investigation Nairne obstructed by refusing to produce documents. Arrested for contempt of the Commons House, he posted bond and fled to England between December 1708 and April 1709 to make his case to the proprietors.[473]

The Scotsman found a different proprietary board from the one that had ratified the Test in 1704. Most significantly, Lord Granville had died and his share had passed to his wife, Rebecca, while the heir of the earl of Craven had become Palatine. With Granville gone, Nairne's London visit brought him ready vindication and restored normal service between the proprietors and the foes of the Goose Creek men: the Lords removed Sir Nathaniel as governor in favor of Edward Tynte and named Nairne as an admiralty judge.[474] These changes seem to have been sufficient to nullify the treason charge and Nairne duly returned to Charles Town in 1711. By that time, his adversary, Johnson, had contracted dysentery and retired from public life.[475]

The departure of the last first-generation Goose Creek man may have promised, yet again, an end to political strife and, correspondingly, peace and prosperity. Almost routinely, the proprietors instructed Tynte, as they had his predecessors, to work to reconcile their colonists and to eliminate their partisan bickering so that Carolina might at last fulfill its hopeful promise.[476]

As it was, the situation of both society and religion remained precarious. On the Church of England side, Le Jau's parishioners had passed a tax of one shilling and three pence upon themselves to maintain their minister while the number of communicants had increased from 30 to 50. Even so, those still opposed to Establishment—and apparently seeking to "introduce ways like those of New England"—had "infected" the parish with their principles.[477]

This report, one of many filed by the Church of England clergy with their superiors indicates that, in addition to continued strife all over Carolina's religious and political landscape, it had become apparent that the province's geography remained unhealthy and, oftentimes, dangerous: outbreaks of dysentery, malaria, yellow fever and other diseases routinely beset the colony. Tynte himself died on June 26, 1710 after just seven months in the province; as had happened with Kyrle in 1684, the colonial climate nipped proprietary plans in the bud.[478]

The governor's demise predictably generated a new round of wrangling, as the colonists contrived to choose two governors—Johnson's son-in-law, Broughton (a deputy and surveyor in his own right), and Robert Gibbes (son of Goose Creek man, Thomas, as well as deputy and provincial chief justice)—to replace him. Fears of violence, encouraged by the appearance of Gibbes's party in arms, only receded when Broughton, although the clergy's favorite for the post, agreed to give way until the proprietors made their pleasure known.[479]

By coincidence, the proprietary board, to which the colonists turned for further guidance at this time, suffered its own difficulties in the wake of Granville's demise. The vagaries of biology that had always placed a heavy hand on the enterprise reemerged. From its inception, at least one proprietor of some prominence—from Albemarle to Ashley to Craven to Bath to Granville—had maintained an interest in the proprietorship. Granville's death, though, created a vacuum in the partnership that had already been weakened by untimely death and the repeated (and illegal) sales of shares in the venture. This resulted in a shortage of leadership at a time when the colony was undergoing its greatest crisis since its early days.

Lady Granville acquired her husband's share under the terms of his will. However, as the newcomer and as a woman, she could scarcely command preeminence given the prevailing attitudes of the day. Then, the Palatine, Lord Craven, died suddenly aged 43 leaving a minor heir. Minors also held the Blake (formerly Baron Berkeley) and Colleton shares. John Carteret, subsequently earl of Granville, had just come into his majority but had no experience with Carolina or the proprietorship and quickly involved himself in affairs at court. Shaftesbury's heirs spent considerable time abroad and died young. Edward Thornburgh and Thomas Amy had the most familiarity with proprietary affairs, but as commoners lacked the social and political clout both to deal with the Crown and its increasing noise against proprietary colonies and to lend oversight to the fractious colony.[480]

The ambivalent attitude of the Lords toward their province at the time they appointed Tynte appears in their letters. On the one hand, the proprietors encouraged their government to "seriously consider of the best and most proper Methods for improving all the Products and Manufactures of our province (particularly that of Rice and Silk)" in order to promote the colony's welfare.[481] Yet, they admitted that the "indisposition" of their secretary, James Griffiths, to whom they had delegated the responsibility for handling Carolina's affairs had caused "some neglect."[482]

It would be a mistake, though, to charge the proprietors—especially considering that a number of them were handicapped by age and gender, that others were deeply involved in English politics, and that their colonists were a contentious, short-sighted lot—with neglecting the problems of their province after the royal disallowance of the Test and Establishment Acts. For example, early in 1713, they commissioned Francis Nicholson, a person with considerable American experience and the former governor of New York, Maryland, and Virginia, to "enquire into disorders that have lately happen'd in [Carolina]."[483]

Indeed, when Lady Granville followed her husband to the grave in 1711, it seemed that these proprietary difficulties might be resolved. She left her share to her son, Henry Somerset, second duke of Beaufort, and one of the up and coming aristocrats of the day, who, the colonists expected, would employ his vigor and influence to good effect in the metropolis and to ride herd on the province's factions.[484] When Beaufort succeeded as Palatine, the Carolinians responded by promptly naming the new settlement at Port Royal in his honor.

On November 30, 1710, in light of the disorder following Tynte's death, the reconstituted Lords appointed a relation of Beaufort's predecessor, Charles Craven, as their new governor.[485] And two months later, having read more reports on the Broughton–Gibbes dispute, they found the latter guilty of bribery and ordered him to pay over to Craven (in "fine rice") the salary he had collected since he had taken office.[486]

The new governor came to Charles Town with two advantages: he, like Tynte, was an outsider and, unlike Tynte, he had a family connection to the proprietors. The Lords particularly wanted Craven to sort out the still-raging land grant problem in light of their concerns over "Exorbitant & Illegal Grants of the Lands of Our said Province." Thus, they gave him specific instructions, following from their January 1710 prohibition against future land sales "Except by Our immediate Order" to watch the payment of rents and make sure public instructions and warrants for land were recorded. Persons who wished to buy land once again had to appear personally before the proprietary board, although one month later they seem to have changed their minds about the practicality of this policy instead notifying grantees to take up their lands within six months or risk forfeiture of their claims. At the same time, they reminded their officers that vigorous rent collection served their interests since the rents paid their salaries; they were to send any surplus "in Rice or Money" to London quarterly.[487]

The proprietors continually had to balance the need to pay their own rent (and arrears) to the Crown, the need to pay their officials, the need to maintain attractive terms for settlement, and the need to discourage thinly spread plantations when determining policy. Hence, they changed their minds about grants again in January 1711. Complaining again about "Illegal and Exorbitant Grants of Lands" in Carolina, they noted that they had ordered that no land should be sold without their special warrant signed in London. However, "to give all due Encouragement to such persons as shall come to settle themselves" in the province, they repealed that requirement and allowed warrants to be issued once again out of the secretary's office in the colony so long as those grants did not exceed 500 acres.[488]

For their part, the colonists also expressed faith that Craven would, finally, put affairs on an even keel. The continuing cycle of war, debt, and political-religious upheaval had made life difficult for many. Thus, in July 1710, the Church of England commissary Gideon Johnston lamented "my Salary here, has never hitherto enabled me to procure [my family] bare food and raiment; and were it not for the help my Wife has given me, and the Charity of some, and the little Credit I have with the Bakers, Butchers, & Shopkeepers, I must have starved in such an excessive dear place as this is." Although the Commons House had been made aware of his plight, the great debts of some £15,000 created by the costs of fortification and defense against the French and Spaniards left no money for the relief for the clergyman or, apparently, for much else.[489]

Of course, Carolina's less attractive qualities remained all-too-evident and the great expectations for the colony, yet again, failed to materialize. On the proprietary front, Beaufort had inherited an estate encumbered with immense debts and proved to have neither interest in nor time for American colonization. In his will, written shortly after receiving this legacy, he left his share in Carolina to three executors "In Trust to sell the same for the best price that can be gotten" in order to fulfill the obligations created by his marriage contract. The duke then compounded the problems both of his estate and of Carolina by dying on May 24, 1714 leaving his own minor heir.[490]

In the meantime, the situation on the Carolina frontier changed abruptly as war broke out with the Tuscaroras in September 1711. As with prior Indian wars, observers generally laid the blame for the outbreak of hostilities on the shoulders of the slave traders.[491] However, after some initial setbacks, by February 1712, a Carolinian army, led by John Barnwell and James Moore, Jr., had destroyed their enemies and calm seemed to have settled once again over relations between Charles Town and its indigenous neighbors and trading partners.[492] With the surviving Tuscaroras moving to the asylum provided by their Iroquois cousins in New York, Craven finally in his place, and political tempers again cooling, it seemed as 1715 began that, after so many disappointments, the colony had finally put many of its problems behind it. Instead, though, the most devastating of the colony's frontier conflicts, and perhaps the major event of the whole proprietary period, broke out.

The Yamassee War was the bitter culmination of Carolina's 45-year history. Having assisted the Goose Creek men in the Indian slave trade since the 1670s, the Yamassees had contrived to amass a sizeable debt to their partners. They were well aware of the consequences of failing to meet these obligations, which the fate of many of the Tuscaroras had hammered home. At the same time, the sparse settlement of the colony, generated by political upheaval and the inhospitable environment, and in disregard of repeated proprietary warnings made it a tempting target for a desperate Indian attack.[493]

The economic and demographic results of this war, as every student of early Carolina history knows, were dire: only a timely alliance with the Cherokees averted disaster. Still security (and its costs) preoccupied the surviving colonists.[494] Moreover, the Yamassee attack also exposed the problems related to the concept of a proprietary colony, particularly Carolina, from an imperial perspective. Craven duly reported the Indian attack to the Board of Trade on May 23, 1715 seeking its immediate help, and they promptly relayed the news on to the proprietors on July 8, 1715.[495] Four days later, Sir John Carteret, guardian also of the minor duke of Beaufort, and Sir John Colleton wrote the Board of Trade that the Lords could not provide the requisite supplies to defend their province and asked George I's government to provide troops and arms in exchange for "sufficient security" for the repayment of the expenditures. In the meantime, Francis Nicholson had informed the proprietors that the province needed 300 barrels of powder, 1,500 muskets with bayonets, 2,000 cutlasses, and 40 mortars to defend itself, that trade of arms and ammunition with Indians in all the colonies should be prohibited, and that assurances be received from the French and Spanish ministers that their colonies would issue similar prohibitions.[496]

Two days after Carteret and Colleton's report, the Lords advised that they had ordered all their "Goods and Effects as our Receiver has in his hands [approximately £2,000]" to be used to acquire arms and ammunition for the colony and that the assembly had sent the equivalent of £2,500 sterling to

New York and New England for arms and ammunition which was on its way. They offered to give a mortgage on their Carolina lands (but no claim to the provincial government) to the king for any money the Crown advanced.[497]

Since 1663, a great deal had changed. When the proprietorship had been created, the government of Charles II lacked the resources and, generally, the inclination to pursue colonization. Only a combination of prominent and wealthy individuals had the means to engage in colony-building. Just over a half-century later, the private interests involved in Carolina had, thanks to the vagaries of inheritance, not substantially improved—if anything, they were less weighty than the individuals involved in the proprietorship originally. Even more significantly—but for reasons that only had to do with "empire" secondarily—the ability of the English (and, by 1715, British) government to pursue imperial aims had increased immeasurably. The flight of James II from his thrones in December of 1688 and the willingness of the subsequent Convention Parliament to attach itself to the fortunes of William of Orange meant, as students of the Williamite period well know, unprecedented success for the government in levying and collecting taxation in order to fight wars against James in Ireland and against James's protector, Louis XIV, on the Continent. Fuelled by the fear of a Jacobite restoration, England, for the first time since the reign of Henry VIII, became a European power supported by institutions, such as the Bank of England (founded in 1694). The desire of the sort of efficiency that was displayed in the formation of the Bank and toward the collection of revenue to wage war against the "Sun King" came to be more forcefully applied against perceived anomalies such as proprietorships.[498]

To compound this situation, even the Lords knew they could not readily muster the required munitions to preserve their colony from a determined assault. Carolina's agents in London also knew this. They brought their own memorial directly to the Board of Trade—itself another manifestation of new governmental vigor at this time—"relating to the miserable Condition of that province by the Insurrection of the Indians & to Relief necessary to be sent thither." These representatives of the colony's planters and merchants noted the threat to their own situations but concentrated on the prospect of "the Ruine of so flourishing so hopeful a province" that had provided a stream of customs revenue to the Crown through its trade in rice, pelts, and naval stores with no charge to the Exchequer. Now, they warned, the attack by the Yamassees and their allies, undoubtedly encouraged by the Spanish and the French, made likely, in addition to the the death and torture of many English subjects, a domino effect: "Carolina being the Frontier of all the other English Settlements upon the Continent, If that should miscarry, all the other Colonys would soon be involv'd in the same Ruin & ye whole English Empire, Religion & Name be extirpated in America," unless the Crown immediately attended to the province's defensive needs.[499]

The Board of Trade itself saw the chance, thanks to apparent proprietary inability or disinclination to relieve the colonists, to encourage the Lords to hand over their government to royal authority, especially since their "neglect" had already cost England control of the Bahamas. Yet, the Carolinians did not escape imperial censure, as the Board also determined that the debts of the Indians generated by unregulated trade with Charles Town had caused the war to break out in the first place. Thus, in the short term, the Board passed on to Secretary of State Stanhope the province's military requests, noting that while the Lords had one ship of 100 tons standing by to sail for Charles Town, they had only one shipment of rice, hopefully worth £400, to pay for its sailing and they refused to hand their charter back to the Crown without compensation.[500]

Significantly, though, the crisis of the Yamassee War caused both imperial officials at the Board of Trade and colonial leaders in Charles Town to bypass the Lords, who were kept informed of events largely after the fact, as they strived for a resolution. At the same time, the colony had become too important to risk. In the natural interest of self-preservation, Carolinians began to appeal to the central government (and adopted an imperial perspective in their petitions) while, in the interests of empire, the Board of Trade's view of the proprietorship as an anachronism came into clearer focus.

The colonists encouraged this attitude. Joseph Boone and Richard Beresford, provincial agents, provided a supporting memorial to the Board of Trade which surveyed the destruction wrought by the war: the hundreds of thousands of pounds worth of property lost while "numbers of its Inhabitants have been destroy'd by Fire & Sword & many more have deserted the place." Boone and Beresford made another presentation on August 9, 1715 and a committee of the House of Commons responded with an address to the king asking him to send relief to Charles Town. George I did commit "a sufficient Quantity of arms & ammunition but the unnatural rebellion [the landing of the 'Old Pretender' in Scotland, 'the "15"'] obstructed sending Men." Thus, the memorialists lamented, the exhausted Carolinians still wanted the requisite men and money to avoid the loss of their province, especially as long as the Spaniards at St. Augustine remained capable of making mischief (these provokers of Indians and "runaway" slaves merited severe punishment). Their agents also petitioned to have defeated Jacobites sent to Carolina.[501]

The impotence of the proprietorship to repulse Indian attack, to deal with Spanish "insolence," or to warn off the French posed a grave problem. Thus, when further grievances emerged between the Lords and their colonists after 1716, the latter had little difficulty casting off their allegiance while the Crown, although not eager to succor a movement that amounted to rebellion, ultimately, despite various misgivings, agreed to assume control of the colony.

Chapter 10 ~

Conclusions

Of course, the proprietorship did not shrivel up and die immediately notwithstanding the misgivings about it held at both Whitehall and Charles Town. But the Yamassee War, following on the heels of the unexpected death of the duke of Beaufort, left the Lords, like their colony, in considerable disarray. The proprietors, for their part, carried on with John Carteret now occupying the Palatine's chair. Yet, although eminently capable, this ambitious young nobleman, who became one of the most prominent subjects of the first Hanoverian monarchs, had his eyes on far bigger things than Carolina. He, and his fellow proprietors, fulfilled their duties, but of necessity they continued to rely heavily on their agents to run the colony while the minority status of several proprietors further hampered the administration of the province after 1715.[502] In particular, the Lords seem to have come to favor individuals who had earlier forged close connections with the late Sir Nathaniel Johnson: Sir Nathaniel's son, Robert, served as the last proprietary governor of the colony, while William Rhett and Nicholas Trott, prominent supporters of the 1704 Test, occupied a variety of offices from receiver to chief judge up until the end of 1719 when the proprietary government collapsed.

These choices, however, did not turn out for the best. In the critical period after the Indian war, the problems of distance, distractions, and incapacity became exacerbated by the perception, which became pervasive among Carolinians, that these agents had blocked the points of contact to the proprietors and had used their position solely to aggrandize themselves. Trott and Rhett, although they attached themselves to the proprietors, neglected to follow the example of their old patron, Sir Nathaniel, of cultivating a base of support in the colony. Thus, the unfavorable perception became prevalent and spawned a professed fear of tyranny and "enslavement" in colonial minds that culminated in the rebellion against proprietary rule.

It did not have to turn out this way. After the colony and its Cherokee allies had driven off the Yamassees and their confederates, Carolina's prospects, once again, brightened. The defeated Indians had withdrawn themselves to St. Augustine and other points further south and west. This result opened a wide swath of territory to settlement and, almost immediately, various people began planning the "peopling" (and "re-peopling") of the area between the Edisto and Altamaha Rivers. But the proprietors received considerable criticism over their handling of the lands seized from the Indians, so a re-examination of their attitudes and policies in this regard seems to be in order.[503]

Shortly after the announcement of peace, the Lords informed Craven that they intended to set out "the Yammasee Settlement" in "proportions not exceeding two hundred acres" to persons already in or planning to migrate to Carolina. Grantees would take their land rent-free "for the first five years" and, then, could either purchase or continue to rent.[504] The proprietors also sold 5,000 acres of this land "at the usual rates" to one William Hodgson and made him a landgrave.[505]

In June 1717, the proprietors agreed to sell their lands between the Altamaha and Savannah Rivers to Sir Robert Montgomery, the son of Sir James Montgomery of Skelmorlie, who had partnered Lord Cardross and William Dunlop back in the 1680s.[506] Claiming to have inherited his father's desire to further colonization in Carolina and hearing of the advantages of Port Royal, Sir Robert sought to establish a "Margravate of Azalia" in the newly opened territory on the southernmost fringe of the proprietary grant. It is possible, of course, to argue that the grant of this sizeable chunk of land constituted a symptom of a collective proprietary desire to be rid of the colony. Considering the extent of the proprietary investment in the colony by 1717 and the expenses expected to accrue in the aftermath of the Yamassee War, it is unsurprising that the Lords seized on a chance to reduce their obligations. However, their willingness to sell off "uninhabited" territory should not be taken necessarily as evidence that they were "fed up with [Carolina's] problems and no longer committed to governing" the colony. "Azalia" might have served as a buffer between their province and Florida.[507] Unfortunately, though, for Sir Robert and the proprietors, the attorney general ruled that the Lords, under the terms of their charter, could not alienate any part of their domain, a determination that rendered the scheme stillborn.[508]

Thus, in the end, Montgomerie's cameo appearance made little impact on the history of Carolina. Far more significant for the province's long-term prospects, the departure of "ye treacherous Yamassees" in the wake of their war put paid to the Indian slave trade. The chief players on the indigenous side of this commerce—the people who had fought the wars that had created the slaves since the 1670s—had left their old partners, the "dealers in Indians," to fend for themselves. Without such connections—guides and interpreters, as well as warriors—the Goose Creek men could not hope to maintain a functioning operation. Moreover, the physical removal of most Indians from the Lowcountry after 1716 shrank the pool of prospective slaves; provoking wars and buying slaves farther in the interior would have entailed considerably more risk and more costs.[509]

The demise of the Indian slave trade coupled with the general recognition that the Indian slavers had provoked the war meant, at last, the disappearance of the Goose Creek men, ironically at what proved to be the end of the proprietary period; after 1716, they suddenly disappear from the historical record in which they had previously figured so prominently. Following the Yamassee War, Charles Town finally placed its Indian trade under governmental regulation free of Goose Creek interference. At the same time, the surviving remnants of the faction seem to have gone their own ways: Rhett and Trott continued to curry favor with proprietary patrons while James Moore, Jr., George Logan, and Arthur Middleton came to pursue different courses.

The reduction of the "dealers in Indians" and the trade that had supported them meant that the colony had yet another chance to put its political house in order. And, notwithstanding the cruel exposure of its limitations by the war, the proprietary regime continued to function after the restoration of peace, although on November 3, 1716, Governor Craven, whose "affairs acquiring his continued presence in England," bade farewell to the colony he had helped save. The Lords chose Robert Johnson, as his successor.[510]

At the same time that they appointed Johnson, the proprietors sought to underscore their belief that matters of provincial finance and government should remain grounded in the locality and to demonstrate their continuing concern for their colony within their power.[511] Hence, they again ordered the collection of rent arrears and the application of those funds for public use as determined by the governor, council, and assembly (after deducting the costs of government and £200 owed to Craven). They also made an additional present of £1,000 (Carolina) to the departing governor from land sales.[512]

The proprietors attempted to stress their continuing commitment to their colony in their responses to a series of queries presented by the Board of Trade in 1717. First, they proclaimed that peace had been made with the Indians thanks to the assistance they had received from London as well as by the alliance with the Cherokee.[513] In addition, they observed, the terms of the peace treaty provided for the return of captives and horses taken by the Indians, while the Lords had paid out "several hundred pounds" in arms and ammunition for their province since the outbreak of hostilities. Seeking to ease the burden of debt that the war had placed on their colonists, the proprietors, "very ready to do everything for the further security of the Province," had ordered Governor Johnson to apply all of their quitrent arrears to public use (of course, this order might not have come from entirely altruistic motives since the proprietors may have viewed it as a means of putting the collection of rents in order).[514]

Even in the period following the Yamassee War, Lords and colonists continued to cooperate. A good deal, for instance, has been made of a colorful comment made by Rhett in 1712 upon his receipt of his commission as receiver—"This is but Lords proprietors Government and I wou'd wipe my Arse with the Commission"—that Craven duly relayed to the Lords.[515] Yet, although the proprietors "highly resented" Rhett's insult, they provisionally restored him to his place as receiver since they perceived that his remarks came out inadvertently or from a passion: if he agreed to submit to the governor, he would receive a pardon. Rhett apparently did so since we have no evidence that he ever lost proprietary favor.[516]

Moreover, a basis existed for this continued proprietary faith in clients. By this time, the Lords had accepted the accounts of quitrents Rhett had submitted to them in January 1711. Indeed, three years later, this erstwhile inmate of the Fleet and confederate of the "High Church party" in the convulsions of 1704–06, actually produced a rent-roll that listed the names of holders along with the location and quantity of their lands.[517] Rhett also shipped rice worth £470 12s 10d to the Lords which, among other things, covered the £80 they owed for two years of secretary Robert Shelton's salary, £10 for a year's salary owed to their former clerk, and £30 owed for three year's salary to their present clerk, as well as £50 "Dividends" due to each of the proprietors.[518] The Lords also approved Rhett's account (and "method in keeping the account") from July 31, 1711 to May 1, 1712 with a balance due (payable in rice) of £1,031 2s 5d.[519]

For his part, Trott gained favor with the Lords although they continually denied his claim to a share of the proprietorship and, even though he was related to the proprietor, Thomas Amy, he never cemented his position in the province to the extent that he desired. The Dissenters consistently, as we have seen, complained about his ambitions and submitted a number of petitions and remonstrances "relating to a Riot Committed on the Chief Justice" to the Lords in 1708. Joseph Boone, who represented the Dissenters against Trott's "Church party" and later served as Charles Town's agent, petitioned the proprietors for the chief justice's removal on the grounds that he held too many offices.[520] Significantly, when the Assembly objected to Trott's pretended power to appoint a Provost Marshal, the Lords, out of respect for the representatives (although possibly expressed as sarcasm) revoked the power even though they "thought it reasonable that Our Said Chief Justice should have the nomination."[521]

Rhett and Trott, with secretary Shelton at the metropolitan end, ultimately became the scapegoats for the breakdown in the relationship between the proprietors and their colonists. In retrospect, it is not hard to see why. They had made lasting enemies of the Dissenters and the other opponents of the 1704 Test, such as Boone (still in London in the late 1710s but acting now as agent for the Commons House of Assembly), for their behavior over the previous decade. However, they had also broken, for reasons that remain unclear, with their old associates from Goose Creek.[522]

Consequently, whether the duo realized it or not, they occupied a vulnerable position. They may have counted on their friends on the proprietary board, but they should have known from experience that any help from that quarter would have been, at best, belated. They apparently also reckoned without the strong anti-proprietary sentiment at the Board of Trade. Thus, when their behavior and accumulation of offices alarmed South Carolinians like Morton, Jr., Boone, and Francis Yonge (the client of Palatine Carteret), the old Goose Creek men—Moore, Jr., Middleton, and Logan—joined new allies and rode again under a different banner. Ultimately, getting rid of Trott and Rhett came to mean getting rid of the proprietary government: a concept that no one felt strongly enough by the end of 1719 to fight over.[523]

Thus, the perception of misbehavior was more important than reality. The Charles Town rebels created a pair of narratives after their *coup d'etat* to justify their actions. These accounts, composed in the mid-1720s when the Carolinians were combating the possibility that proprietary rule might be restored, provide the bulk of what we know about the "revolution" against the proprietors. Consequently, they stress the malfeasance of Trott, Rhett, and Shelton, who engrossed offices and influence and prevented information from reaching proprietary notice. Whether or not these documents are reliable evidence as to the motives of the rebels or an *ex post facto* justification, must remain unknown at this point. Some other evidence, though, does exist to support the implied conclusion of the authors of these narratives that the rebellion of 1719 stemmed from conditions after the Yamassee War and not from any inherent defects or "widespread anti-proprietary sentiment," although the proprietors contributed to their demise by relying on these unpopular, arguably venal, agents.[524]

Of course, disputes between the proprietors and their colonists, especially over land, existed. Notwithstanding Rhett's efforts cited above, the Lords remained generally unsatisfied about land grants and quitrents.[525] They complained to their colonists in September 1718 that their lands continued to be conveyed "without our knowledge or Consent" while previous grants remained "in such a disorderly & confus'd condition" as to render a reasonable accounting or calculation of rents impossible. Thus, they again prohibited the creation of further grants without their consent.[526]

Yet, a little over one month later, the proprietors flip-flopped and agreed to grant 50-acre headrights for every migrant along with another 50 acres granted for each person accompanying the head of household in exchange for a peppercorn rent for the first three years and, thereafter, an annual rent of one penny per acre. This policy was to continue in force for seven years.[527]

A year on, though, the Lords found that abuses in the issuance of land grants continued. Persons with no authority to do so, they observed, had made "Exorbitant Grants of Land." As a result, quitrents remained in "a Disorderly & confused Condition" for which no satisfactory assurances could be offered for the future. Consequently, they halted land sales in the colony once again; prospective grantees now had to apply directly to the proprietors.[528]

This ongoing concern over quitrents and irregular settlement, no doubt, came to affect proprietary attitudes toward the Yamassee lands. Again, the issues here constituted far more than the degree of proprietary "control" over the colony or even the collection of rents. As anyone who had familiarity with the colony's history in the fall of 1718 should have (at the least) known, the combination of colonial disregard of instructions from London, exorbitant land grants, and resulting scattered settlements had created a recipe for disaster in the Yamassee War. To the Lords and their officials, then, it is quite possible to argue, the settlers seemed to have learnt nothing from that near-death experience: it was *déjà vu* as opposed to "tyranny."

Thus, the close call of the Yamassee War generated a further argument over the lands that had been taken from the Indians. In the aftermath, the Assembly passed two acts that appropriated the newly acquired territory for new migrants and "to such other Persons qualify'd as therein mentioned." These granted "several Privileges, Exemptions and Incouragements" to British and Irish Protestants to move to the province. The Lords, though, naturally disallowed these laws as an improper "Encroachment" on their title and their sole right to dispose of their own lands as they saw fit.[529] The Assembly then passed another act "relating to the payment of the Lords Rents & the Sale of their Lands" which the proprietors similarly disallowed.[530]

Apparently, in response to the news of the legislation, a "Mr Wilson" brought 200 families to Carolina from Belfast. By the time they arrived in the colony, though, the proprietors had disallowed the settlement act. Curiously, for people so keen on expanding settlement, the Commons House of Assembly seems to have regarded this veto as an excuse to avoid any obligations that the law may have created on the part of the colony. Thus, these Ulster migrants received no money from the province on their arrival and were left to fend for themselves to Wilson's "very great loss." He sought redress from the Charles Town government but in vain, leaving the proprietors, not for the first time, to clean up a mess left by their colonists: they ordered their governor and council to "do all the Justice that is in their power to Mr Wilson."[531]

Perhaps regarding the Wilson affair as further evidence of the flightiness, at best, or disingenuousness, at worst, of their colonists, the proprietors, in November 1718, received drafts and "plans of Lands" that Thomas Broughton and William English had laid out in 1711. These surveys included 48,000 acres near Port Royal, 24,000 acres to the north of Charles Town, patents of 12,000 and 10,000 acres on Craven River in Craven County, a draft of 12,000 acres in Craven County near Winyaw Sound, and a draft of 21,000 on Hilton Head Island, a total of 119,000 acres that included the Yamassee lands. The proprietors then determined that these lands should be divided amongst themselves into 12,000-acre baronies.[532] Then, in April 1719, they instructed their surveyor, Francis Yonge, to lay out fifteen baronies for themselves out of these lands with one-fourth of each barony fronting a river.[533]

The Carolinians made a great deal of the motives suggested by the colonists in their post-rebellion narratives for the proprietary reservation of the baronies: that the Lords "instead of granting Land for the Publick Use of the Garrisons, they gave strict Orders that no more Land should be granted to any Person whatsoever," yet kept the 15 baronies "to be laid out for their own Private Use." In the meantime, although their charter charged them with encouraging "His Majesty's Subjects to go over, and settle there, and to extend his Dominions, and they had just before promis'd it in Tracts of 200 Acres to new Comers" and "several Hundreds had come from Ireland" in reliance on that promise, the Lords had granted no land "notwithstanding the Country had been put to the Expence of paying some Thousands of Pounds for their Passages to Carolina." As a result, "the Number of Inhabitants could not be increas'd or their Frontiers strenghten'd." This view has received scholarly sanction, as noted above.[534]

Yet, rather less attention has been accorded to the explanation for their actions offered by the proprietors. Ten years after the rebellion, as their venture was winding up, they told the Privy Council that they believed that laying out the baronies at that time "might lend to the better peopling the Province by engaging the Proprietors separately to cultivate and improve their own lands," which would have meant bypassing the colony's land office, the source of so much of the historical difficulty surrounding rents and grants. In any event, though, the proprietors observed, "by reason of the disorders of the Colony, these lands were never entred upon except one Barony by Sir John Colleton's son who went over above a year since to settle the same."[535]

While these debates went on, the Charles Town government also had to continue to deal with the economic consequences brought on by the

Yamassee War. The costs of the conflict to the economy, which had still not recovered from the severe blow dealt to it by Moore's expedition against St. Augustine, nearly finished off what the Indians did not. The province was compelled to attempt to retire at least some of its debt and apply some order to its currency. Unsurprisingly, most of the members of the Commons House seem to have intended that the burden of economic reform fall on other shoulders than their own: merchants doing business, but not necessarily resident, in the colony. Equally unsurprising, those who found themselves bearing the burden strenuously objected to these policies.

Thus, the proprietors received irate petitions from merchants in doing business in both Charles Town and London against several new laws designed to raise revenue from the collection of excise duties. These laws placed, inter alia, a £10 duty on all goods of British manufacture imported into Carolina, a duty on "Liquors, Goods & Merchandize &c," and a £40 per head duty "upon all Negroes that shall be imported after 8 June 1719"; this last act was also designed "for the better ordering & governing of Negroes & all other Slaves."[536]

The Lords disallowed all of these statutory schemes. One, the duty on British goods—"of pernicious consequence to Trade and repugnant to the Laws and Customs of Great Britain"—ran afoul of the Crown which directed the proprietors to repeal it.[537] A second, having an adverse effect on the trade of Great Britain, created an improper distinction between British and Carolinian traders and no "greater Duties should be impos'd on Ships built in Great Britain than on Ships built in Carolina."[538] Finally, the import duty on "Negroes" seemed prejudicial to merchants and the Lords intended to repeal it, "But upon the Report of the Danger the Country might be in from too great Number of Negro Slaves," they were willing to defer any action. However, they did advise the Carolina government "that if the Country at present be in no real Danger from the great Number of Negroes," the act should be repealed in favor of another that would compel each planter "to have one White Man for every Ten Negroes" on their land. In addition, they noted that the king had ordered all colonial governments to pass no acts with respect to trade or shipping until further notice.[539]

Needless to say, the disallowance of these laws did not please those who had passed them.[540] The dispute between the planters and the merchants, which arose from the attempt to foot the latter with the bill for the war as well for the longstanding debt and currency problems, together with the contention over the Yamassee lands left Governor Johnson and the proprietors stuck between two stools: imperial policy concerning trade and colonial desire to avoid paying the freight for 40 years of provincial mismanagement. In the summer of 1719, the Lords wrote Johnson expressing their continued support but also their surprise that he had opted to please the Carolinians by accepting three additional bills, which again sought to raise money through excises and to control the rental and sale of proprietary lands.[541] Faced with intransigence on these and other matters, the proprietors (with the Board of Trade and Parliament now taking a closer interest in their affairs), in July 1718, rejected the proposed legislation and dissolved the Commons House, noting dryly "We are very well pleas'd to fine by the Behaviour of the House of Assembly that the affairs of the province are such as do not require Our Bounty or assistance."[542]

Naturally, all of these disputes came to center around control of the Commons House of Assembly. Elections in the colony for the membership of this body had always been held at Charles Town, and the Goose Creek men had consistently availed themselves of this reality in prior decades. Now, the assembly finally passed legislation to conduct elections in the various counties apparently, according to the post-rebellion narratives, to break the power of Rhett and Trott in the provincial capital.

Although previous generations of Lords had supported localizing elections as part of the effort to rein in the Goose Creek men, they repealed this 1719 legislation as "void in it self, because it breaks thro an Act made by the Assembly & confirmed by the Lords Proprietors, & never repeal'd by the same authority." The same day, they wrote Trott thanking him for his defense of their powers and prerogatives.[543]

That very summer, the proprietors also sought to increase the power of the council by expanding its membership to 12. Among the appointees, in addition to the ubiquitous Trott, were the proprietary surveyor, Yonge, and secretary, Charles Hart, two Huguenots, and the ex–Goose Creek man, Ralph Izard.[544] Unfortunately, the news of this "novelty" in the government, combined with fear of an impending Spanish attack, and underlying apprehensions that sinister forces were at work to place the colony under tyranny while the proprietors were incapable of dealing with emergencies, galvanized a number of planters into action. At the end of November 1719, they converted the Commons House Assembly into a convention parliament, apparently following the example of England at the "Glorious Revolution," to consider their next move.

By December 17, matters had come to a head when, with the exception of Rhett and Trott, the provincial leadership refused to recognize Governor Johnson's authority under the proprietors. "At a time when [the colony] lay under [the] greatest questions imaginable, by the illegal and Arbitrary Proceedings of the Lords Proprietors" the Convention selected Moore, Jr., as the temporary governor when Johnson, following family precedent, declined to forswear his oath of obedience.[545]

Fearing "imminent danger" from a "daily" threat of another invasion by the Spanish and Indians, the *coup* leaders promptly submitted a petition to the Privy Council for a royal takeover of the colony. They had no other choice, they insisted: "the impossibility we are under of defending ourselves from our Enemies under a Proprietary Government, together with the unspeakable Hardship we have receiv'd from the Lords Proprietors of this Province have obliged us to throw off their unsuportable Yoak and fly to your Majesty's immediate Protection."[546]

In doing so, of course, the Convention members had to lay out clearly the reasons for their rebellion. In particular, they charged the Lords with having "taken upon themselves to repeal several Laws made for the support of this Government & duly ratified & confirmed by their deputys according to the Powers granted to them by their Charter." These laws had included the acts to settle the Yamassee lands, as well as legislation to "ascertain the Manner & Form of Electing Members to represent the Inhabitants" and another that levied "an Imposition on Negroes, Liquors & other Goods & Merchandizes." Even more seriously, the petitioners argued, the proprietors, by disallowing the laws, had assumed a double negative in legislative matters: on the one hand, their deputies on the colony had oversight over bills while, in the metropolis, the Lords had a second chance to act on statutes.[547]

Then, according to the Convention, the proprietors had illegally sought to modify the government by appointing 12 deputies rather than the eight permitted them by their charter at an obvious time of danger from foreign enemies and Indians. Even worse, this new threat came at a time when a hurricane had ruined the colony's defenses while the proprietary obstructions of their legislative policies had destroyed the colony public credit. Thus, the petitioners asked that the three acts should be restored on the procedural grounds that the Council had illegally issued the writs for Assembly elections in the names of the proprietors, and to choose their governor and other officials in their role "as guardians of the Province" until "his Majestys pleasure be known."[548] The Convention also moved against their nemesis, Chief Justice Trott, removing him from office and sending 31 articles against him to London.[549]

According to a justification of the rebellion published in London seven years later, Johnson made some effort to restore proprietary authority.[550] He remained in the province and took a number of opportunities, especially with regard to religion, to remind everyone of his presence to the consternation of the rebels/Convention. Provisional governor Moore, for instance, became indignant at a report that a minister had married a couple under a license issued by Johnson and the Church of England clergy continued to recognize the proprietary governor into the summer. The other proprietary officials, though, subsided fairly quietly. Indeed, Yonge, who composed one of justifications of 1726, moved to the forefront of the rebellion, while Rhett, as we shall see, accepted office from the provisional government. Trott, for his part, went to England to plead his case to the proprietors and anyone else who would listen. In the meantime, the agents of the *coup* awaited the outcome of their petition for royal relief. Significantly although left unmentioned in their petitions and remonstrances, the proprietor–planter relationship had deteriorated to the point that many of those who had joined opposite sides in previous squabbles—Boone and Moore Jr., for instance—now found themselves in alliance.[551]

The political combination that underpinned the Convention, the failure of Johnson to regain control of the situation, and the recurring realization—which the proprietors and their governor even admitted in their correspondence—that the Lords were fundamentally incapable of dealing with the new imperial world of 1720 led to the conclusion that the proprietorship had reached the end of its useful life. On the other hand, undoubtedly tired of dealing with their fractious colony, the news of the rebellion against their governor may well have been the last straw for the proprietors: they drafted an agreement to sell their interests to John Falconer, David Barclay, and Thomas Hyam.[552]

This maneuver blew up in their faces as news of the proposed sale, which ultimately fell through, confirmed the uncaring attitude of the Lords to unsympathetic imperial officials. Naturally, it also sparked outrage when it reached Carolina where the supporters of the Convention screamed, without irony, of the injustice of being "sold as slaves" by uncaring overlords.[553] On top of all this, the prospective buyers then attacked the proprietary charter in order to secure a better deal.[554]

The petitions of the Convention, bolstered by the aborted sale of the proprietorship, eventually bore fruit. Francis Nicholson, veteran of American affairs, arrived in Charles Town in May 1721 (undoubtedly to the bemusement of his former employers, the Lords Proprietors) with a royal commission to serve as provisional governor to which Moore and his Assembly happily acquiesced. This event sounded the death knell for proprietary rule in South Carolina. However, for the next eight years, the Lords made enough noises about their rights to arrears of quitrents and to dispose of their lands that the Carolinians never could be quite sure that their rebellion had taken until the Act of Parliament that bought out the proprietors finally received the Royal Assent at the end of July 1729.

Indeed, between 1721 and 1727, the Lords with some persistence tried to recover the situation and maintain a semblance of the status quo ante. They were convinced that the planters would not have made their "false insinuations and Invectives against the Proprietors Government had not the Arrears of Quit Rents and other dues been very considerable which they were so weak to imagine a Governor from the Crown would discharge them of."[555]

In the meantime, they ordered their receiver Rhett, to pay Johnson his salary from August 11, 1719 until Nicholson's arrival,[556] and they continued to complain about lack of action on the quitrents, especially after the Treasury dunned them for their own overdue rent payments to the Crown dating from 1708.[557] In addition, they asked the king—and pressed the suggestion subsequently—to appoint Colonel Samuel Horsey in their name as governor to succeed their former advisor, Nicholson, with authority to collect their quitrents, to restore their damaged property, and to stop trespass on their lands.[558] Finally, they continued to grant patents to new landgraves.[559] Incredibly, people still remained interested in joining the proprietorship.[560]

The Lords also, at least occasionally and with some defiance, continued to encourage people to go to Carolina, if only to remind the Privy Council and the Carolinians that they still existed. In November 1726, they made a grant to Thomas Taylor of Dublin who intended to move to South Carolina with "several Planters Handicrafts Artificers and other persons of his own proper Costs and Charges." In return for this undertaking, Taylor received 1,000 acres in consideration of 12d for every 100 acres payable yearly at Michaelmas; the proprietors directed their surveyor to lay out a tract.[561] The response of the provisional government to this transaction remains unknown but Taylor did go to Charles Town with 30 people in 1727.[562]

A potentially significant opportunity for the Lords to demonstrate their continued affection for their colony (and, correspondingly, torment the provisional government) arrived in January 1725 when Jean-Pierre Purry proposed a scheme to "transport 600 switzers who would greatly strengthen the province of South Carolina." The proprietors promptly conveyed Sir Robert Montgomery's moribund barony to Purry "conditionally, that he transport 300 people (within one year from the date of the patent) at his own charges," and agreed to grant the Swiss "another barony of 12,000 acres when there shall be 1200 people settled by him in that part of the province."[563] Purry's venture, though, did not really get underway until after the royal takeover of the province.[564]

So far from furthering reconciliation between Lords and colonists around a purported common interest in "peopling," though, the proposed Swiss colony heaped fuel on the flames, perhaps demonstrating continuing nervousness in the minds of the Carolinians in this period. One pamphleteer railed against these potentially "dangerous Guests" who "may perhaps be Papists and Jacobites," even as he lamented the ruined state of a colony sunk in debt, with defenses ruined by storms, and where "the White People are averse to Proprietor-Governors." Dependent upon the newly secured good will of the Indians and "this Weakness known to our implacable Neighbours the Spaniards," the Carolinians "possessing above forty thousand Negroes besides Cattle" absolutely required continued royal protection.[565]

This continued activity of the proprietors compelled the Carolinians to undertake a final offensive to eliminate the prospect of the *ancien regime*, however remote, once and for all. They sent Francis Yonge, the proprietary surveyor and client of the Palatine, John Carteret, earl of Granville, to London in 1726 to oppose the selection of Horsey, to remove any threat that proprietary government would be resumed, and to terminate proprietary land rights. Unsurprisingly, the appearance of their former surveyor who had neglected to provide them with a promised account of their colonists, rankled the Lords, as did the memorial he submitted to the Privy Council against a restoration of proprietary government—yet another justification in a history full of them and the account that has dominated subsequent understanding of the rebellion.[566]

Faced with the determined opposition of the rebels and the imperial desire to quiet this important frontier, the Lords subsided. Indeed, it is possible that the proprietors and the Crown may have reached some sort of "buyout" agreement in 1727. On May 31, the proprietors—being "sensible of the great disorder, the Inhabitants are in, and the great difficulties they labour under"—petitioned the king to take "the unhappy condition of" the province "into your royall consideration in order to settle it upon a sure and lasting foundation."[567] On October 12, the Lords, complaining to the Privy Council again about infringement upon their rights again, claimed to have offered to surrender their power of appointment to the Crown.[568]

This reminder was probably necessary because the death of George I in that year had intervened. This meant a new parliamentary session and, so, a new bill to terminate the proprietary rights had to be introduced and passed. On March 5, 1728, the Lords formally petitioned the new monarch, George II, to surrender all of their rights in exchange for £2,500 apiece in lieu of the outstanding quitrents.[569]

Not that it particularly mattered in the end but in reality, of course, the Carolinians, especially the Goose Creek men, had brought practically all of the colony's problems upon themselves. It was they, after all, who had provoked the Yamassee War. Moreover, these more immediate difficulties stemmed from long-standing issues that the colonists had also generated. It had been they who had taken it upon themselves to attack St. Augustine in 1702 that created the huge debt that, in turn, generated the issuance of nearly worthless paper money that nearly ruined the economy and left the government unable to fend for itself. When the proprietors directed the colony to retire these bills of credit, merchants and planters united in the Convention. It was the colonists who had perpetrated the fierce factional battles that had continually upset the political equilibrium and disturbed settlers. It was they who also persisted, against constant proprietary warnings, in laying out the plantations in a disorderly and straggling sort of way, and it was they who prepared a tinderbox for frontier explosion of 1715 by their persistence in enslaving Indians. The Lords, hampered by minority, distractions, and disinterest in some cases, lacked the capacity to handle these complex and overwhelming problems.[570]

At the same time, the "revolution" against the proprietors did not translate into any fundamental change for what had come to be called South Carolina. Yes, the responsibility for appointing officials now came from the Crown rather than the proprietors. But, to a remarkable degree, the people in charge of the colony remained the same: both proprietary governor Johnson and secretary Hart returned to their duties under royal auspices. Even the supposedly hated quitrent system remained in place.[571] Even more significantly but unsurprisingly, the province's sociopolitical system—staple agriculture, slave labor, the pursuit and maintenance of estates—that suited both Crown and white colonists remained in place.

Then, under the new royal government, South Carolina benefited from several new developments that the Convention had not conceived of ten years before and really had nothing to do with the character of the proprietors or their regime. First, as the petitioners had requested since it was first listed in 1705, Parliament removed rice from the list of enumerated commodities in 1731. Then, Johnson introduced the relatively successful "township" program that began to attract settlers from other colonies to the colony's backcountry. This policy extended settlement westward (impossible in Maurice Mathews's time) and increased the number of whites in the colony (which promoters of the colony had always fervently desired).[572] Finally, factional difficulties, the colony's curse since the mid-1670s, abated. With the royal government in place and the Goose Creek men a memory, the lines of patronage at both the local and imperial levels now cleared. The result was prosperity and peace.

Of course, the "revolution" of 1719 was an English revolution with its "Convention" and its petitions.[573] Indeed, it would be difficult to characterize this event in any other way. From the founding of Carolina, the colony's elite regarded themselves as English and consistently looked to London for patronage, for a public forum to express their positions, for socioeconomic ideas—whatever support they needed while sharing the "Old World" sentiment that locality should come first. The planters, in turn, by exporting commodities not only augmented their own estates and local positions, contributed—as they grew so fond of relating—their small but vital share to Britain's imperial greatness politically and economically.[574] An estate-based society, nudged along by proprietary encouragement but entailing—through a tragic pragmatism in the bitterest of ironies—the enslavement of Africans and Indians, prevailed with the plantation substituting for the manor. Unfortunately, it had to if the colony was to survive, since no acceptable alternative framework for constructing a society existed in the minds of early modern English folk—but Anglo-Carolinian tendencies to self-destruction made survival, let alone prosperity, a close-run thing.

Having survived, what, then, does the case of proprietary Carolina reveal about the character of the early modern British Empire and of Anglo-American settlement? In the first instance, for all of the recent scholarly fascination for studying "state formation" and "Atlantic history," the record confirms that this colony and its inhabitants serve as an example of the weakness of the Anglo-British state and its enduring reluctance, even in the 1720s, to assume a direct role in "empire-building," let alone conduct imperial policy. The geographical interests of the British Empire may have extended to Bombay by 1729 (as opposed to Calais 200 years before), but Whitehall seems not to have kept up with the times. In any case, by the end of the proprietorship, this colony, situated on the boundary of hostile French and Spanish claims and with its still valuable Indian (non-slave) trade and profitable rice cultivation, required a rebellion to provoke an interest from the metropolitan government. Only after the collapse of the proprietary regime, seventy years after the colony's founding, did the Board of Trade commission a survey of the economic and social character of the province.[575]

Finally, the colony's early history itself provides an excellent demonstration of the inherent ambiguity of what we call today the "early modern" period. On the one hand, England, most particularly, achieved territorial gains, became increasingly commercialized, experienced increasing population and movement of people, withstood deep convulsions in its political nation, centralized its governmental authority, and reformed its religion. On the other, many English people—at the "periphery," as well as the "center"—while divided in matters of religion and in the constitution of the national government, remained drawn to an agrarian, locally based, hierarchical society of the sort that reflected the spirit, if not the precise formula, of the Fundamental Constitutions. How this came to play out peculiarly in South Carolina after 1730 is another story.

Abbreviations ~

Add. MS.	Additional Manuscripts
BL	British Library
Bodl. Lib.	Bodleian Library, University of Oxford
CO	Colonial Office
CRNC	William L. Saunders, ed., *The Colonial Records of North Carolina*, 10 vols. (Raleigh, NC: P.M. Hale, 1886–90)
CSP AWI	H.N. Sainsbury and J.W. Fortescue, eds., *Calendar of State Papers, America and West Indies Series* (London: H.M. Stationers Office, 1896–1905)
DeBeer	E.S. DeBeer, *The Correspondence of John Locke*, 9 vols. (Oxford: Oxford University Press, 1968)
HMC	Historical Manuscripts Commission
JGC	A.S. Salley, Jr., ed., *Journal of the Grand Council of South Carolina*, 3 vols. (Columbia, SC: South Carolina Department of Archives and History, 1907)
Johnston	Frank J. Klingberg, ed., *Carolina Chronicle: the Papers of Commissary Gideon Johnston, 1707–1716* (Berkeley, CA: University of California Press, 1955)
Le Jau	Frank J. Klingberg, ed., *The Carolina Chronicle of Dr. Francis Le Jau, 1706–1717* (Berkeley, CA: University of California Press, 1956)
Lesser	Charles H. Lesser, *South Carolina Begins: The Records of a Proprietary Colony, 1663–1721* (Columbia, SC: South Carolina Department and Archives, 1995)
NAS	National Archives of Scotland, Edinburgh
NLS	National Library of Scotland, Edinburgh
PRO	Public Record Office of Great Britain, Kew
Rivers, Appendix	William J. Rivers, *A Sketch of the History of South Carolina to the close of the Proprietary Government by the Revolution of 1719*, Appendix (Spartanburg, SC: Historic Reprints Co., 1972 [Charleston, 1856])

RPCS	P. Hume Brown, ed., *The Register of the Privy Council of Scotland*, 3rd ser., 12 vols. (Edinburgh: H.M. General Register House, 1915)
Salley, *Narratives*	Alexander S. Salley, ed., *Narratives of Early Carolina, 1650–1708* (New York: Barnes & Noble, 1967 [1911])
SCDAH	South Carolina Department of Archives and History, Columbia
SCHM	*South Carolina Historical Magazine* (formerly *South Carolina Historical and Genealogical Magazine*)
SCHS	South Carolina Historical Society, Charleston
Shaftesbury Papers	South Carolina Historical Society, *The Shaftesbury Papers* (Charleston: Tempus Press, 2000) (reprint of Langdon Cheves III, ed., *The Shaftesbury Papers and Other Records Relating to Carolina*, Collections of the South Carolina Historical Society, V [Charleston, 1897])

Notes ∼

Acknowledgments

1. Louis H. Roper, "The Unraveling of an Anglo–American Utopia in South Carolina," *The Historian*, 58 (1996), 277–88.

Introduction

2. Cf. Bernard Bailyn, "The Idea of Atlantic History," *Itinerario*, 20 (1996), 19–44; Nicholas Canny, "Writing Atlantic History; or, Reconfiguring the History of Colonial British America," *The Journal of American History*, 89 (1999), 1093–1114; idem, "Atlantic History: What and Why?" *European Review*, 9 (2001), 399–411.

3. Cf. Russell R. Menard, "The Africanization of the Lowcountry Labor Force, 1670–1730," in Winthrop D. Jordan and Sheila L. Skemp, eds., *Race and Family in the Colonial South* (Jackson, MS and London: University Press of Mississippi, 1987), pp. 81–103 at 83; David Hackett Fischer, *Albion's Seed: Four British Folkways in America* (New York: Oxford University Press, 1989); Karen Ordahl Kupperman, *Providence Island, 1630–1641: The Other Puritan Colony* (New York: Cambridge University Press, 1993).

4. Joyce Appleby, "A Different Kind of Independence: The Postwar Restructuring of the Historical Study of Early America," *William and Mary Quarterly*, 3rd ser., 50 (1993), 245–67; Fred Anderson and Andrew R.L. Cayton, "The Problem of Fragmentation and the Prospects for Synthesis in Early American Social History, ibid., 299–310; Ian K. Steele, "Exploding Colonial American History: Amerindian, Atlantic, and Global Perspectives," *Reviews in American History*, 26 (1998), 70–95.

5. J.C.D. Clark, "The Strange Death of British History? Reflections on Anglo-American Scholarship," *Historical Journal*, 40 (1997), 787–809; Joyce E. Chaplin, "Expansion and Exceptionalism in Early American History," *Journal of American History*, 89 (2003), 1431–55; David Armitage, "Greater Britain: A Useful Category of Historical Analysis?," *American Historical Review*, 104 (1999), 427–45; Ian Tyrrell, "American Exceptionalism in an Age of International History," ibid., 96 (1991), 1031–55.

6. Chaplin, "Expansion and Exceptionalism in Early American History," 1453–55.

7. Robert Olwell, *Masters, Slaves, and Subjects: The Culture of Power in the South Carolina Low Country, 1740–1790* (Ithaca: Cornell University Press, 1998). All of the accounts of the introduction of slavery and the lives of slaves in proprietary South Carolina, which emphasize "the crude and egalitarial intimacies inevitable on a frontier," rely on flimsy evidence, such as the seemingly poignant story of the Huguenot Elias Horry working "on a Whip saw" opposite "a Negro man", first related by Horry's grandson over 40 years after the "fact." They also rely on a characterization of the colony's political history that the present analysis refutes, Peter H. Wood, *Black Majority: Negroes in Colonial South Carolina from 1670 through the Stono Rebellion* (New York: W.W. Norton Co., 1975 [1974]), p. 97; the anecdote recurs in Olwell, *Masters, Slaves, and Subjects*, p. 44, in Philip D. Morgan, *Slave Counterpoint: Black Culture in the Eighteenth-Century Chesapeake and Lowcountry* (Chapel Hill: University of North Carolina Press, 1998), p. 6, and Ira Berlin, *Many Thousands Gone: The First Two Centuries of Slavery in North America* (Cambridge: Harvard University Press, 1998), p. 66n.

8. The standard work remains James H. Merrell, *The Indians' New World: Catawbas and Their Neighbors from European Contact through the Era of Removal* (Chapel Hill: University of North Carolina Press, 1989).

9. Jack P. Greene, *Pursuits of Happiness: The Social Development of Early Modern British Colonies and the Formation of American Culture* (Chapel Hill: University of North Carolina Press, 1988), pp. 7–27, 141–51; Michael J. Braddick, *State Formation in Early Modern England, c.1550–1700* (Cambridge: Cambridge University Press, 2000); Jonathan Scott, *England's Troubles: Seventeenth-Century English Political Instability in European Context* (Cambridge: Cambridge University Press, 2000).

10. Jack P. Greene, *The Intellectual Construction of America: Exceptionalism and Identity from 1492 to 1800* (Chapel Hill: University of North Carolina Press, 1993), pp. 6–7.

11. Bernard Bailyn, *The Peopling of British North America: An Introduction* (New York: Vintage, 1986), pp. 7–8.

12. Wood, *Black Majority*, pp. 16–62; M. Eugene Sirmans, *Colonial South Carolina: a Political History, 1663–1763* (Chapel Hill: University of North Carolina Press, 1966), pp. 17–18, 30, 75–100; Robert M. Weir, " 'Shaftesbury's Darling': British Settlement in the Carolinas at the Close of the Seventeenth Century" in Nicholas P. Canny, ed., *The Origins of Empire: British Overseas Enterprise to the Close of the Seventeenth Century*, vol. 1 in Wm. Roger Louis, ed., *The Oxford History of the British Empire* (Oxford: Oxford University Press, 1998), pp. 375–97 at 384–85 and 392; Richard S. Dunn, "The English Sugar Islands and the Founding of South Carolina," *SCHM*, 72 (1971); Jack P. Greene, "Colonial South Carolina and the Caribbean Connection" in Greene, ed., *Imperatives, Behaviors & Identities: Essays in Early American Cultural History* (Charlottesville, VA: University of Virginia Press, 1992), pp. 68–86; John P. Thomas, Jr., "The Barbadians in Early South Carolina," *SCHM*, 31 (1930), 75–92; Richard Waterhouse, "England, the Caribbean, and the Settlement of South Carolina" in *Journal*

of American Studies, 9 (1975), 259–81; Waterhouse, *A New World Gentry: The Making of a Merchant and Planter Class in South Carolina, 1670–1770* (New York: Garland Publishing, 1989), pp. 10–17, 38–39, 44–45; Weir, *Colonial South Carolina: A History* (Columbia, SC: University of South Carolina Press, 1997 [Millwood, NY, 1983]), pp. 62, 77, 90–99, 101–03.

13. Meaghan N. Duff, "Creating a Plantation Province: Proprietary Land Policies and Early Settlement Patterns" and Gary L. Hewitt, "The State in the Planters' Service: Politics and the Emergence of a Plantation Economy" in Jack P. Greene, Rosemary Brana-Shute, and Randy J. Sparks, eds., *Money, Trade, and Power: The Evolution of Colonial South Carolina's Plantation Society* (Columbia: University of South Carolina Press, 2001), pp. 1–25 and 49–73.

14. *Greene, Pursuits of Happiness*, pp. 166–69. Since South Carolina survived and prospered as a colony, unlike, for instance, Roanoke, it is difficult to see how its development could be otherwise described.

15. Weir, " 'Shaftesbury's Darling,' " pp. 395–96.

16. Alan Gallay, *The Indian Slave Trade: The Rise of the English Empire in the American South, 1670–1717* (New Haven, CT: Yale University Press, 2002); William L. Ramsay, " 'All & Singular the Slaves': A Demographic Profile of Indian Slavery in Colonial South Carolina" in Greene, Brana-Shute, and Sparks, eds., *Money, Trade, and Power*, pp. 166–86; James L. Axtell, *The Indians' New South: Cultural Change in the Colonial Southeast* (Baton Rouge: Louisiana State University Press, 1997), especially pp. 41–44. None of these studies, though, considers the slave trade between Carolina and the West Indies nor have they provided an alternative analysis of South Carolina politics with which the slave trade was intertwined.

17. Thomas J. Little, "The South Carolina Slave Laws Reconsidered, 1670–1700," *SCHM*, 94 (1993), 86–101.

18. Mathews arrived with the first fleet from England in 1670, *Shaftesbury Papers*, 135. This analysis builds on suggestions made by Kinloch Bull, "Barbadian Settlers in Early Carolina: Historiographical Notes," *SCHM*, 96 (1995), 329–39.

19. For example, Edmund White to Joseph Morton, February 29, 1688, *SCHM*, 30 (1929), 1–5, reprinted in part in Wood, *Black Majority*, p. 331.

20. James Horn, *Adapting to a New World: English Society in the Seventeenth-Century Chesapeake* (Chapel Hill: University of North Carolina Press, 1994).

21. Daniel W. Fagg, Jr., "Carolina, 1663–1683," endorses this view but does not address events after the death of Shaftesbury.

22. Cf. Weir, *Colonial South Carolina*, pp. 62, 77, 90–92. Duff's error-strewn essay imagines a "proprietary land policy" where none existed, "Creating a Plantation Province," passim.

23. John M. Murrin, "Political Development" in Jack P. Greene and J.R. Pole, eds., *Colonial British America: Essays in the New History of the Early Modern Era* (Baltimore: Johns Hopkins University Press, 1984), pp. 408–56; Horn, *Adapting to a New World*, pp. 368–80; Patricia U. Bonomi, *A Factious People: Politics and Society in Colonial New York* (New York: Columbia University Press, 1971); idem, *The Lord Cornbury Scandal: The Politics of Reputation in British America* (Chapel Hill: University of North Carolina Press, 1998);

Brendan McConville, *These Daring Disturbers of the Public Peace: The Struggle for Property and Power in Early New Jersey* (Ithaca, NY: Cornell University Press, 1999); Charles M. Andrews, *The Colonial Period of American History*, 4 vols. (New Haven, CT: Yale University Press, 1937), III, pp. 307–11, 316–21; Richard S. Dunn, *Sugar and Slaves: The Rise of the Planter Class in the English West Indies, 1624–1713* (New York: W.W. Norton, 1973), pp. 143–46.

24. Bernard Bailyn, "Politics and Social Structure in Early Virginia" in James Morton Smith, *17th-century America* (Chapel Hill: University of North Carolina Press, 1959), pp. 90–115 at 115.

25. Gordon S. Wood, "The Creative Imagination of Bernard Bailyn" in James A. Henretta, Michael Kammen, and Stanley N. Katz, eds., *The Transformation of Early American History: Society, Authority, and Ideology. How the writings of Bernard Bailyn have changed our understanding of the American past* (New York: Alfred A. Knopf, 1991), pp. 16–50 at 23.

26. Greene, *Pursuits of Happiness*, pp. 1–5, 28–54, 101–23, 200–09; idem, "Early South Carolina and the Psychology of British Colonization" in idem, *Imperatives, Behaviors & Identities*, pp. 87–112 at 88, 96, 100–01, 111–12; Bailyn, *The Peopling of British North America*, pp. 20, 36–38; Bailyn, *Voyagers to the West: A Passage in the Peopling of America on the Eve of the Revolution* (New York: Vintage, 1988), pp. 3–5, 189–203, 635–37.

For Maryland, another colony with a proprietor who planned to implement a manorial system, Lois Green Carr, Russell R. Menard, Lorena S. Walsh, *Robert Cole's World: Agriculture & Society in Early Maryland* (Chapel Hill: University of North Carolina Press, 1991), pp. 8–20 at 9 and 11, 115–37. For Pennsylvania and the similar plans of William Penn, Gary B. Nash, *Quakers and Politics, 1681–1726* (Princeton, NJ: Princeton University Press, 1968), pp. 90–91, 97.

27. Such Anglo-American hierarchies also readily developed, of course, in the West Indies, the Chesapeake, and New York, Dunn, *Sugar and Slaves*; James R. Perry, *The Formation of a Society on Virginia's Eastern Shore, 1615–1655* (Chapel Hill: University of North Carolina Press, 1990); Horn, *Adapting to a New World*.

28. Jack P. Greene, ed., *Selling New World: Two Colonial South Carolina Pamphlets* (Columbia, SC: University of South Carolina Press, 1989), pp. 64–65, 126–31.

29. Samuel Wilson, *An Account of the Province of Carolina* [London, 1682] in Salley, *Narratives*, pp. 164–76 at 174; Little, "The South Carolina Slave Laws Reconsidered."

30. Greene has given the per capita for the Charles Town area in 1774 at £ 2,337.7, *Pursuits of Happiness*, p. 147.

31. In 1708, some 9,580 persons resided in South Carolina, of which "42.6% were whites, 42.8% were Negroes, and 14.6% were Indians," Robert V. Wells, *The Population of the British Colonies in America before 1776: A Survey of the Census Data* (Princeton, NJ: Princeton University Press, 1975), p. 167; Menard, "Africanization of the Lowcountry Labor Force," 85–87. For the colony's rice production, John J. McCusker and Russell Menard, *The Economy of British America, 1607–1789: Needs and Opportunities for Study* (Chapel Hill: University of North Carolina Press, 1991 [1985]), pp. 175–79;

on the increasing importation of slaves into the colony as the eighteenth century wore on, Wood, *Black Majority*, pp. 131–66. Wood has found that the slave population almost doubled the free white population by 1740, at 152. The provincial government devised a series of efforts to recruit whites dating from the "township" scheme of the 1730s to address the "problem" of racial imbalance, Robert L. Meriwether, *The Expansion of South Carolina, 1729–1765* (Kingsport, TN: Southern Publishers, 1940).

32. Henry Steele Commager and Elmo Giordanetti, *Was America a Mistake?: An Eighteenth-Century Controversy* (New York: Harper & Row, 1967); Anthony Pagden, *Lords of all the World: Ideologies of Empire in Spain, Britain and France, c. 1500–c.1800* (New Haven, CT: Yale University Press, 1995), pp. 156–77.

33. Instead of the "best poor man's country," as its competitor, Pennsylvania, came to be styled, the malarial lowcountry, further handicapped by its tumultuous politics, quickly lagged behind in the demographic derby. Greene gives the white population of South Carolina in 1710, 40 years after the colony's founding, at 6,783. By comparison, in the Chesapeake, the white population of Virginia in 1660, 53 years after the founding of Jamestown, was 26,070 while proprietary Maryland had 7,668 whites less than 30 years after its founding; Massachusetts, 30 years after the establishment of Boston, contained 22,062 whites; Barbados, benefiting from its sugar boom, had 26,200 white inhabitants in 1660; Pennsylvania, founded almost ten years after South Carolina had 22,875 whites in 1710; that same year, 14,220 whites lived in North Carolina, a colony that neither received proprietary attention nor undertook systematic recruitment and lacked a port like Charles Town to facilitate in-migration, *Pursuits of Happiness*, pp. 178–79.

34. Wood, *Black Majority*, pp. 131–326.

35. The proprietors specifically complained that the Goose Creek men had cost the colony 10,000 Scots and a steady stream of English migrants in 1690, Lords Proprietors to Andrew Percival, October 18, 1690, *CSP AWI*, XIII, no. 1,117, p. 331. All dates from the sources are rendered Old Style but with the year taken to begin on January 1.

Prologue

36. Sir Robert Harley to Sir Edward Harley, October 31, 1662, *HMC*, Series 29 (3), 14th rpt. (iii), p. 268.

37. Charles McLean Andrews, for one, found, mostly on faith, Colleton at the center of organization, *The Colonial Period of American History*, III, pp. 182–87, a view followed by subsequent studies, Weir, *Colonial South Carolina*, pp. 48–49.

38. On Sir William Berkeley's earlier activities and intermittent interest in the future North Carolina as an appendage of Virginia, see Warren M. Billings, "Sir William Berkeley and the Carolina Proprietary," *North Carolina Historical Review*, 72 (1995), 329–42 at 329.

39. For the connection between Albemarle and Ashley, see, e.g., George Monk to Sir A.A. Cooper, June 4, 1659, in W.D. Christie, ed., *Memoirs, Letters, and*

Speeches of Anthony Ashley Cooper, First Earl of Shaftesbury, Lord Chancellor, from his Birth to the Restoration (London, 1869), pp. 132–33.

40. Edward, earl of Clarendon, *The Life of Edward, Earl of Clarendon, Lord High Chancellor of England, and Chancellor of the University of Oxford: in which is included A Continuation of his History of the Grand Rebellion*, 2 vols. (Oxford: Oxford University Press, 1857), II, p. 463.

41. Ronald Hutton, *Charles II: King of England, Scotland, and Ireland* (Oxford: Oxford University Press, 1989), pp. 157–60, 214–15.

42. Quoted in Andrews, *Colonial Period in American History*, III, p. 186n.

43. BL Add. MS. 36,270, f. 104.

44. A copy of the first charter to the Lords Proprietors of Carolina may be found in *CRNC*, I, pp. 20–33.

45. Paul E. Kopperman, "Profile of Failure: the Carolana Project, 1629–1640," *North Carolina Historical Review*, 59 (1982), 1–23.

46. *CRNC*, I, pp. 14–16 ("Maltravers Patent"), 42–43 (minutes of the Privy Council, August 12, 1663), 102–14 ("Second Charter Granted by King Charles the Second, to the Proprietors of Carolina," June 30, 1665); Andrews, *Colonial Period of American History*, III, pp. 182–91.

47. George, duke of Albemarle, to Colonel Thomas Modyford and Peter Colleton, Esqr, August 30, 1663, *CRNC*, I, pp. 46–47; Albemarle to Lord Willoughby of Parham, August 31, 1663, *CRNC*, I, pp. 47–48.

48. Minutes of a meeting of the Lords Proprietors of Carolina, May 23, 1663, CO 5/286/1, Minutes of a meeting of the Lords Proprietors of Carolina, May 23, 1663, CO5/286/2–3, "Instructions for Sir William Berkeley Governor & Captain Generall of Virginia in relation to ye setling & planting some parts of ye province of Carrolina," [September 1663], CO 5/286/5–6, PRO.

49. Lords Proprietors to Sir William Berkeley, September 8, 1663, CO 5/286/6–7, PRO.

50. "Proposealls of Severall Gentlemen of Barbadoes" and Sir Thomas Modyford and Sir Peter Colleton to Lords Proprietors, August 12, 1663, *CRNC*, I, pp. 39–42.

51. "A Declaration & Proposealls to all yt will plant in Carolina," August 25, 1663, in Rivers, Appendix, pp. 335–37, summarized in "An Answer to Certine Demands and Proposealls made by severall Gentlemen and Persons of Good Quallity in the Island of Barbados to the Lord Propryetors of the Province of Carolina," *CRNC*, I, pp. 57–59.

52. Lords Proprietors to Sir John Yeamans, January 11, 1665, *CSP AWI*, VI, no. 912, pp. 269–70.

53. "Articles of Agreement between the Lords Proprietors and Major William Yeamans on behalf of the Barbados Adventurers," January 7, 1665, *CRNC*, I, pp. 75–92.

54. Ships required a license, such as the one granted to the *Great Charles*, bound for Barbados "with servants, provisions, and horses" from the Admiralty in order "to be free from imprest" (signed *inter alia* by Albemarle, Ashley, and Sir John Berkeley), December 2, 1664, *CSP AWI*, no. 871, p. 259.

55. Hutton, *Charles II*, pp. 219–24, 231–34.

56. Governor Sir William Berkeley to [Secretary Lord Arlington], August 1, 1665, *CSP AWI*, VI, no. 1,030, p. 316.

57. "Humble desires of Lord Willoughby to be presented to the King," [1666?] *CSP AWI*, VI, no. 1,188, p. 379.

58. *A Relation of a Voyage on the Coast of the Province of Carolina* [London, 1666], by Robert Sandford, in Salley, *Narratives*, pp. 83–84.

59. Henry Vassall to Lords Proprietors, August 15, 1666, *CRNC*, I, pp. 144–45; Instructions from the Lords Proprietors of Carolina to Samuel Stephens, October 1667, *CRNC*, I, 162–75; Lords Proprietors of Carolina to Sam. Stephens, Governor, and to the Council of Albemarle County, [1670], *CSP AWI*, VII, no. 141, p. 52.

60. The *Shaftesbury Papers*, transcribed from bundle 48 (and bits of bundles 47 and 49) in the Shaftesbury Papers in the PRO (PRO 30/24), constitute the bulk of the record for Carolina's history between 1669 and 1675.

61. Salley, *Narratives*, pp. 106–07.

Chapter 1

62. These manorial court records are found in MSS. Craven f. 142 (Berks II, 1422–1764), Bodl. Lib.

63. E.A. Wrigley and R.S. Schofield, *The Population of England, 1541–1871* (Cambridge, MA: Harvard University Press, 1981), has placed the English population at 2,984,576 in 1561, 4,109,981 in 1601, 5,091,725 in 1641, 4,982,687 in 1671, and 5,057,790 in 1701, at pp. 208–09. They estimate that births exceeded deaths by 7.411 million between 1541 and 1801, at p. 227.

64. Burials continually outpaced baptisms in London from 1550 to 1799, according to Wrigley and Schofield. Between 1650 and 1674, there were 520,463 burials and 293,635 baptisms; between 1675 and 1699, 546,312 burials and 364,847 baptisms, *The Population History of England*, p. 167.

65. Richard Hakluyt, *A Discourse on Western Planting* [London, 1584] in E.G.R. Taylor, ed., *The Original Writings and Correspondence of the Two Richard Hakluyts*, 2 vols. (London: Hakluyt Society, 1935), I, pp. 233–39.

66. Richard Greaves, *Deliver Us from Evil: The Radical Underground in Britain, 1660–1663* (Oxford: Oxford University Press, 1986); idem, *Enemies Under His Feet: Radicals and Nonconformists in Britain, 1664–1667* (Stanford, CA: Stanford University Press, 1990).

67. The nation's population continued to grow from 5,230,371 in 1711 to 5,350,465 ten years later to 6,146,857 by 1761 to 7,042,140 in 1781 to 8,664,490 by 1801, *The Population History of England*, pp. 208–09.

68. [Anonymous], *Some Reasons Humbly Offered to the Consideration of the Parliament for the Continuance of the Writs of Capias, and Process of Arrest, in Actions of Debt, &c.* (London, 1671).

69. Keith Wrightson, *English Society, 1580–1680* (New Brunswick, NJ: Rutgers University Press, 1990 [1982]), pp. 121–82.

70. Peter Clark and David Souden, "Introduction" in Clark and Souden, eds., *Migration & Society in Early Modern England* (Totowa, NJ: Barnes & Noble,

1987), pp. 11–48, and Paul Slack, *Poverty and Policy in Tudor and Stuart England* (London: Longman, 1988). The latter study does not consider colonization.

71. We have countless anecdotes: Lionel Cranfield, James I's Lord Treasurer and prominent City of London merchant, retired from commerce at his first opportunity, buying an estate, entering government and accepting the title of earl of Middlesex while William Hutton of Birmingham served an apprenticeship to a stocking maker then achieved success as a bookbinder, before acquiring his estate and retiring. He died "an aged and respectable figure" in 1815, Clark and Souden, eds., *Migration and Society in Early Modern England*, pp. 11–12.

72. Bailyn, *The Peopling of British North America*, p. 7; Greene, *Pursuits of Happiness*; Wrightson, *English Society*, pp. 40–57; Alan Macfarlane, *The Origins of English Individualism: The Family, Property and Social Transition* (Oxford: Oxford University Press, 1978), pp. 7–61; Perez Zagorin, *Rebels and Rulers, 1500–1660*, 2 vols. (Cambridge: Cambridge University Press, 1982), I, pp. 87–139.

73. In addition to the Carolina pamphlets discussed below, John Hammond, *Leah and Rachel, or, The Two Fruitfull Sisters, Virginia and Mary-Land* [London, 1656] in Clayton Colman Hall, ed., *Narratives of Early Maryland, 1633–1684* (New York: Barnes & Noble, 1953 [New York, 1910]), pp. 277–308 at 288–300; Willliam Penn, *A Further Account of the Province of Pennsylvania* [London, 1685] in Albert Cook Myers, ed., *Narratives of Early Pennsylvania, West New Jersey, and Delaware* (New York: Charles Scribner's Sons, 1912), pp. 255–78 at 262–65.

74. "Captain Halsteds Instructions," May 1, 1671, *Shaftesbury Papers*, pp. 318–22 at 321.

75. Jack P. Greene, ed., *Selling a New World: Two Colonial South Carolina Promotional Pamphlets* (Columbia, SC: University of South Carolina Press, 1989), pp. 1–30.

76. H.N. Sainsbury, ed., *Documents in the British Public Record Office Relating to South Carolina*, 5 vols. (Atlanta, 1928–47), I, pp. 82–83.

77. Although early modern English people generally recognized landed estates as the barometer of status and the platform for liberties, some of the advertised advantages of Carolina, such as liberty of conscience and ballots in elections, reflect an apparent influence of the republican political theorist, James Harrington, J.G.A. Pocock, *Harrington: The Commonwealth of Oceana and A System of Politics* (Cambridge: Cambridge University Press, 1996 [1992]), pp. 11, 13, 100–01, 114–18, 126. See also the fragment endorsed by Locke, "Carolina, A draught of some laws," a copy of which was graciously provided to me by the late Peter Laslett. Crucially, of course, the province remained part of the English monarchy.

78. Several of Ashley's fellow proprietors expressed similar thoughts about a government that would prove attractive to settlers while improving the wealth of the realm, John, Lord Berkeley, *A Treatise about Government* [London, 1660?], Sloane MS. 3828, ff. 81–91, BL; Sir William Berkeley, *A Discourse and View of Virginia* [1662?], Egerton MS. 2395, ff. 354–57, BL; Sir William Berkeley to [?], March 28, 1663, Egerton MS. 2395, ff. 361–63, BL.

79. Same to same, March 30, 1663, Egerton MS., 2395, ff. 364–65, BL; same to Lord Anthony Langston, April 10, 1663, Egerton MS. 2395, f. 366, BL.
80. Sir Francis Bacon, "On Plantations" in C.W. Eliot, ed., *Essays, Civil and Moral and New Atlantis* (Danbury, CT: Grolier Enterprises Corp., 1988 [1909]), pp. 85–87 at 85; Thomas Woodward to Lords Proprietors, June 2, 1665, in *CRNC*, I, pp. 99–101 at 100.
81. Wrightson, *English Society*, pp. 108–18.
82. Lords Proprietors to Colonel Thomas Modyford and Sir Peter Colleton, August 30, 1663, CO 5/286/8–9, PRO. Cf. Wood, *Black Majority*, p. 13.

Chapter 2

83. Shaftesbury to Mr. Maurice Mathews, June 20, 1672, *Shaftesbury Papers*, pp. 398–99 at 399.
84. John Milton, "John Locke and the Fundamental Constitutions of Carolina," *Locke Newsletter*, 21 (1990), 111–33, provides the latest and clearest examination of the degree of Locke's involvement in the original production of the Constitutions.
85. Vicki Hseuh, "Giving Orders: Theory and Practice in the *Fundamental Constitutions of Carolina*," *Journal of the History of Ideas*, 63 (2002), 425–46, although riddled with errors, notes this at 425–29. Cf. Weir, *Colonial South Carolina*, pp. 71–2; Sirmans, *Colonial South Carolina*, pp. 7–9; David Wootton, ed., *Political Writings of John Locke* (New York: Penguin, 1993), p. 42; Wesley Frank Craven, *The Southern Colonies in the Seventeenth Century, 1607–1689* (Baton Rouge: Louisiana State Univeristy Press, 1949), p. 340. Aside from giving too much credit to Locke in the drafting of the constitutions, Barbara Arneil, *John Locke and America* (Oxford: Oxford University Press, 1996), pp. 118–31, mistakenly characterizes the document as a reflection of a proprietary "objective of ensuring the rights of the individual citizens particularly in terms of their religious freedom," at 128.
86. In 1669, the notion of a written constitution was naturally associated with the Levellers (*The Agreement of the People* (1647), *The Instrument of Government* (1653), *The fundamental lawes and liberties of England claimed* (1653)) and Harringtonians (*A model of a democraticall government* (1659), one of the possible authors of which was Ashley's associate, Major John Wildman), Perez Zagorin, *A History of Political Thought in the English Revolution* (London: Routledge & Kegan Paul, 1954), pp. 132–45, 155–63; S.R. Gardiner, *Constitutional Documents of the Puritan Revolution, 1625–1660*, 3rd ed. (Oxford: Oxford University Press, 1962 [1906]), pp. lii–lx, 405–17.
87. In terms of "Harringtonian" effects on the Fundamental Constitutions, there can be no question that Ashley regarded hereditary aristocracy as the keystone of constitutional government and codified that belief in the Fundamental Constitutions, D. McNally, "Locke, Leveller and Liberty: property and democracy in the thought of the first Whigs," *History of Political Thought*, 10 (1989), 17–40.

88. Lords Proprietors to Governor Joseph Blake and Council, October 19, 1699, CO 5/289/78, PRO. The point had to be made clear since some observers claimed that colonization actually detracted from the nation's wealth and trade, Roger Coke, *A Discourse of Trade* (London, 1670).

89. Samuel Wilson, *An Account of the Province of Carolina in America. Together with An Abstract of the Patent, and several other Necessary and Usefull Particulars, to such as have thoughts of Transporting themselves thither* [London, 1682], in Salley, *Narratives*, p. 166.

90. R[obert] F[erguson], *The Present State of Carolina with Advice to the Setlers* (London, 1682), p. 23.

91. All references to the Fundamental Constitutions, unless otherwise indicated, are to the March 1, 1670 version reprinted in Wootton, ed., *Political Writings of John Locke*, pp. 210–32.

92. Lords Proprietors to Sir Nathaniel Johnson, June 18, 1702, CO 5/289/93, PRO.

93. Wootton, ed., *Political Writings of John Locke*, pp. 43–44.

94. Weir, *Colonial South Carolina*, p. 54.

95. Ashley to Andrew Percival [1672], Shaftesbury Papers, PRO 30/24/48, pt. 2 #55, ff. 127–33, PRO.

96. In addition to the provisions of the Fundamental Constitutions, see also the more obscure, but significantly titled, Agrarian Laws that the proprietors substituted for the constitutions, *Shaftesbury Papers*, p. 405. Cf. McNally, "Locke, Leveller and Liberty," 22–25; Zagorin, *A History of Political Thought in the English Revolution*, pp. 135–37.

97. Most recently, Meaghan Duff has claimed that the Fundamental Constitutions "maximized the feudal nature of their administration," "Creating a Plantation Province" in Greene, Brana-Shute, and Sparks, eds., *Money, Trade, and Power*, p. 1.

98. M.E.E. Parker, *North Carolina Charters and Constitutions, 1578–1698* (Raleigh: North Carolina Department of Archives and History, 1963), p. 212.

99. For all of the incentives to migrate spelled out in the Fundamental Constitutions and in the promotional literature, there can be little doubt that the proprietors had little objection (and may have foreseen) to the importation of African slave labor into their colony. In the first place, all of the original proprietors, save Clarendon and Sir William Berkeley, joined the list of "Royal Adventurers of England Trading to Africa" in 1667, Elizabeth Donnan, ed., *Documents Illustrative of the History of the Slave Trade to America*, 4 vols. I, pp. 169–72. In addition, Sir Peter Colleton, one of the more active Lords, also played an active role in the African slave trade for at least 20 years, ibid., pp. 88, 304–05, 308n. Hence, the proprietors quickly clarified the Barbadian "mistake": they did intend to grant headrights for imported slaves as well as servants, Lord Ashley, &c. to Sir John Yeamans, May 1670, *Shaftesbury Papers*, pp. 164–65 at 164; cf. Wood, *Black Majority*, pp. 18–20, which characterizes this letter as a "turnabout" in proprietary attitudes. Even before the colony came into existence, then, African slavery constituted a means to "independence" for English planters, a perception underscored by every promotional pamphlet published after 1670; e.g., Wilson,

An Account of the Province of Carolina, p. 172, John Norris, *Profitable Advice for Rich and Poor in a Dialogue, or Discourse Between James Freeman, a Carolina Planter and Simon Question, a West-Country Farmer* [London, 1712], in Greene, ed., *Selling a New World*, pp. 86–87, 107–08.

100. Cf. Steve Pincus, "Neither Machiavellian Moment nor Possessive Individualism: Commerical Society and the Defenders of the English Commonwealth," *American Historical Review*, 103 (1998), 705–36. Shaftesbury's co-proprietors, Lord Berkeley and Carteret, had codified religious toleration in their other province of New Jersey in 1665, John E. Pomfret, *Colonial New Jersey: A History* (New York: Charles Scribner's Sons, 1973), pp. 22–23.

101. Wilson, *An Account of the Province of Carolina in America* (London, 1682), p. 10; R.F., *The Present State of Carolina*, p. 22.

102. R.F., *The Present State of Carolina*, p. 5; Wilson, *An Account of the Province of Carolina*, p. 17.

103. Edmund White to Paul Grimball, January 29, 1688 in William Dunlop Papers, MS. 9250, NLS (microfilm in SCHS), reprinted in *SCHM*, 30 (1929), 1–5.

104. R.F., *The Present State of Carolina*, pp. 7, 9–10, 13, 21.

105. H.R. Merrens and G.D. Terry, "Dying in Paradise: Malaria, Mortality, and the Perceptual Environment in Colonial South Carolina" in *Journal of Southern History*, 50 (1984), 533–50 at 534; A.J. Schmidt, ed., "Hyrne Family Letters," *SCHM*, 63 (1962), 150–57; Timothy J. Silver, *A New Face on the Countryside: Indians, Colonists, and Slaves in South Atlantic Forests, 1500–1800* (Cambridge: Cambridge University Press, 1990), pp. 156–57.

106. Slack, *Povery and Politics in Tudor and Stuart England*, pp. 188–204.

107. Wrigley and Schofield, *Population History of England*, p. 186. Unfortunately, we have no figures on the number of seventeenth-century arrivals, African or European, to Carolina.

108. Peter Clark, "Migration in England During the Late Seventeenth and Early Eighteenth Centuries" in Clark and Souden, eds., *Migration & Society in Early Modern England*, pp. 213–52 at 233–34.

109. Clark, "Migration in England," pp. 236–42.

110. Lords Proprietors to Grand Council and Parliament, May 13, 1691, CO 5/288/180, PRO.

111. "Temporary Laws of Carolina," CO 5/286/66–67, PRO.

112. Parker, *North Carolina Charters and Constitutions*, p. 94.

113. Lords Proprietors to Governor, Council and Assembly, May 13, 1691, CO 5/288/180, PRO.

114. Cf. Alison Games, "Migration" in David Armitage and Michael J. Braddick, eds., *The British Atlantic World, 1500–1800* (Baskingstoke and New York: Palgrave Macmillan, 2002), pp. 31–50; Bailyn, *Voyagers to the West*; Horn, *Adapting to a New World*; Jon Kukla, "Order and Chaos in Early America: Political and Social Stability in pre-Restoration Virginia," *American Historical Review*, 90 (1985), 275–98.

115. James, duke of Ormonde, to Capt. G. Mathew, February 5, 1687, *HMC Ormonde*, Series 36, N.S., pt. 7, pp. 482–83.

116. Governor and Council to Board of Trade, December 7, 1709, CO 5/1291/84–85, PRO.

117. David Ramsay, *The History of South-Carolina, From the First Settlement in 1670, to the Year 1808*, 2 vols. (Charleston, 1809), II, pp. 413–15. The Lowcountry tourist of today may visit Middleton Place, Boone Hall, and the Manigualt House in Charleston and drive past plantations in private hands, all testimony to the importance of "estate" in past, yet relatively recent, times.

Chapter 3

118. "Articles of Agreement between the Lords Proprietors of Carolina in order to the speedy settlement of the said Province," April 26, 1669, *CSP AWI*, VII, no. 54, p. 19. L284 12s. 3d. of this sum had gone to "arms and ammunition towards the settlement of Port Royal" that had been destroyed by storm in late 1665, while 106l. 11s. had been spent "for charges of the Carolina patent" passing the seals. "A Dr. and Cr. Account with the Lords Proprietors of Carolina," June 1663 to April 1666, *CSP AWI*, VI, no. 1192, p. 379; Lesser, p. 14; "Memorial of 'the persons concerned in Carolina' to the King," March 24, 1668/69, *CSP AWI*, VII, no. 41, p. 13; "The Accompt of the Costs of the Ship Carolina and her setting to Sea," etc., August 17, 1669, *Shaftesbury Papers*, pp. 143–52; "Temporary Laws of Carolina," CO 5/286/66–67, PRO; "Coppy of Instructions Annexed to ye Commission for ye Governor & Council," July 27, 1669, *Shaftesbury Papers*, pp. 119–23; "Instructions from the Lords Proprietors of Carolina to Joseph West 'about our plantation,'" July 1669, *Shaftesbury Papers*, pp. 125–27; "Instructions from the Lords Proprietors of Carolina to Joseph West, storekeeper," July 1669, *Shaftesbury Papers*, pp. 127–29.

119. This figure, of course, excludes African and Indian slaves who receive no mention in the documents of the early 1670s. Joseph Dalton to Lord Ashley, January 20, 167, *Shaftesbury Papers*, pp. 376–83.

120. Lord Ashley to Joseph West, November 1, 1670, *Shaftesbury Papers*, pp. 208–10.

121. "Provisions at Ashley River, [September 1670?], *Shaftesbury Papers*, p. 178.

122. Walter Edgar, *South Carolina: A History* (Columbia: University of South Carolina Press, 1998), pp. 82–108, and Sirmans, *Colonial South Carolina*, pp. 17–34, provide the general account.

123. Weir, *Colonial South Carolina*, p. 53; *Shaftesbury Papers*, p. vi.

124. Ashley to Sir Thomas Lynch, October 29, 1672, *Shaftesbury Papers*, pp. 414–15 at 414.

125. Peter Laslett, ed., *John Locke: Two Treatises of Government* (Cambridge: Cambridge University Press, 1988), p. 28.

126. "Carolina: A draught of some laws"; "Temporary Laws of 1672" and "Agrarian Laws," June 21, 1674, *Shaftesbury Papers*, pp. 403–05, 450–51; cf. Zagorin, *A History of Political Thought in the English Revolution*, p. 136.

127. To scratch the surface of this voluminous correspondence, Governor Sayle and Council at Ashley River to the Lords Proprietors, [September 1670],

Shaftesbury Papers, pp. 175–76; Joseph Dalton to Anthony, Lord Ashley, Chancellor of the Exchequer, September 9, 1670, ibid., pp. 182–85; Florence O'Sullivan to [Lord Ashley], September 9, 1670, ibid., pp. 188–90; Stephen Bull to [same], September 12, 1670, ibid., pp. 192–96; Joseph West to Lord Ashley, September, 1670, ibid., pp. 202–04; Henry Brayne to Lord Ashley, November 9, 1670, ibid., pp. 214–17; Sir John Yeamans to Lord Ashley, November 15, 1670, ibid., pp. 220–21.

128. Earl of Shaftesbury to Sir Peter Colleton, November 27, 1672, *Shaftesbury Papers*, pp. 416–18.

129. Weir, *Colonial South Carolina*, pp. 58–61. Yeamans was removed over the vociferous objection of Sir Peter Colleton, who Ashley believed had connived with Sir John (although the proprietors continued as partners and, apparently, as friends and political allies), Shaftesbury to Sir John Yeamans, June 20, 1672, *Shaftesbury Papers*, 397–98; same to Sir Peter Colleton, November 27, 1672, *Shaftesbury Papers*, pp. 416–18; Sir Peter Colleton to John Locke, July 22, 1674, DeBeer, I, no. 289, pp. 404–05.

130. *Shaftesbury Papers*, p. 349; Sirmans, *Colonial South Carolina*, pp. 27–29.

131. *Shaftesbury Papers*, pp. 134–35 (first fleet passengers), 350.

132. Mathews's role in this war remains unclear; an unknown village (probably the Westos whom he had also visited) had made him a cacique sometime before June 20, 1672 and, as a member of the Grand Council and proprietary deputy, he certainly knew, at the least, what was happening, *Shaftesbury Papers*, pp. 399, 271n (for Fitzpatrick's relationship with Godfrey), 338, 351 (for the murder of the Indian and reactions). William Robert Snell, "Indian Slavery in Colonial South Carolina, 1671–1795" (Ph.D. diss., University of Alabama, 1972), offers a discussion of the war and its outbreak at pp. 8–13, but makes no mention of the Fitzpatrick incident finding "provocations by both sides," at 10. Cf. Amy Ellen Friedlander, "Indian Slavery in Proprietary South Carolina" (M.A. thesis, Emory University, 1974), pp. 7–9. Friedlander notes the importance of the "Goose Creek men" and the enslavement of Indians but regards them as "Barbadians." We have a glimmer as to both of the number of Indians taken for slaves by Carolinians and of the number of Indian slaves living in Carolina during the proprietary period, but we have no firm notion as to the numbers sold to the West Indies and New England, Snell, "Indian Slavery in Colonial South Carolina," pp. 125–32.

Purportedly, Moore, Mathews's lieutenant, both came from Barbados himself and married a woman who was either the widow or daughter of Sir John Yeamans; these beliefs have underpinned the enduring, but misleading, portrayal of the Goose Creek men as "Barbadian Anglicans," Sirmans, *Colonial South Carolina*, p. 17; Weir, *Colonial South Carolina*, p. 65; Edgar, *South Carolina*, pp. 84–85. Unfortunately, however, no evidence (at best) exists to support Barbadian origins for Moore, while his wife, Margaret, was the posthumous daughter of the Barbados planter, Benjamin Berringer (apparently a rival in love of Yeamans) and Margaret Forster. Thus, Moore seems to have had connections with the Berringer family (members of which lived in Carolina as well as Barbados) but not necessarily with the West

Indies, Bull, "Barbadian Settlers in Early Carolina," 331–39; P.F. Campbell, ed., *Chapters in Barbados History, First Series* (Barbados: The Barbados Museum and Historical Society, 1986), pp. 49–53.

133. John Locke to Captain Kingdon, April 29, 1672, *Shaftesbury Papers*, p. 392.

134. *CSP AWI*, VII, no. 918, p. 404.

135. Earl of Shaftesbury to Stephen Bull, August 13, 1673, *Shaftesbury Papers*, p. 427.

136. MS. Locke c. 30, Bodl. Lib. (photocopy in SCDAH) provides minutes of the proprietors' meetings between 1671 and 1675.

137. Richard Ashcraft has argued that Shaftesbury learned of the "secret" treaty whereby Charles II agreed, *inter alia*, to convert publicly to Catholicism in exchange for a subsidy sometime in 1673, *Revolutionary Politics & Locke's Two Treatises of Government* (Princeton: Princeton University Press, 1986), pp. 115–16.

138. K.H.D. Haley, *The First Earl of Shaftesbury* (Oxford: Oxford University Press, 1968), pp. 287–347.

139. Hutton, *Charles II*, p. 303.

140. [Sir Peter Colleton] to John Locke, May 28, 1673, *Shaftesbury Papers*, pp. 422–24; Sir Peter Colleton to John Locke, [October 1673], DeBeer, I, no. 279, pp. 392–96 at 394–95; Joseph West to John Locke, June 28, 1673, *Shaftesbury Papers*, pp. 424–25; Sir Peter Colleton to John Locke, March 3, 1674, DeBeer, I, no. 287, p. 403.

141. Extract Governor & Council to ye Lds Proprietor, December 26, 1674, Extract of the people's address to the Governor & Grand Council, December 22, 1674, MSS. Locke c. 30, f. 6, Bodl. Lib.

142. Commission from the Lords Proprietors of Carolina to Joseph West, April 25, 1674, *CSP AWI*, VII, no. 1265, p. 575.

143. Extract of Joseph West to Lords Proprietors, September 22, 1674; West to Proprietors, December 30, 1674, MSS. Locke c. 30, ff. 6–7, Bodl. Lib.

144. Articles of Agreement between the Lords Proprietors of Carolina, May 6, 1674, *Shaftesbury Papers*, pp. 431–35; Lords Proprietors of Carolina to the Governor and Council at Ashley River, May 18, 1674, ibid., pp. 435–38.

   Undoubtedly, as discussed above, Shaftesbury conceived of the concept of leet-men as poor relief both for England and Carolina: "What can become of the poor people there that have no stocks, unless they will become leetmen to some that are able to support them," he observed, especially since "The Lords Proprietors are resolved only to supply those who can pay, and to lay out their money in procuring skilful men and fit materials for the improvement of the country in wine, silk, oil, &c." "Instructions for Mr Andrew Percivall," May 23, 1674, *Shaftesbury Papers*, pp. 440–45.

145. Earl of Shaftesbury to Governor and Council at Ashley River, June 10, 1675, *Shaftesbury Papers*, pp. 466–68. West, feeling underpaid and under-appreciated by the proprietors and wary of the trustworthiness of his fellow colonists, expressed strong reservations about this plan, Joseph West to Lords Proprietors, September 4, 1676, DeBeer, I, no. 318, p. 457.

146. For example, Edgar, *South Carolina*, p. 83.
147. Sir Peter Colleton to John Locke, July 22, 1674, DeBeer, I, no. 289, pp. 404–05.
148. Earl of Shaftesbury to Joseph West, May 23, 1674, *Shaftesbury Papers*, pp. 446–47.
149. Locke neither sought permission from his Oxford college for his departure nor did he go to Oxford to collect belongings for his trip, Ashcraft, *Revolutionary Politics*, pp. 116–23.
150. Haley, *The First Earl of Shaftesbury*, pp. 416–17.
151. Once Shaftesbury had assumed the leadership of the venture, his partners, not for the last time, found themselves at something of a loss when he was unavailable. At the proprietary meeting of March 29, 1674, for instance, Baron Berkeley presented a petition from Captain Halstead of the *Blessing* "but they would not read it but ordered a letter to be drawn to ye Earle of Shaftesbury to desir his advice what they should doe ther in & in the rest of the affairs of Carolina wherein they desired his assistance to put businesse in the right cause he having as they think a perfect scheme of it in his head." The Lords (Berkeley, Craven, and Sir George Carteret) then adjourned for a week. On December 4, the trio (along with Locke) reconvened having received a response from Shaftesbury (now lost). Minutes of meeting of the Lords Proprietors of Carolina, March 29, 1674, MS. Locke, c. 30, f. 6, Bodl. Lib.

Chapter 4

152. The dubious Atkin Williamson constituted the only known clerical presence in Carolina prior to the mid-1690s, although the records we have date from twenty years after. These accounts indicate that the "Reverend" Williamson provided an appropriate spiritual example for the Goose Creek men. Apparently ordained in Ireland (with his papers conveniently in Dublin), he allegedly, in a drunken stupor, christened a bear brought to him by James Moore in a tavern. This story continued to make the rounds in the early 1700s to the scandal of more reputable Church of England clergy, *Johnston*, 57; A.S. Salley, ed., "A Letter by the Second Landgrave Smith," *SCHM*, 32 (1931), 61–63; *Le Jau*, pp. 72–73.
153. Cf. Waterhouse, *A New World Gentry*, pp. 10–17, 35–46.
154. Wrightson, *English Society*, pp. 23–28.
155. Lesser, pp. 46, 48, 179, 186, 204, 206, 414, 418.
156. Cf. Sirmans, *Colonial South Carolina*, p. 30; Weir, *Colonial South Carolina*, pp. 65, 75.
157. Many contemporaries regarded Shaftesbury's political career as particularly slippery even by the slippery standards of the day. The royal brothers, Charles II and James, duke of York, dubbed him "Little Sincerity" while Dryden memorably portrayed his switching of political sides and appeals to the English nation as the dangerous machinations of a disingenuous advocate of anarchy in *Absalom and Achitophel* (1681).

158. Lords Proprietors to Council, April 10, 1677, CO 5/286/125–28, PRO.

159. Sirmans, *Colonial South Carolina*, p. 31. However, no evidence exists to support his claim that these grants constituted "a major attraction for many immigrants" although some did receive lands in excess of 1,000 acres.

160. Lords Proprietors of Carolina to Governor and Council of Ashley River, May 19, 1679, *CSP AWI*, X, no. 992, p. 360.

161. Sirmans, *Colonial South Carolina*, p. 31.

162. Cf. Sirmans, *Colonial South Carolina*, p. 33; Weir, *Colonial South Carolina*, p. 62.

163. Maurice Mathews to Lord Ashley, August 30, 1671, *Shaftesbury Papers*, pp. 332–36; Lord Ashley to Maurice Mathews, December 15, 1671, ibid., pp. 362–63; earl of Shaftesbury to Maurice Mathews, June 20, 1672, ibid., pp. 398–99; same to same, May 23, 1674, ibid., p. 448; same to same, June 9, 1675, ibid., 465–66; Maurice Mathews to Sir Peter Colleton, 1681, folder 30–04, "Mathews, Maurice," SCHS (photocopy of ms. in Pinckney Papers, Library of Congress); Maurice Mathews, "A Contemporary View of Carolina in 1680," *SCHM*, 55 (1954), 153–59; Joel Gascoyne, "A Plat of the Province of Carolina in North America: The South Part, A Quality Survey By Mr Maurice Mathews" ([1693]), Add. MS. 5414.24, BL.

164. For the enmity between Mathews and the Colleton family, J.G. Dunlop and Mabel L. Webber, eds., "Letters from John Stewart to William Dunlop," *SCHM*, 32 (1931), 81–114 at 106.

165. Samuel Wilson to Anthony, second earl of Shaftesbury, March 7, 1683, PRO 30/24/48/101, PRO.

166. Percival, as noted above, had been "admitted to" the Whig Green-Ribbon Club on May 2, 1680 while in England, "Journal of the Green-Ribbon Club," Pepys MS. Miscellany, VII, f. 483, Pepys Library, Magdalene College, Cambridge University. As such, he rubbed elbows with people who became implicated in various plots against the government: in addition to Shaftesbury and Wilson, Slingsby Bethel, Aaron Smith, Lord Grey of Wark, Sir William Waller, Anthony Shepherd, and John Trenchard, "Journal of the Green-Ribbon Club," ff. 489–91. There is no evidence that he joined some of these individuals in informing against co-conspirators; however, as will be discussed later, the Goose Creek men did have connections with James II's government.

167. Samuel Wilson to second earl of Shaftesbury, December 21, 1683, PRO, 30/24/48/103, PRO; "Deed of Sale of the stock and effects, servants and slaves at St Giles Plantation by the Trustee of the Earl of Shaftesbury's Estate to Andrew Percival," May 2, 1685, Papers of the Lords Proprietors in the Malmesbury Collection, Hampshire Record Office (photocopy in Special Files, SCDAH).

168. Dunlop and Webber, eds., "Letters from John Stewart to William Dunlop," 96.

169. Lords Proprietors to Andrew Percival, October 18, 1690, in Rivers, appendix, pp. 412–14 at 414.

170. Lesser, p. 148; *Shaftesbury Papers*, p. 471.

171. "Ledger of quit rents collected by John Archdale in Carolina" (1696), CO5/288/124 (loose sheets in back of entry book), PRO.

172. Copy of Edward Randolph to Lords of Trade, March 22, 1699, CO 5/1287/218–22, PRO.
173. Edward J. McCrady, *History of South Carolina under the Proprietary Government* (New York: Macmillan), pp. 720–21.
174. A "Robert Quarry" is listed as Lieutenant of Captain Francis Jones's company of foot. *HMC, MSS. Ormonde*, N.S. 36, pt. 1, 14th rpt., vii, I, p. 224.
175. Lords Proprietors to Grand Council and Parliament, May 13, 1691, CO 5/288/180; same to same, April 12, 1693, CO 5/288/228–31, both PRO; Lords Proprietors to Governor Joseph Morton, February 15, 1686, *CSP AWI*, XII, no. 568, pp. 153–54. Quarry received a grant of 650 acres on May 6, 1686, Salley, ed., *Warrants for Lands in South Carolina, 1680–1692* (Columbia, SC: South Carolina Department of Archives and History, 1911), p. 192.
176. Minutes of a Palatine's Court held at Charlestown, Carolina, October 10, 1685, *CSP AWI*, XII, no. 395, p. 100; Lords Proprietors to Governor Joseph Morton, April 22, 1686, *CSP AWI*, XII, no. 639, pp. 178–79.
177. Ibid.; Lords Proprietors to Governor James Colleton, September 16, 1686, *CSP AWI*, XII, no. 866, p. 243.
178. Sir Nathaniel received 560 acres on October 9, 1683 for transporting 13 servants and 200 additional acres on January 1, 1684 for transporting another four servants. He also acquired five "town lots" in Charles Town on April 10, 1684, Salley, ed., *Warrants for Lands, 1680–1692*, pp. 107, 116, 149–50.
179. Dunlop and Webber, eds., "Letters from John Stewart to William Dunlop," *SCHM*, 32 (1931), 1–33 at 6, 16–17; 81–114 at 85–86, 110.
180. Conceivably, although no evidence exists to support this idea, the government enlisted Johnson's help in the matter of the "black box" noted briefly in chapter 3. This alleged receptacle, containing "proof" of the marriage of Charles II and Lucy Walter, mother of the duke of Monmouth, was supposed to have been housed somewhere in Newcastle.
181. It should be noted that although the case stemmed from apolitical matters, Charles II favored an acquittal and it seems arranged for Johnson's appearance. The other three defendants, whom Conigsmark had engaged to kill his rival in love, Thynne, were found guilty and hanged. For reasons that still remain unclear, the Crown failed to present sufficient evidence to convict Conigsmark. "The Trial of George Borosky alias Boratzi, Christopher Vratz, John Stern, and Charles John Count Conigsmark, at the Old-Bailey, for the Murder of Thomas Thynn, esq. 34 Charles II. A.D. 1682," in T.B. Howell ed., *A Complete Collection of State Trials and Proceedings of High Treason and Other Crimes and Misdemeanors from the Earliest Period to the Year 1783, with Notes and Other Illustrations*, 21 vols. (London, 1816), IX, pp. 7, 11, 63–66. John Stewart offered double hearsay testimony in 1690 that Sir Nathaniel "in Antego brag'd at open table how he had impos'd on Count Coningsmark's Jury" to bring a not guilty verdict and received £10,000 in reward. Dunlop and Webber, eds., "Letters from John Stewart to William Dunlop," 114.
182. Sloane MS. 3299, f. 211, BL.

183. Governor Sir Nathaniel Johnson to [?], April 25, 1689, *CSP AWI*, XIII, no. 88, p. 31.

184. Governor Sir Nathaniel Johnson to Lords of Trade and Plantations, May 24, 1689, *CSP AWI*, XIII, no. 143, p. 43; Lieutenant-General Christopher Codrington to Lords of Trade and Plantations, July 31, 1689, *CSP AWI*, XIII, no. 312, pp. 111–12.

185. Dunlop and Webber, eds., "Letters from John Stewart to William Dunlop," 32, 99–100. Richard Dunn has found that Sir Nathaniel "alarmed" planters in the Leewards, especially St. Christopher (now St. Kitts, which had a sizeable population of Irish Catholic servants), by pursuing "cordial relations with the French at Martinique." According to Dunn, the intercepted letter from the French island, compounded by the assault in May 1689 on plantations by Irish servants on St. Christopher and the invasion of that island by the French in July made the governor's position untenable. St. Christopher surrendered one week later, Richard S. Dunn, "The Glorious Revolution and America," in Canny, ed., *The Origins of Empire*, pp. 445–66 at 455, 457.

186. In addition to the 760 acres he already owned, Johnson received an additional 500 for "tenn Negroes" on October 12, 1689 and 1,200 more for "servants & Negroes at Sundry times" on April 27, 1691, Salley, ed., *Warrants for Lands, 1680–1692*, pp. 212, 215.

187. As late as April 12, 1693, the proprietors, including the Tory earl of Craven, warned their colonists about Johnson's ambitions, Lords Proprietors to Colonel Philip Ludwell, April 12, 1693, CO 5/288/227–31 at 229, PRO.

188. Dunlop and Webber, eds., "Letters from John Stewart to William Dunlop," 106.

189. Dunlop and Webber, eds., "Letters from John Stewart to William Dunlop," 103.

190. Dunlop and Webber, eds., "Letters from John Stewart to William Dunlop," 104–05.

191. Instructions from Lord Shaftesbury to Henry Woodward, May 23, 1674, *Shaftesbury Papers*, pp. 445–46.

192. Extract, Mr. Percival to Lords Proprietors, December 26, 1674, MS. Locke c. 30, f. 7, Bodl. Lib.

193. "A Faithfull Relation of my Westoe Voiage, by Henry Woodward," December 31, 1674, in Salley, *Narratives*, pp. 130–34; Dr. Henry Woodward to John Locke, November 12, 1675, DeBeer, I, no. 305, p. 431.

194. "Robert Sandford's Relation" and "Henry Woodward's Westoe Voyage" in Salley, *Narratives*; "Account of Henry Woodward and the Earl of Shaftesbury, 1674–1680," Wimborne St. Giles, Dorset (photocopy in Special File, SCDAH).

195. Minutes of the Grand Council, September 3, 1673, *JGC*, I, p. 63.

196. Articles of Agreement between the Earl of Shaftesbury and Andrew Percival, April 23, 1674 and June 2, 1680, Papers of the Lords Proprietors in the earl of Malmesbury Papers, Hampshire Record Office (photocopy in Special File, SCDAH); Joseph West to Lords Proprietors of Carolina, September 4, 1676, DeBeer, I, no. 318, p. 457.

197. Minutes of the Grand Council, September 3, 1673, *JGC*, I, p. 63.

198. Minutes of the Grand Council, October 4, and October 7, 1673, *JGC*, I, p. 64.

199. Minutes of the Grand Council, July 25, and August 3, 1674, *JGC*, I, pp. 69–70.

200. Woodward received payments of £112 12s. 4d. from St. Giles Edisto in 1680, £40 paid on June 11, 1676, £34 on April 30, 1676, and £56 on March 31, 1676, "Joynt account belonging to the Rt. Honble Anthony Earl of Shaftesbury and Mr. Andrew Percival [1674–1680]," June 6, 1680, and Percival received £227 19s. 10d. on July 16, 1678, £259 16s. 11d. on May 11, 1679, and £156 12s. on January 23, 1679/80, "Account of Henry Woodward and the Earl of Shaftesbury, 1674–1680."

201. Abstracts of Grants, SCDAH, II, p. 23; earl of Shaftesbury to Andrew Percival, June 6, 1682, PRO 30/24/7/505, PRO. This letter, bundled separately from the mass of Carolina papers in Bundle 48 of the Shaftesbury Papers at the PRO, was not included in the *Shaftesbury Papers* and thus appears to have escaped the attention of prior investigations.

202. "Letters of Thomas Newe," in Salley, *Narratives*, p. 182.

203. The Westo War has been customarily portrayed as a manifestation of settler dissatisfaction with the proprietary monopoly on the Indian trade. Gallay, *The Indian Slave Trade*, pp. 48–69 (and for general proprietary failure to control the Indian slave trade); Sirmans, *Colonial South Carolina*, pp. 33–34. Since the Carolinians involved already controlled the trade and profited from it under proprietary authority, this argument does not make much sense. J. Leitch Wright, *The Only Land They Knew*: The Tragic Story of the American Indians in the Old South (New York: Free Press, 1981), provides a discussion of the Westo War that blames the conflict on Westo dependence on Virginia traders which purportedly "provoked Woodward and other Carolinians to exterminate" that people. However, Wright cited a 1674 letter from Woodward to Shaftesbury to support his view, at p. 107.

204. Minutes of Grand Council, July 14, 1677, *JGC*, I, pp. 82–83. It should be noted that only one of the Carolinians mentioned—Sir John Yeamans's agent, Godfrey—came from the West Indies. Boone came to the province from New York, *Shaftesbury Papers*, pp. 386n, 469n.

205. Lords Proprietors to the Governor, Council, and other inhabitants of Carolina, *CSP AWI*, X, no. 176, p. 60.

206. Articles of Agreement between the Lords Proprietors of Carolina, *CSP AWI*, X, no. 177, pp. 60–61.

207. Minutes of the Grand Council, June 1, 1680, *JGC*, I, pp. 83–85.

208. Minutes of the Grand Council, June 4, 23, and 24, 1680, *JGC*, I, p. 85.

209. Anthony, earl of Shaftesbury, to Andrew Percival, June 6, 1682, PRO 30/24/7/505, PRO. Percival, as noted below, was in England in 1680. However, he certainly benefited from the outcome of the Westo War.

210. Mathews, "A Contemporary View of Carolina in 1680," at 158.

211. "Letters of Thomas Newe" in Salley, *Narratives*, p. 183.

212. Lords Proprietors to Andrew Percival, February 21, 1681, CO 5/286/155, PRO; Commission from the Lords Proprietors of Carolina to Joseph West, May 17, 1680, *CSP AWI*, X, no. 1356–57, pp. 525–26. Percival, after Shaftesbury's death, sued Woodward to stop the doctor from taking proceeds from the earl's estate in Carolina, Samuel Wilson to second earl of Shaftesbury, December 21, 1683, PRO 30/24/48/103, PRO.

213. "Instructions for the Commission appoynted to heare and determine differences between the Christians and the Indians," May 17, 1680, CO 5/286/150–52, PRO.

214. Lords Proprietors to the Governor and Council of Ashley River, February 21, 1681, *CSP AWI*, XI, no. 27, p. 12.

215. Lords Proprietors to Governor and Council of Ashley River, March 7, 1681, *CSP AWI*, XI, no. 37, pp. 16–17.

216. *CSP AWI*, XI, no. 518, p. 236. Meanwhile, Woodward and six associates had moved deep into the interior where their presence alarmed the Spanish authorities in Florida, Herbert S. Bolton, "Spanish Resistance to the Carolina Traders in Western Georgia (1680–1704)," *Georgia Historical Quarterly*, 9 (1925), 115–30 and 120–22. Professor Bolton, like the Spanish, believed that Woodward was an agent of the Charles Town government, which, given the history, seems unlikely.

217. Lords Proprietors to Governor and Council, September 30, 1683, CO 5/287/72, PRO. Percival, one of the big winners, naturally maintained a different perspective, Percival to Locke, August 22, 1682, DeBeer, II, no. 729, p. 543.

Chapter 5

218. Locke did not discuss the particulars or the timing of these discussions in his diaries. However, Rene Petit and Jacob Guerard were in England by January 1679 trying to arrange for the transportation of their group to Carolina. Locke did not return to England until April 1679 (Ashcraft, *Revolutionary Politics*, p. 137). Since Shaftesbury had been in the Tower for much of the time his physician had been abroad, it seems most likely that Sir Peter Colleton handled this matter on the proprietary end, especially since he took charge of subsequent proprietary facilitation of the migration of Huguenots.

219. "A humble proposition addressed to the King and Parliament to give retreat to Protestant and proselyte foreigners in his American colonies and particularly in Carolina," [January 1679?], *CSP AWI*, X, no. 875, p. 321; "Petition of Rene Petit and Jacob Guerard to the Lords of Trade and Plantations," [March 1679], *CSP AWI*, X, no. 918, p. 336; "Report of the Lords Proprietors of Carolina on the Petition of Rene Petit and Jacob Guerard," March 6, 1679, *CSP AWI*, X, no. 919, pp. 336–37; "Humble Proposals for Carolina," [March 1679], *CSP AWI*, X, no. 920, p. 337; Commissioners of the Customs to Lords of the Treasury, April 14, 1679, *CSP AWI*, X, no. 967, p. 351; Lords Proprietors of Carolina to the Governor and Council of Ashley River, May 19, 1679, *CSP AWI*, X, no. 992, p. 360; Lords

Proprietors of Carolina to the Governor and Council of Ashley River, December 17, 1679, *CSP AWI*, X, no. 1233, p. 455.

For the most thorough study of the Huguenot migration to South Carolina, see Bertrand Van Ruymbeke, *From New Babylon to Eden: The History of the Huguenot Migration to Proprietary South Carolina, 1680–1720* (Columbia, SC: University of South Carolina Press, forthcoming).

220. Landgrave Axtell received a grant of 3,000 acres which was entered on December 13, 1680, his wife, Dame Rebecca, received 2,900 acres at the end of 1686, Salley, ed., *Warrants for Lands, 1680–1692*, pp. 23, 196.

221. Wilkinson never went to Carolina. Arrested for debt on board his ship in the Thames, he was taken to the Tower where the government, including Charles II personally, sought unsuccessfully to secure his testimony against Shaftesbury, *Animadversions on Capt. Wilkinson's Information being highly conducive to the better informing and disabusing the Minds of Men, and tending to the publick Peace and Safety. (He that is first in his own Cause seems just, but his neighbour comes and searches him out, Prov. 18.17)* (London, 1682).

222. Haley, *First Earl of Shaftesbury*, pp. 629–31, 642–51.

223. Earl of Longford to duke of Ormonde, September 15, 1681, *HMC Ormonde*, Series 36, pt. 6, p. 154; Narcissus Luttrell, *A Brief Relation of State Affairs*, 6 vols. (Oxford, 1857), I, p. 136; Haley, *First Earl of Shaftesbury*, pp. 667–68.

224. William Bird to Secretary Jenkins, August 22, 1681, Stowe MS. f. 49, BL. For Wilson's movements in the autumn of 1681, see Sir James Hay to Secretary Jenkins, [September 1681], Stowe, MS. f. 48, BL; Information of Sir James Hay against Samuel Wilson, [October 1681], Stowe MS. 186 f. 46, BL; Sir James Hay to Secretary Jenkins, September 19, 1681, Stowe MS. f. 48, BL, and J. Coates to Secretary Jenkins, September 17 and 19, 1681, Stowe MS. f. 49, BL; Tim Taylor to "Mr. Herne," September 30, 1681, Stowe MS. 186 f. 41, BL; Taylor to "Mr. Herne," September 30, 1681, Stowe MS. 186 f. 43, BL; Taylor to "Mr. Herne," October 5, 1681, Stowe MS. 186 f. 42, BL; Taylor to "Mr. Herne," October 5, 1681, Stowe MS. 186 f. 44, BL.

Andrew Percival was in England at this time and we have evidence that he also dabbled in politics: he was "admitted to" the Whig Green-Ribbon Club on May 2, 1680, "Journal of the Green-Ribbon Club," Pepys MS. Miscellany, VII, f. 483, Pepys Library. Percival left Carolina for Barbados sometime in 1679 taking ship for London on December 23 of that year, "Tiketts Granted by the Secretary of Barbadoes to Persons for Departure to Other American Ports," 12/102/2, Langdon Cheves III Papers, SCHS. However, he must have returned to the colony by November 1681 when his commission as secretary and as Shaftesbury's deputy were recorded, Lesser, pp. 165–66. He probably left London in August or September. It should be noted that this trip to England coincided with the final phase of the Westo War.

225. Luttrell, *A Brief Relation of State Affairs*, I, pp. 138, 146.

226. "Instructions to Joseph Moreton, Governor of the Province South and West of Cape Fear," *CSP AWI*, XI, no. 498, p. 230.

227. Lords Proprietors to Andrew Percival, October 18, 1690, *CSP AWI*, XIII, no. 1,117, p. 331; Gilbert Burnet, *The History of My Own Time*, 2 vols. (Oxford: Oxford University Press, 1897–1900 [London, 1721]), II, pp. 332, 355–56; John Archdale, "A New Description of that Fertile and Pleasant Province of Carolina" [London, 1707] in Salley, *Narratives*, pp. 282–311 at 295. Benjamin Blake received two grants totaling 2,090 acres on March 29, 1683, Salley, ed., *Warrants for Lands, 1680–1692*, pp. 84–85.

228. R[obert] F[erguson], *The Present State of Carolina with Advice to the Setlers.*

229. *True Protestant Mercury*, no. 125, March 15 to March 18, 1682, and no. 126, March 18 to March 22, 1682.

230. Luttrell, *A Brief Relation of State Affairs*, I, pp. 179–80.

231. Minutes of a meeting of the Lords Proprietors, July 1, 1681, CO 5/287/173.

232. Articles of agreement Indented and made between the [Lords Proprietors of Carolina] And ye Honourable Sir John Cochran and Sir George Campbell," [July 31, 1682], CO 5/287/15–19, PRO.

233. These versions appear in Parker, ed., *North Carolina Charters and Constitutions*, pp. 186–207 (version of January 12, 1682) and 208–33 (version of August 17, 1682).

234. Parker, ed., *North Carolina Charters and Constitutions*, p. 196.

235. Parker, ed., *North Carolina Charters and Constitutions*, p. 202.

236. Parker, ed., *North Carolina Charters and Constitutions*, p. 227.

237. Lords Proprietors to Governor, Council and Parliament of Carolina, September 30, 1683, CO 5/287/76–77, PRO. Sections 30 and 81 of the August 17, 1682 version governed the removal of councilors and Sections 66–73 provided for the selection of juries by lot. See also Lords Proprietors to Governor Joseph Morton and Deputies, May 30, 1682, Commissions and Instructions from the Lords Proprietors, 1685–1715 MS., SCDAH.

238. Parker, ed., *North Carolina Charters and Constitutions*, pp. 195–96.

239. Parker, ed., *North Carolina Charters and Constitutions*, pp. 223–25.

240. "Proclamation of thanksgiving for the preservation of the king and the duke of York for preservation from the Rye-House Plot," August 7, 1683, *RPCS*, VIII, pp. 209–13 at 213.

241. Robert Wodrow, *The Sufferings of the Church of Scotland from the Restoration to the Revolution*, 3 vols. (Edinburgh, 1721), III, p. 230.

242. Ashcraft, *Revolutionary Politics*, pp. 354, 363, 367–69; Richard L. Greaves, *Secrets of the Kingdom: British Radicals from the Popish Plot to the Revolution of 1688–1689* (Stanford: Stanford University Press, 1992), pp. 163–64. None of the Covernanters interested in Carolina, though, was a "personal emissary" of Argyll nor did the duke himself have any apparent interest in the province, cf. Stephen Saunders Webb, *Lord Churchill's Coup: The Anglo-American Empire and the Glorious Revolution Reconsidered* (New York: Alfred A. Knopf, 1995), p. 59; Linda G. Fryer, "Documents Relating to the Formation of the Carolina Company in Scotland, 1682," *SCHM*, 99 (1998), 110–34; Peter Karsten, "Plotters and Proprietaries,

1682–83: The 'Council of Six' and the Colonies: Plan for Colonization or Front for Revolution," *The Historian*, 38 (1970), 474–84.

243. Wodrow, *Sufferings of the Church of Scotland*, III, p. 230.

244. For earlier Scottish interest in Carolina, see Charles, duke of Lauderdale to Sir John Nisbet, July 10, 1671, GD 205/40/10/13/3 (Ogilvy of Inverquharity Muniments), NAS; Minutes of the Privy Council of Scotland with a Memorial, February 21, 22, 26, 1681, *RPCS*, VIII, pp. 651–72. For Shaftesbury's sympathies with the Presbyterians, see his speech on the "The true interest of Scotland" (1678), PRO 30/24/6A/325, PRO.

245. Fryer, "Documents Related to the Carolina Country," 129.

246. *RPCS*, vol. VII, pp. 655–56, 664–72.

247. Wodrow, *Sufferings of the Church of Scotland*, I, p. 270; II, pp. 374, 395–96, 443; III, pp. 124–26, 228 (after the Lanark Declaration, the council banished some rebels "and made Recruits in the Army in Flanders, some were sold as slaves in Carolina and other Places in America, in order to empty the full Prisons"); *RPCS*, VII, pp. 525–36.

248. *RPCS*, VII, pp. 294–95.

249. Cardross, William Dunlop, and Walter Gibson, the Glasgow merchant who conveyed the colonists all subscribed to the Carolina Company, Fryer, "Documents Related to the Carolina Company," 131–32.

250. For centuries, admirers of the Whigs argued that the Rye-House Plot itself had been a figment of the imagination of Charles II and his government since, they believed, people like Shaftesbury and Locke (most of all) would not have dirtied their hands in such matters as assassination. Ashcraft has laid that shibboleth to rest, *Revolutionary Politics*, passim. The plotters intended to kill the royal brothers as they returned to London from the races at Newmarket and their scheme derives its name from the house where the attempt was to be made.

251. "A.M." [Alexander Munro?] to Sir George Campbell of Cessnock, April 28, 1682, *HMC*, xiv (iii), p. 113.

252. Unsigned letter, July 22, 1682, GD 158/846 (Hume of Marchmont Papers), NAS.

253. Approval came on August 15, 1682 but was not recorded in Edinburgh until November 30; *RPCS*, VII, pp. 599–600; Sir George Mackenzie to George Gordon, earl of Aberdeen, [September 1682], in *Letters of Public Affairs of Scotland, Addressed by Contemporary Statesmen to George, Earl of Aberdeen, Lord High Chancellor of Scotland. MDCLXXI–MDCLXXXIV* (Aberdeen, 1851), pp. 68–69.

254. James, duke of Albany, to duke of Queensberry, October 10, 1682, GD 224/171/37–40 (Buccleuch Muniments), NAS.

255. Contract between Sir John Cochrane of Ochiltree and Sir George Campbell of Cessnock and the other undertakers, September 15, 1682, Wod.Qu. XXXVI, ff. 130–32, Wodrow Papers, NLS.

256. Sir John Cochrane of Ochiltree to Governor Joseph Morton, [September, 1682], GD 158/847 (Hume of Marchmont Papers), NAS; Charles Charters to Sir George Campbell of Cessnock, August 2, 1682, *HMC*, xiv (iii),

p. 114; Sir Patrick Hume of Polwarth to Sir John Cochrane and Sir George Campbell, October 2, 1682, *HMC,* xiv (iii), pp. 114–15; [John Crafford], *A New and More Exact Account of the Fertile and Famous Colony of Carolina (On the Continent of America)* (Dublin, 1683) (reprinted by Nathan Tarrant (Belfast, 1684)).

257. Sir John Cochrane to earl of Aberdeen, in *Letters to Aberdeen,* pp. 58–60.

258. *True Protestant Mercury,* no. 183, October 4 to October 7, 1682; no. 186, October 14 to October 18, 1682; no. 187, October 21, 1682. According to the Lord Advocate in Scotland, "the Carolina project encourages much our fanaticks, thinking they ar now secur of a retreat," Sir George Mackenzie to George, earl of Aberdeen, [September 1682], *Letters to Aberdeen,* pp. 68–69.

259. Lords Proprietors to Governor Morton, November 21, 1682, *CSP AWI,* XI, nos. 807–09, pp. 338–39.

260. If so, his signature on the letter to the Scottish Carolina Company would have been among his last public acts.

261. Ashcraft, *Revolutionary Politics,* pp. 357–59. Shaftesbury, obviously, then did not sign the instructions sent by the proprietors to Morton about granting land to the Scots and the implementation of new Fundamental Constitutions, Lords Proprietor to Governor Joseph Morton, November 21, 1682, *CSP AWI,* XII, no. 1284, pp. 805–09.

262. Luttrell, *A Brief Relation of State Affairs,* I, pp. 273–74, Rev. Walter MacLeod, *Journal of the Hon. John Erskine of Carnock, 1683–1687* (Edinburgh, 1893), pp. 21–22.

263. Walcot's disaffection had come to the attention of the government in 1672, "The Information of Thomas Cullen taken before the Earl of Thomond," November 5, 1672, *HMC Ormonde,* Series 36, N.S., pt. 3, p. 321.

264. "Further information of Robert West of the Middle Temple," June 26, 1683, in Thomas Sprat, *Copies of the Informations and Original Papers of the Horrid Conspiracy Against the Late King, His Present Majesty and the Government* (London, 1685), p. 35; "The Further Examination of Robert West of the Middle-Temple, Barrister at Law," June 27, 1683, in Sprat, *Copies of the Informations,* p. 48; "Colonel Romzey's further information," June 25, 1683, in Sprat, *Copies of the Informations,* p. 16; "The Information of Thomas Shepherd, taken by the Right Honourable the Earl of Sunderland, &c, June the 27th 1683" in Sprat, *Copies of the Informations,* pp. 9–10; the "Information of Zechariah Bourne," July 6, 1683, in Sprat, *Copies of the Informations,* p. 55; "Examination of Mr. Steil and Andrew Oliver anent Mr. Aaron Smith's coming to Scotland & his going to Sir J. Cockram's House at Ochiltree," December 11, 1683, in Sprat, *Copies of the Informations,* 103–04; Burnet, *History of My Own Time,* II, pp. 331–32; Howell ed., *State Trials,* VIII, 846, 851–52; idem, X, 671, 674; "Trial of Captain Thomas Walcot," idem, IX, 554 (when Walcot testified that he had come from Ireland at Shaftesbury's behest to become governor of Carolina, the Lord Chief Justice, Sir Francis Pemberton, interjected cryptically, "That design was a great while ago frustrated"); James Ferguson, *Robert Ferguson the*

Plotter or The Secret of the Rye-House Conspiracy and the Story of a Strange Career (Edinburgh, 1887), pp. 68, 160; "The Deposition of Mr. William Carstares, when he was Examined before the Lords of Secret Committee, given in by him, and renewed upon Oath, upon the 22d of December 1684 in presence of the Lords of His Majesty's Privy-Council," September 8, 1684, in Sprat, *Copies of the Informations*, pp. 125–28 at 127–28; "Deposition of Commissarie Monro" in *Acts of the Parliament of Scotland*, 9 vols. (London, 1820), VIII, appendix, pp. 33–35; "Deposition of William Carstares" in idem, VIII, appendix, pp. 35–36; "Deposition of Robert West" in idem, VIII, appendix, pp. 51–52.

265. "Deposition of Commissary Monro" in *Acts of Parliament of Scotland*, VIII, appendix, p. 35.

266. *Acts of Parliament of Scotland*, VIII, appendix, p. 60.

267. Howell, ed., *State Trials*, VIII, pp. 1026–27.

268. "Trial of Robert Baillie of Jerviswood," Howell, ed., *State Trials*, X, pp. 671–74.

269. Sir John Cochrane of Ochiltree to earl of Aberdeen, June 15, 1683, in *Letters to George, Earl of Aberdeen*, pp. 127–28.

270. GD 238/3/4/1–10x (Baird of Saughtonhall Muniments), NAS, and AC7/7/1–3, Admiralty Court Records, NAS. Patrick Crawford's case did not end until 1691.

271. "Memoir of Mrs William Veitch" in *Memoirs of Mrs William Veitch, Mr Thomas Hog of Kiltearn, Mr Henry Erskine, and Mr John Carstares* (Edinburgh, 1846), pp. 7–8.

272. "Memoir of Mr Thomas Hog of Kiltearn" in *Memoirs of Mrs William Veitch, Mr Thomas Hog of Kiltearn, Mr Henry Erskine, and Mr John Carstares*, pp. 105–07.

273. *RPCS*, VII, 672 for Stewart; John Dick to [Thomas Linning?], April 22, 1684, Wod.Qu. XXXVI, f. 195, Wodrow Papers, NLS.

274. MacLeod, ed., *Journal of the Hon. John Erskine of Carnock*, pp. 21–22, 62–63 (for imprisonment of the Cessnocks and their confederates and other trials of the "godly"), 39 (for taking for soldiers).

275. Bishop of Derry to duke of Ormonde, December 12, 1682, *HMC Ormonde*, Series 36, pt. 1, xiv (vii), p. 56.

276. Ezekial Hopkins, bishop of Derry, to Ormonde, January 16, 1683, *HMC Ormonde*, Series 36, N.S., pt. 6, pp. 512–13.

277. William, bishop of Raphoe, to duke of Ormonde, August 15, 1683, *HMC Ormonde*, Series 36, pt. 1, xiv (vii), p. 57; Viscount Mountjoy to duke of Ormonde, July 3, 1683, *HMC*, Ormonde MSS., pt. 7, pp. 59–60; same to same, August 17, 1683, *HMC*, Ormonde MSS., pt. 7, pp. 107–08; same to same, January 13, 1684, *HMC*, Ormonde MSS., pt. 7, pp. 180–81.

278. Duke of Albany to duke of Queensberry, August 4, 1683, *HMC*, xv (viii), pp. 195–96.

279. Luttrell, *A Brief Relation of State Affairs*, I, p. 289.

Chapter 6

280. MacLeod, ed., *Journal of the Hon. John Erskine of Carnock*, p. 72.

281. Lords Proprietors to Andrew Percival, October 18, 1690, *CSP AWI*, XIII, no. 1,117, p. 331; Lords Proprietors to Governor and Council, July 11, 1684, CO 5/288/38, PRO.

282. MacLeod, ed., *Journal of the Hon. John Erskine of Carnock*, pp. 68–71.

283. Account of the voyage of transportees to Carolina, [1690?], Wod.Qu. XXXVI, ff. 223–24, Wodrow Papers, NLS; Testimony of John Mathieson, MS 2832, NLS; James McLintock to Thomas Linning, June 1684, Wod.Qu. XXXVI, ff. 204–06, Wodrow Papers, NLS. The names of Dick and McLintock appear on the list of prisoners (to be "carried in shackles and put aboard" ship) for whom Walter Gibson and Dunlop gave bond to the Scottish Privy Council on June 20, 1684, RPCS, IX, p. 208. The evidence indicates that Dunlop, as an associate of the Gibsons, could not have been ignorant of their business or their methods. The alleged behavior of the future Principal of the University of Glasgow on this voyage has been studiously ignored for three centuries as his reputation has been carefully guarded first by Wodrow, his friend and kinsman and, later, by subsequent generations of descendants, such as J.G. Dunlop.

284. MacLeod, ed., *Journal of the Hon. John Erskine of Carnock*, p. 139. Cf. George Pratt Insh and J.G. Dunlop, eds., "Arrival of the Cardross Settlers," *SCHM*, 30 (1929), 69–80, contains the letter from Cardross and Dunlop to Sir Peter Colleton of March 27, 1685; p. 72 contains their report that of "148 persons" on their ship "none dide at sea except one after our arrivell."

On hostility between the Cameronians (also known as the United Societies and the Societies for Prayer and Correspondence in Scotland), such as Thomas Linning (before 1690) and Presbyterians, such as Dunlop, who, as compounders with the government, they regarded as traitors to the cause, see Elizabeth Hyman Hannan, "A church militant: Scotland, 1661–1690," *Sixteenth Century Journal*, 26 (1995), 49–74 and [William Dunlop] to Robert Wyllie, January 15, February 19, April 28, 1679, Wod.Fol. XXVI, ff. 252–59, Wodrow Papers, NLS. Transportation would not have presented an issue for the moderates such as Dunlop.

285. Sir Peter Colleton to Sir Richard Kyrle, June 28, 1684, CO 5/287/130, PRO.

286. M.E.E. Parker, "The First Fundamental Constitutions of Carolina," *SCHM*, 71 (1970), 78–85; R.S. Green, ed., "The South Carolina Archives Copy of the Fundamental Constitutions," *SCHM*, 71 (1970), 86–100.

287. Lords Proprietors to Governor James Colleton, March 3, 1687, CO 5/288/118, PRO.

288. Parker, *North Carolina Charters and Constitutions*, pp. 153–64. Revised Article 71 considered the proprietary veto power, at 161–62.

289. Lords Proprietors to Governor James Colleton, March 3, 1687, CO 5/288/118, PRO.

290. Ibid.

291. Lords Proprietors to Governor and Council, March 13, 1685, CO 5/287/108, PRO.
292. Dunlop and Webber, eds., "Letters from John Stewart to William Dunlop," 13–14.
293. Ibid.; Lords Proprietors to Grand Council and Parliament, May 13, 1691, CO 5/287/180, PRO.
294. Irish army muster list, May 5, 1662, *HMC Ormonde*, N.S. 36, pt. 1, xiv (vii, Part I), p. 350, company commanders February 18, 1665, *HMC Ormonde*, N.S. 36, pt. 1, xiv (vii, Part I), p. 325.
295. Irish army muster roll, *HMC Ormonde*, N.S. 36, pt. 1, xiv (vii, Part 2), p. 224.
296. Lords Proprietors of Carolina to Governor Sir R. Kyrle, June 3, 1684, *CSP AWI*, XI, no. 1722, pp. 645–47 at 646.
297. Lords Proprietors to Sir Richard Kyrle, June 9, 1684, *CSP AWI*, XI, no. 1733, p. 650.
298. Same to same, June 28, 1684, CO 5/287/130, PRO.
299. Lords Proprietors to Grand Council, March 13, 1685, CO 5/288/50–51, PRO. Since the proprietors had suggested to Sir Richard Kyrle that he might appoint Quarry as a sort of deputy governor, it could be argued also that the council meant to act in accordance with proprietary wishes—or, at least, on the pretext of doing so, Lords Proprietors to Sir Richard Kyrle, June 3, 1684, *CSP AWI*, XI, no. 1,722, pp. 645–47 at 646.
300. Lords Proprietors to Governor and Council, March 13, 1685, CO 5/287/107–12, PRO; Lords Proprietors to Joseph West, March 13, 1685, CO 5/287/113–15, PRO. Cf. Sirmans, *Colonial South Carolina*, pp. 35–45. According to Weir, the creation of "seven different administrations during the decade of the '80s and five more during the first five years of the '90s suggests that the proprietors were initially as persistent as they were frustrated with the Goose Creek men, *Colonial South Carolina*, pp. 65–66. Unfortunately, the chronology fails to support such an interpretation: the Lords commissioned Morton as governor on May 18, 1682 but did not order the removal of Mathews and his confederates until March 13, 1685, Lords Proprietors to Governor and Council, CO 5/287/113–115 at 114, PRO. Although Morton and others came to oppose the Goose Creek men, they did not constitute a "proprietary party." Moreover, Scottish interest in Carolina stemmed from Scottish interest in colonization and concern about religious persecution, see later. Migration in this period emerged from English, Scottish, and French contexts not in response to the political situation in Carolina. Also, there seem to have been only five governors in the 1680s (West and Morton each served on two different occasions). Of these, Kyrle died almost upon his arrival in the colony (succeeded temporarily by West, Quarry, and Morton in accordance with local determination and proprietary instructions), leaving Morton's first term and James Colleton. For the 1690s, the tenure of Seth Sothell can scarcely count as a proprietary initiative while Joseph Blake also served temporarily. The proprietors

appointed Philip Ludwell to clean up the mess made by Sothell and his "Goose Creek friends," Lesser, pp. 176–77.

301. Lords Proprietors to Governor Joseph Morton, September 9, 1685, CO 5/288/64–66, PRO.

302. Insh and Dunlop, eds., "Arrival of the Cardross Settlers," at 72–73.

303. Insh and Dunlop, eds., "Arrival of the Cardross Settlers," 73.

304. To that end, the Scots declared their readiness to abide by their deal with the Lords. However, to encourage the "flourishing" of this "noble plantation" and make them "be mor for the lords proprietors' trew Intrest then any in Carolina," the Stuarts Town leaders asked the Lords for the right to choose deputies among "persones receiding amongst us, and who shall have plantations here," Insh and Dunlop, eds., "Arrival of the Cardross Settlers," 74–76.

305. Ibid., 72; Sir Peter Colleton to Lord Cardross, [1687], in J.G. Dunlop, ed., *The Dunlop Papers, v. 3, Letters and Journals, 1663–1689* (Frome and London: Butler & Tanner Ltd., 1953), pp. 45–46.

306. Insh and Dunlop, eds., "Arrival of the Cardross Settlers," 75–76.

307. Lord Cardross to [Governor Morton], January 10, 1685, *CSP AWI*, XI, no. 2,043, p. 760.

308. Caleb Westbrook to [Colonel Godfrey?], February 21, 1685, *CSP AWI*, XII, no. 28, pp. 5–6. By this time, the Yamassees had become the most prominent of the coastal tribes using the Spanish and English to their advantage, Verner W. Crane, *The Southern Frontier, 1670–1732* (Ann Arbor: University of Michigan Press, 1956 [1929]), p. 33.

309. Dr. Henry Woodward to Deputy-Governor John Godfrey, March 21, 1685, *CSP AWI*, XII, no. 83, p. 19.

310. Depositions of Ruben Wills, George Franklin, William Parker, Dr. Henry Woodward, John Edenburgh, and "of severall Yamassee Indians" before Maurice Mathews, Robert Quarry, John Godfrey, Robert Gibbes, and John Moore, CO 5/287/137–40, PRO.

311. Cardross to Governor and Council of Charlestown, March 25, 1685, *CSP AWI*, XII, no. 92, pp. 22–23; same to Robert Quarry, July 17, 1685, *CSP AWI*, XII, no. 286, pp. 67–68.

312. "The declaration of twelve members of ye commons Mett in Parliament Chamber at Charles Town and Excluded theire this 20th day of November 1685," CO 5/287/144–47; Lords Proprietor to Governor James Colleton, March 3, 1687, CO 5/288/118; same to Grand Council and Parliament of Carolina, CO 5/288/180, all PRO.

313. Coincidentally or not, Morton, Axtell, and Grimball were all staunch opponents of Mathews and the Goose Creek men, J.G. Dunlop and Mabel L. Webber, eds., "Paul Grimball's Losses by the Spanish Invasion," *SCHM*, 29 (1928), 231–37; idem, "Spanish Depredations, 1686," *SCHM*, 34 (1933), 81–89.

314. William Dunlop to Sir James Montgomery of Skelmorie, October 21, 1686, GD3/E2/115, NAS (photocopy in SCDAH).

315. William Dunlop to Sir James Montgomery of Skelmorie, November 21, 1686, GD3/E2/116, NAS (photocopy in SCDAH).

316. "Memorial of the hostilities committed in the Province of Carolina by the spaniards Represented by Major William Dunlop who is commissioned to that effect," [1689], GD26/7/277, NAS (photocopy in SCDAH).

317. Lords Proprietors to Governor James Colleton, October 10, 1687, CO 5/288/121, PRO; Dunlop and Webber, eds., "Spanish Depredations, 1686," 81–89. For relations between Charles Town and Stuarts Town, Cardross to Governor and Council at Charles Town, March 25, 1685, *CSP AWI*, XI, no. 92, p. 22; same to Robert Quarry, July 17, 1685, *CSP AWI*, XI, no. 286, p. 67. Weir, *Colonial South Carolina*, argues that this "otherwise puzzling remark" makes sense in the context of the concerns the Lords had about attacks on Spanish shipping made by pirates based in their Bahamas colony. Such activity violated the proprietary charter and, hence, their "repeated instructions" to their officials to clamp down on piracy (some of which will be discussed later). Having "pirates on the brain," Weir contends, the proprietors naturally became alarmed at the planned attack on St. Augustine of 1687, at pp. 87–88.

     This characterization suffers from a number of problems. In the first place, as Weir himself notes, England and Spain were at peace at this time. An attack on a friendly power amounted to treason; hence the Lords' observation as to the fate avoided by the backers of the campaign. Moreover, James Colleton, arriving by coincidence, suppressed the plan, not the proprietors. Finally, Weir's account of the proprietary period does not discuss the letters in the Dunlop Papers and elsewhere (nor does it consider evidence in John Stewart's letters that it does discuss in other places) upon which the account here is based. These documents clearly indicate that all of the activity that surrounded the Scottish colony centered on threats to Goose Creek control of the Indian trade.

318. [Sir Peter Colleton] to Lord Cardross [1687], in Dunlop, ed., *The Dunlop Papers, vol. 3*, pp. 45–46; Lords Proprietors to Governor and Council, October 10, 1687, CO 5/288/121, PRO.

319. Dunlop and Webber, eds., "Letters from William Dunlop," 25, 32, 102–03.

320. Captain Thomas Spragg to Samuel Pepys, April 17, 1688, MS. Rawlinson A 186, f. 265, Bodl. Lib. This letter is bundled with other documents pertaining to the movements of other enemies of Pepys in America.

321. Landgrave Thomas Smith to Major William Dunlop on board *HMS Drake*, February 5, 1688, Dunlop Papers, MS. 9250/63, NLS.

322. Ashcraft, *Revolutionary Politics*, pp. 428–29.

323. Dunlop and Webber, eds., "Letters from John Stewart to William Dunlop," p. 5.

324. Lords Proprietors to Andrew Percival, October 18, 1690, *CSP AWI*, XIII, no. 1,117, p. 331.

325. Lords Proprietors to Grand Council and Parliament, May 13, 1691, CO 5/287/180, PRO.

326. Edmund White to Joseph Morton, February 29, 1688, *SCHM*, 30 (1929), 1–5.

Chapter 7

327. The Lords commissioned Colleton on August 30, 1686, *CSP AWI*, XII, no. 835, p. 233.

328. Earl of Craven to Lords of Trade and Plantations, May 27, 1684, *CSP AWI*, XI, no. 1707, p. 642. The sole work to treat this subject in any depth for South Carolina remains Shirley C. Hughson, "The Carolina Pirates and Colonial Commerce, 1670–1740," *Johns Hopkins University Studies in Historical and Political Science*, Twelfth Series, V-VI-VII (Baltimore, 1894), pp. 241–370. Lynch's complaint signaled a change in governmental attitude toward pirates that came to spread throughout Anglo-America, even in Carolina. Piracy, actively supported by governors from the Bahamas to South Carolina to New York, thrived at the expense of legitimate commerce through the seventeenth century until policy began to shift, Robert C. Ritchie, *Captain Kidd and the War against the Pirates* (Cambridge, MA: Harvard University Press, 1986).

329. Lords Proprietors to Sir Richard Kyrle, June 3, 1684, CO 5/288/30, PRO.

330. Instructions to James Colleton, March 3, 1687, *CSP AWI*, XII, no. 1,165, p. 338; Lords Proprietors of Carolina to Governor James Colleton, September 16, 1686, *CSP AWI*, XII, no. 865, p. 243; The proprietors ratified this law on March 3, 1687, CO 5/288/112, PRO. Lords Proprietors to Governor Joseph Morton, April 22, 1686, *CSP AWI*, XII, no. 639, pp. 178–79.

331. Lords Proprietors to Governor James Colleton, March 3, 1687, *CSP AWI*, XII, no. 1,161, pp. 336–37. Colleton apparently had some success since some pirates had been "taken in Carolina" by the fall of 1687 and "the goods taken from" them were supposed to go to the proprietors. Lords Proprietors to Governor James Colleton, October 17, 1687, *CSP AWI*, XII, no. 1,464, p. 453, and same to Paul Grimball, October 17, 1687, *CSP AWI*, no. 1,465, p. 453.

332. Although the proprietors had dismissed Mathews from favor for enslaving Indians, they remained so much in ignorance of his activities that they granted him 1,000 acres of land "in consideration of his having purchased the lands from the Indians" on November 2, 1686, *CSP AWI*, XII, no. 961, p. 271.

333. Notably the Barbados planter and merchant, Edward Thornburgh, whose family came to participate in the proprietorship, Dunlop and Webber, eds., "Letters from John Stewart to William Dunlop," 106.

334. Dunlop and Webber, eds., "Letters from John Stewart to William Dunlop," 7, 23–27, 94–95.

335. For the Huguenots, see Bertrand Van Ruymbeke, "L'emigration huguenote en Caroline du Sud sous le regime des Seigneurs Proprietaires" (Ph.D. diss., Universite de Sorbonne-Nouvelle, 1995). For connections between the Goose Creek men and the government of James II, see Landgrave Thomas Smith to Major William Dunlop, February 5, 1688, and Thomas Spragg to Samuel Pepys, April 17, 1688. The sons of the Huguenot leader, Jacob Guerard, associated with Mathews, Dunlop and Webber, "Letters from John Stewart to William Dunlop," 108.

336. Bertrand Van Ruymbeke, "*Les Seigneurs de Manoir de Caroline*: An Aspect of the Rise and Fall of the Manorial System in Early Proprietary Carolina" (paper presented at the 1999 Annual Meeting of the Organization of American Historians), 6.

337. Cf. Weir, *Colonial South Carolina*, p. 65.

338. Dunlop and Webber, eds., "Letters from John Stewart to William Dunlop," 96–97; cf. Weir, *Colonial South Carolina*, pp. 66–67, Sirmans, *Colonial South Carolina*, pp. 45–49.

339. They apparently tried the same trick on a subsequent governor, Lords Proprietors of Carolina to Governor Philip Ludwell, April 12, 1693, *CSP AWI*, XIII, no. 269, pp. 82–84 at 83.

340. Dunlop and Webber, eds., "Letters from John Stewart to William Dunlop," 32, 105.

341. Dunlop and Webber, eds., "Letters from John Stewart to William Dunlop," 101–02.

342. Dunlop and Webber, eds., "Letters from John Stewart to William Dunlop," pp. 9, 103–04. Neither Sirmans nor Weir noted this alleged Goose Creek plot to betray the colony to the French.

343. A justification compiled after the fact and presented to the proprietor Seth Sothell says that How read the letter in parliament on February 14, "87," which would actually have predated the letter of March 3, 1687. Stewart wrote about the February 1690 parliament so 1690 seems the most likely date for the reading of the letter, "Petition to the Right Honorable Seth Sothell, One of the Lords and absolute Proprietors of the Province of Carrolena,—Chancellor, Governor and Comander in Cheefe of all theire Majesties Forces in the said Province," [1690], Rivers, Appendix, pp. 418–30 at 419; Dunlop and Webber, eds., "Letters from John Stewart to William Dunlop," 13, 87.

344. Rivers, Appendix, pp. 418–19. According to the justification offered in the form of a petition to Seth Sothell three years later, the other proprietors (who were named), either because of the relative brevity of their tenure or the distractions of other matters, could not be blamed. Leaving Sir Peter's name out of this document also enabled the petitioners to avoid a libel suit as well any other unpleasantness caused by publicly questioning a "superior."

345. Lords Proprietors to James Colleton, Landgrave and Governor, March 3, 1687, CO 5/ 288/118, PRO.

346. *Shaftesbury Papers*, p. 439.

347. *Shaftesbury Papers*, p. 453.

348. A neat move since the Goose Creek men had gone to some lengths to resist the ratification of the 1682 version.

349. Dunlop and Webber, eds., "Letters from John Stewart to William Dunlop," 12–13, 104–05. As these were private communications—as opposed to the public justifications and explanations offered in other instances in the history of proprietary South Carolina—they should receive a relatively high degree of credibility. Certainly, Stewart had no apparent reason to deceive his compatriot.

350. Dunlop and Webber, eds., "Letters from John Stewart to William Dunlop," pp. 9–11, 13–15, 27–29, 87–89, 98, 105–09.

351. Dunlop and Webber, eds., "Letters from John Stewart to William Dunlop," 114.

352. Dunlop and Webber, eds., "Letters from John Stewart to William Dunlop," 109.

353. Cf. Sirmans, *Colonial South Carolina*, pp. 39–49; Weir, *Colonial South Carolina*, pp. 62–67: "The proprietors thought Colleton's recourse to martial law excessive even though they believed the governor had acted within the scope of proprietary rights granted by the charter"; Lords Proprietors to Andrew Percival, October 18, 1690, *CSP AWI*, XII, no. 1,117, p. 381.

354. CO 5/286/146, PRO.

355. *Acts of the Privy Council (Colonial)*, Charles II, v. 16 (June 1, 1680–May 31, 1683), pp. 3–5.

356. Lords Proprietors to Seth Sothell, May 13, 1691, and unsigned petition to Sothell [1691] in Rivers, Appendix, pp. 416–17, 418–30.

357. Cf. Sirmans, *Colonial South Carolina*, p. 46.

358. This letter actually said, in reviewing the "additions and alterations" to the March 1, 1670 document, that these changes, "being for the greater Liberty, security & Quiet of the people, wee doe not doubt but you will acquiesce in them, which is the reason wee have done it without proposeing of it first unto you"—hardly, it would seem, an imposition, Rivers, Appendix, p. 395. Cf. Sir Peter Colleton to Sir Richard Kyrle, June 28, 1684, CO 5/287/130, PRO. No evidence exists that the proprietors ever instructed Morton to compel parliament to ratify the January 1682 Constitutions. To do so, moreover, would have made little sense anyway since the Lords themselves had amended this version.

359. "The declaracon of twelve members of ye commons Mett in Parliament Chamber at Charles Town and Excluded theire this 20th day of November 1685," CO 5/287/144–47 at 144, PRO. We have no evidence that Morton produced these orders and no letters containing such instructions have been found. It may, therefore, be significant that the "declaracon" found its way into the proprietary entry books at the PRO: Morton's enemies may have tried to show his high-handedness even as they disputed the Fundamental Constitutions, Rivers, Appendix, pp. 422–24. Curiously, the petition makes no mention of the war with France.

360. Rivers, Appendix, pp. 424–25.

361. Rivers, Appendix, pp. 425–26. Since only Mathews, Moore, Boone, and Arthur Middleton were put out of office for enslaving Indians and other misdemeanors, this passage confirms the "Goose Creek" perspective of the petition's author(s).

362. Rivers, Appendix, pp. 426–27.

363. Rivers, Appendix, p. 427.

364. Rivers, Appendix, p. 422.

365. Lords Proprietors to Governor Joseph Morton, September 9, 1685, CO 5/287/64–66, PRO.

366. For supporting the proclamation of martial law that prevented the illegal attack on St. Augustine, Lords Proprietors of Carolina to Seth Sothell, May 12, 1691, *CSP AWI*, XIII, no. 1,488, pp. 444–46.

367. Lords Proprietors to Seth Sothell, May 13, 1691, *CSP AWI*, XII, no. 1,498, p. 447.

368. Lords Proprietors to Governor, Deputies and Officers of South Carolina, May 27, 1691, *CSP AWI*, XII, no. 1,535, p. 457.

369. Same to the Governor or Deputies of South Carolina, 27 May 1691, *CSP AWI*, XII, no. 1,536–1,537, p. 457.

370. Lords Proprietors to Seth Sothell, May 12, 1691, Rivers, Appendix, pp. 430–33.

371. Lords Proprietors to Governor and Council at Ashley River, May 13, 1691, CO 5/287/171, PRO.

372. Lords Proprietors to Governor and Council, CO 5/288/172, PRO.

373. Lords Proprietors to Grand Council, May 13, 1691, Rivers, Appendix, pp. 414–16; Lords Proprietors of Carolina to Governor and Council, May 11, 1693, CO 5/289/1.

374. Dunn, "The Glorious Revolution and America," in Canny, ed., *The Origins of Empire.*

375. Instructions to Colonel Philip Ludwell as Governor of Carolina, November 8, 1691, *CSP AWI*, XII, no. 1,884, pp. 565–66.

376. Private Instructions to Governor Philip Ludwell, November 8, 1691, *CSP AWI*, XII, no. 1,886, pp. 566–67.

377. "Representation of grievances" from the Assembly to Governor Ludwell, November 8, 1692, Rivers, Appendix, pp. 433–35.

378. This consideration promptly generated the fourteenth grievance, Lords Proprietors to Governor and Council, April 7, 1693, Rivers, Appendix, pp. 435–36.

379. Lords Proprietors to Governor and Deputies, April 27, 1694, CO 5/288/15, PRO.

380. Lords Proprietors to Governor and Council, April 10, 1693, Rivers, Appendix, pp. 436–39.

381. "The Humble Petition of the House of Commons" [1693?], Rivers, Appendix, pp. 440–41.

382. "Form of Grant for Land in Carolina," November 21, 1682, Rivers, Appendix, pp. 404–06; cf. Sirmans, *Colonial South Carolina*, p. 39, which erroneously claims that the indenture provided a complete right of reentry.

383. Lords Proprietors to Colonel Philip Ludwell, April 12, 1693, CO 5/288/227–31, PRO.

384. Lords Proprietors to Grand Council and Parliament, May 13, 1691, CO 5/288/180–81, PRO.

385. Lords Proprietors to Governor and Council, October 6, 1690, CO 5/288/166, PRO.

386. Lords Proprietors to Governor Philip Ludwell, April 12, 1693, CO 5/288/227–31 at 228, PRO.

387. Lords Proprietors to Governor Joseph Morton, April 26, 1686, CO 5/288/79–81, PRO.

388. Lords Proprietors to Council and Parliament of Carolina, May 13, 1691, CO 5/288/180–81, PRO.

389. "Enymys" here refers to the opponents of paying rents as opposed to some sort of cabal opposed to the proprietorship.

390. Lords Proprietors to Colonel Philip Ludwell, April 12, 1693, CO 5/288/227–31, PRO.

391. Lords Proprietors to Governor and Council, October 18, 1690, CO 5/288/168, PRO.

392. Lords Proprietors to Council and Parliament of Carolina, May 13, 1691, CO 5/288/180–81, PRO.

393. Lords Proprietors to Colonel Philip Ludwell, April 12, 1693, CO 5/288/227–31, PRO.

394. Lords Proprietors to Mr. Trouillard, Mr. Burecell, Mr. Jacques Serrurier, Mr. Courau, Mr. Vervalt, Mr. De Lisle Cramahe and Mr. Dugue in Carolina, April 12, 1693, CO 5/288/236, PRO.

395. Lords Proprietors of Carolina to Governor Philip Ludwell, April 12, 1693, *CSP AWI*, XIII, no. 269, pp. 82–84.

396. Lords Proprietors to Paul Grimball, April 12, 1693, *CSP AWI*, XIII, no. 271, p. 85.

397. J.G. Dunlop and Mabel L. Webber, eds., "Letters from John Stewart to William Dunlop," *SCHM*, 32 (1931), 170–74; Mathews died in England in 1693, Percival's will was probated in 1697, Lesser, pp. 363, 370.

398. Lords Proprietors to Landgrave Thomas Smith, November 29, 1693, CO 5/288/10–11.

399. Letters Patent of the Lords Proprietors of Carolina, April 12, 1693, *CSP AWI*, XIII, no. 266, p. 82.

400. Thus, Mathews escaped charges for his conspiracy with the Spanish and for enslaving Indians. Sothell returned to England also where he died without having received any apparent sanction. Thomas Amy assumed his proprietary share, Lords Proprietors to Governor and Council, September 29, 1697, on back of loose pages in CO 5/288, PRO.

401. Lords Proprietors to John Archdale, February 10, 1695, CO 5/288/24; same to Paul Grimball, April 12, 1695, CO 5/288/25, PRO.

402. Lords Proprietors to Landgrave Thomas Smith, April 24, 1694, CO 5/288/13.

403. Lords Proprietors to Landgrave Thomas Smith, November 29, 1693, CO 5/288/10–11.

404. Lords Proprietors to Landgrave Joseph Blake, April 25, 1697, CO 5/289/35, PRO; Lords Proprietors to John Archdale and Paul Grimball, June 28, 1695, CO 5/288/28, PRO; Lords Proprietors to Landgrave Smith and Deputies, August 31, 1694, CO 5/288/19, PRO.

405. Lords Proprietors to John Archdale, Esquire, August 31, 1694, CO 5/288/20–21, PRO.

406. "Ledger of quit rents collected by J. Archdale in Carolina" (1696), CO 5/288 (loose sheets folded in back of entry book), PRO.

407. Lords Proprietors to Grand Council and Parliament, May 13, 1691, CO 5/288/180, PRO.

Chapter 8

408. Lords Proprietors to John Archdale, February 10, 1695, CO 5/289/24, PRO.
409. Cf. Sirmans, *Colonial South Carolina*, pp. 55–74.
410. Lords Proprietors to John Archdale, June 17, 1696, CO 5/289/32, PRO.
411. Lords Proprietors to Landgrave Joseph Blake, April 25, 1697, CO 5/289/35, PRO.
412. Lords Proprietors to Governor Joseph Blake, April 11, 1698, CO 5/289/48, PRO.
413. Cf. Sections 123–31 of Locke's Second Treatise on Government, Peter Laslett, ed., *Two Treatises of Government* (Cambridge: Cambridge University Press, 1988), pp. 350–53; Parker, ed., *North Carolina Charters and Constitutions*, p. 235.
414. Parker, ed., *North Carolina Charters and Constitutions*, p. 234.
415. Parker, ed., *North Carolina Charters and Constitutions*, pp. 235–36.
416. Parker, ed., *North Carolina Charters and Constitutions*, p. 236.
417. Parker, ed., *North Carolina Charters and Constitutions*, p. 237.
418. Lords Proprietors to Governor Blake and Council, September 21, 1699, CO 5/289/73–74, PRO.
419. Lords Proprietors to Governor Blake and Council, October 19, 1699, CO 5/289/77–78, PRO.
420. Sirmans, *Colonial South Carolina*, p. 73.
421. Lesser, pp. 166, 182, 437.
422. Lords Proprietors to Governor Joseph Blake, August 16, 1698, CO 5/289/52, PRO. Daniel's role in all this is muddled. By 1700, he was a leading "Goose Creek man."
423. Thornburgh, a London merchant, served as trustee for the Sir William Berkeley share which the proprietors now owned jointly, and acted on behalf of Sir Peter Colleton's minor son. Amy, Sir Peter's cousin and a London druggist, had been involved in the proprietorship for 13 years and owned the Clarendon share in 1698 after Sothell's demise, Lesser, p. 44.
424. Lords Proprietors to Governor Joseph Blake and Council, September 21, 1699, CO 5/289/73–74, PRO. Morton's commission as vice-admiralty judge was entered in London at least over a year earlier, "List of the Admiralty Officers in North and South Carolina" in William Bridgeman to William Popple, February 16, 1698, CO 5/1287/99, PRO.
425. Crane, *Southern Frontier*, pp. 143–44; Sirmans, *Colonial South Carolina*, pp. 82–83; Weir, *Colonial South Carolina*, pp. 82–83.
426. Minutes of the Grand Council, April 12, 1680, *JGC*, II, 83, and chapter 4 herein for hostilities between Moore and Woodward; Dunlop and Webber,

eds., "Letters from John Stewart to William Dunlop," passim, for the close ties between Moore and Maurice Mathews.

427. John Ash, "The Present State of Affairs in Carolina" [London, 1706] in Salley, *Narratives*, pp. 269–76 at 270.

428. For Randolph's career, Michael Garibaldi Hall, *Edward Randolph and the American Colonies, 1676–1703* (Chapel Hill, NC: University of North Carolina Press, 1960).

429. "Copy of a Letter from Mr James Moor Dated in Carolina 22 March 1699 to Mr Randolph," CO 5/1287/221–23, PRO.

430. Edward Randolph to Lords of Trade, March 22, 1699, CO 5/1287/218–21, PRO. Thomas Cutler, another adventurer "intimately acquainted with one Captain Moor a Person of known Experience, judgement and great power among the Indians" further seconded Moore's plan and recommended Crown "encouragement." Otherwise, he claimed, Moore would "run a very great Risque to be prejudiced in his own Affaire in that Country, by this proposall, because of the considerable Post he has in that place and dependence on the Lords Proprietors, who may not possibly think it their Interest to Encourage such discovery, but rather to obstruct it," "The Humble Memorial of Thomas Cutler" to the Lords of Trade [March 22, 1699], CO 5/1287/223, PRO.

431. James Moore to Edward Randolph, March 22, 1699, CO 5/1287/222, PRO.

432. Randolph's report made no mention of the troubles in the Carolina parliament in 1689 and the corresponding accusations that were leveled against the Goose Creek men, Edward Randolph to Lords of Trade, June 28, 1699, CO 5/1287/225–30, PRO.

433. CO 5/289/95, PRO.

434. Blake supposedly sold six barrels of powder to the Indians although the "chief men" had previously complained to Randolph that the Lords had supplied no powder for the defense of the province. Cf. Randolph to Lords of Trade, May 16, 1700, CO 5/1287/233 and same to same, June 28, 1699, CO 5/1287/227, both PRO.

435. Edward Randolph to Lords of Trade, May 16, 1700, CO 5/1287/233–35, PRO.

436. Randolph either did not know that Blake was a Quaker or else did not believe that Blake's religious beliefs would prevent him from selling arms and ammunition to Indians (or he believed that Quakers were so "depraved" as to sell powder to Indians when the colony had none). And once again, it is curious to see the opponents of the Goose Creek men charged with abetting piracy and abuses in the Indian trade, the actual hallmarks of the "dealers in Indians" themselves.

437. Joseph Morton to Board of Trade, September 25, 1701, CO 5/1289/168, PRO; Dr. Newton, Advocate of the Lord High Admiral, to William Popple, February 3, 1702, CO 5/1289/172, PRO; Lords of Trade to Lords Proprietors of Carolina, March 3, 1702, CO 5/1289/193, PRO.

438. Sirmans, *Colonial South Carolina*, pp. 83–84.

439. Ash, *Present State of Affairs*; Salley, *Narratives*, p. 271; Sirmans, *Colonial South Carolina*, pp. 84–85.

440. Wright, *The Only Land They Knew*, pp. 113–15, 140–43.

441. Crane, *Southern Frontier*, pp. 73–77; Sirmans, *Colonial South Carolina*, pp. 84–85. Weir, *Colonial South Carolina*, pp. 80–82.

442. Crane, *Southern Frontier*, pp. 73–77; Sirmans, *Colonial South Carolina*, pp. 84–85.

443. Edward Randolph to Lords of Trade, June 28, 1699, CO 5/1287/225–30 at 230, PRO.

443. Crane, *Southern Frontier*, pp. 77–78; Sirmans, *Colonial South Carolina*, pp. 85–86.

445. Cf. Weir, *Colonial South Carolina*, pp. 76–79, 92–93.

446. CO 5/1290/45, 85, PRO.

447. Robert Quarry to Board of Trade, June 16, 1703, in E.B. O'Callaghan, ed., *Documents Related to the Colonial History of the State of New-York; Procured in Holland, England and France*, 15 vols. (Albany, 1857), IV, p. 1,048.

448. Address from the Commons House of Assembly to the Lords Proprietors of Carolina, December 6, 1,703, CO 5/1290/198, PRO.

449. The text of the statute appears in Thomas Cooper and Daniel J. McCord, eds., *The Statutes at Large of South Carolina*, 10 vols. (Columbia, SC, 1836–41), II, pp. 236–46. Cf. Sirmans, *Colonial South Carolina*, p. 18; Weir, *Colonial South Carolina*, pp. 76–78.

450. Sirmans believed that Johnson "from the time he took office aimed at the establishment of the Church of England," *Colonial South Carolina*, p. 87; Weir, *Colonial South Carolina*, p. 78. Significantly, the leading study of metropolitan politics under Queen Anne makes no mention of South Carolina, Geoffrey Holmes, *British Politics in the Age of Anne* (London: Macmillan, 1967).

451. *Party-Tyranny, or an Occasional Bill in Miniature; as now Practiced in Carolina. Humbly offered to the Consideration of both Houses of Parliament* [London, 1705], Salley, *Narratives*, pp. 224–64 at 248.

452. *The Present State of Affairs in Carolina. By John Ash, Gent. Sent by several of the Inhabitants of that Colony, to deliver their Representation thereof to, and seek Redress from, the Lords Proprietors of that Province: Together with an Account of his Reception, by the Honourable the Lord Granvill, their Palatine, President, or Chief of the Proprietors* in *Papers Relating to Carolina* (London, 1705), reprinted in Salley, *Narratives*, pp. 269–76.

453. A copy of Ash's narrative appears in a set of published *Papers Relating to Carolina*, a copy of which resides in the Early Modern Printed Collections of the British Library, including copies of the second charter, of the Fundamental Constitutions of March 1, 1670, and of the Constitutions dated April 11, 1698 ("Agreed on by all the Lords Proprietors" with "the Original being sent to Carolina by Major Daniel.") Cf. Salley, *Narratives*, p. 268.

454. *The Present State of Carolina*, pp. 29–32, 34–36; *The Case of the Church of England in Carolina, Humbly offer'd to the Consideration of both Houses of*

Parliament (London, 1705), pp. 1–4; Daniel Defoe, *The Case of Protestant Dissenters in Carolina, Shewing How a Law to prevent Occasional Conformity There, has ended in the Total Subversion of the Constitution of the Church and State. Recommended to the serious Consideration of all that are true Friends to our present Establishment* (London, 1706); "To his Excellency John Granvill, Esq; Palatine, and to the rest of the true and absolute Lords and Proprietors of the Province of Carolina. The Representation and Address of Several of the Members of the present Assembly returned for Colleton County, and other the Inhabitants of this Province, whose Names are hereunto subscribed," *Papers Relating to Carolina*, pp. 33–38; "To His Excellency, John Lord Granville Palatine, and to the rest of the true and absolute Lords and Proprietors of the Province of Carolina. 10 May 1704," *Papers Relating to Carolina*, pp. 41–42; "The Letter of Mrs. Blake, Widow of the late Governor to the Lords Proprietors. 16 May 1704" and "The Petition of the Committee of the Pensylvania Company, and divers other Merchants trading to Carolina" in *Papers Relating to Carolina*, pp. 42–43, reprinted in Salley, *Narratives*, pp. 224–64; Archdale, *A New Description of that Fertile and Pleasant Province of Carolina* in Salley, *Narratives*; Alexander Moore, ed., "A Narrative...of an Assembly...January the 2d, 1705/6": New Light on Early South Carolina Politics," *SCHM*, 85 (1984), 181–86.

For Rhett's imprisonment, PRIS 10/157 (Prisoners committed to the Fleet Prison), PRO.

The anti-Establishment pamphleteers complained about voting by slaves, "unqualified Aliens," and other "rabble" voting. South Carolina Huguenots, though, had been naturalized under an act of 1697, Van Ruymbeke, *From New Babylon to Eden*. The tracts also raged against the polling of servants, the poor, and free blacks. Of course, we have no way of being certain that such persons did actually vote in these elections. It does appear clear, though, that, presuming the accuracy of these chronicles, this voting behavior neither reflected "leveling influences" (cf. Wood, *Black Majority*, p. 96) nor an "early example of pure democracy" (cf. Salley, *Narratives*, p. 239n.). In the first place, it is harder to imagine a less likely proponent of levelling tendencies than Sir Nathaniel Johnson. In the second place, the documentation cited here constitutes evidence of how this behavior offended the sensibilities of the authors (and, presumably, the readers) of these tracts not necessarily of what transpired in the colony. A.S. Salley, for one, claimed that these elections had been conducted legitimately (as opposed to having been orchestrated by the Goose Creek men), *Narratives*, pp. 270–72n. Be that as it may, the significance here is that, by this time in the colony's history, the pattern of behavior of the Goose Creek faction, exaggerated or otherwise, had driven their opponents to take their case directly to London and, in the end, over the heads of the proprietors.

455. *An Account of the Fair and Impartial Proceedings of the Lords Proprietors, Governor and Council of the Colony of South Carolina, in Answer to the Untrue Suggestions contained in the Petition of Jos. Boon and others, and of a Paper Intituled The Case of the Church of England in Carolina* (London, 1706), pp. 1–4.

456. The Society for the Propagation for the Gospel voted to send no more missionaries to the province until the "High Commission" was abolished, Frederick Dalcho, *An Historical Account of the Protestant Episcopal Church, in South-Carolina, from the first settlement of the province to The War of the Revolution; with Notices of the Present State of the Church in Each Parish and some account of the Early Civil History of Carolina never before published* (Charleston, 1820), p. 69.

457. Dalcho, *An Historical Account of the Protestant Episcopal Church in South-Carolina*, p. 32; John Robert Moore, "Defoe's 'Queries upon the Foregoing Act': A Defense of Civil Liberty in South Carolina" in Heinz Blum, ed., *Essays in History and Literature Presented by the Fellows of The Newberry Library to Stanley Pargellis* (Chicago: University of Chicago Press, 1965), pp. 133–55 at 140.

458. "Documents Related to the Reverend Samuel Thomas," 51, for Marston's geographical and political origins.

459. Moore, "Defoe's 'Queries upon the Foregoing Act' " at p. 140; Reverend Edward Marston to Society for the Propagation of the Gospel, May 3, 1705, in *Papers Relating to Carolina*, pp. 56–59; Reverend Edward Marston to Lord Granville [1705], in *Papers Relating to Carolina*, pp. 60–64; "The Case of the Reverend Edward Marston, Minister of the Church belonging to the Church of England in Charles-Town, in South Carolina, truly stated" in *Papers Relating to South Carolina*, pp. 64–65. See also the account in Dalcho, *An Historical Account of the Protestant-Episcopal Church in South Carolina*, pp. 54–59; Salley, ed., "A Letter by the Second Landgrave Smith," 61–63; "Letters of Rev. Samuel Thomas, 1702–1710," 226, 228, 284–85; *Le Jau*, pp. 18, 20; Dalcho, *An Historical Account of the Protestant Episcopal Church in South-Carolina*, pp. 80, 85–89; "Documents Related to the Reverend Samuel Thomas," 51–54.

460. Cooper and McCord, *Statutes at Large*, II, pp. 282–94; Mark Kishlansky, *A Monarchy Transformed: Britain, 1603–1714* (London: Penguin, 1996), pp. 331–33.

461. *Le Jau*, p. 17.

Chapter 9

462. *Le Jau*, pp. 22–23.

463. Governor and Council to Society for the Propagation of the Gospel in Foreign Parts, September 19, 1707, SPG MSS. (L.C. Trans.), A 3, pp. 152, 311–13 (quoted in Johnston, 17–18); *Le Jau*, p. 29. Unfortunately, we have little further evidence on this "singular club."

464. *Le Jau*, p. 34.

465. *Le Jau*, p. 35.

466. *Le Jau*, p. 44.

467. *Le Jau*, pp. 39, 41, 55, 61, 63–64; *Johnston*, pp. 19–27.

468. Crane, *Southern Frontier*, pp. 146–47.

469. "Colonial Currency," *SCHM*, 38 (1937), 138–39. On April 20, 1714, Le Jau complained "Things are not in this province as when I came near 8

Yeares ago but our Shopkeepers having contrived to make certain Tickets pass for current Coyn we are come by degrees to See nothing else current which considering how they Sell all things reduce our Sallaries to be very inconsiderable so that 100£ of those tickets is hardly equal to 20£ Sterling," *Le Jau*, p. 138.

470. Sirmans, *Colonial South Carolina*, pp. 90–93.

471. Sirmans, *Colonial South Carolina*, pp. 93–94. Weir, *Colonial South Carolina*, notes Nairne's career as an imperial "visionary" was interrupted by his arrest for treason but never discusses Sir Nathaniel's own checkered political career. The treason case assumed significance, according to Weir, because it "crippled regulation of the trade at a crucial time"—the outbreak of the Tuscarora War in 1712, at p. 83. In actuality, notwithstanding Nairne's appointment, scant evidence appears to exist that the Carolinians ever undertook serious reform of the Indian trade prior to the Yamassee War discussed later. In addition, neither the collapse of the Carolina currency nor the controversy over regulating the Indian trade after 1703 stemmed from a competition between "planters" and "merchants," cf. Hewitt, "The State in the Planters' Service," in Greene, Brana-Shute, and Sparks, eds., *Money, Trade, and Power*, passim.

472. Proprietary minute book, April 14, 1709, CO 5/292/15, PRO; Alexander Moore, ed., *Nairne's Muskhogean Journals: The 1708 Expedition to the Mississippi River* (Jackson, MS: Mississippi Division of Archives and History, 1988), p. 17.

473. For a comprehensive account of Nairne's career, Moore, ed., *Nairne's Muskhogean Journals*, pp. 3–31.

474. Proprietary minute book, December 9, 1708, CO 5/289/158–60, PRO for Tynte's appointment; proprietary minute, book, February 28, 1711, CO 5/292/44, PRO for Nairne's appointment.

475. The occasion of his appeal for approbation from the Commons House of Assembly in 1709. In between his appearances before the proprietors, Nairne composed a promotional tract, the first for the colony in over 25 years (*A Letter from South Carolina* [London, 1710] in Greene, ed., *Selling a New World*, pp. 35–73). "Peopling" remained a vital concept to South Carolina in 1710. Although the proprietors by this time no longer cared to oversee such activity, they certainly had no objection to a prominent colonist keen to advertise the province to prospective migrants especially since Nairne noted their exceedingly fair land policy and encouraged the planters to pay for their land.

No evidence exists to indicate that the proprietors had anything to do with the recruiting of the thousands of "poor Palatines" who arrived in England in 1709 under the misapprehension, supplied by one "Kocherthal," that the Crown would subsidize their migration to Carolina, cf. Philip Otterness, "The 'Poor Palatines' of 1709: The Origins and Characteristics of Early Modern Mass Migration" (paper presented to the International Seminar on the History of the Atlantic World, 1500–1800, Harvard University, 1996).

476. Lords Proprietors to Colonel Tynte, February 9, 1710, CO 5/289/241–42, PRO.

477. *Le Jau*, p. 58. Since congregational control over ministers had been one of the tenets of the first Establishment Act, it is unclear how Le Jau reconciled his devotion toward Sir Nathaniel Johnson and other members of the "High-Church" party with his fervent opposition to "Independency."

478. *Johnston*, pp. 55, 99; *Le Jau*, pp. 83, 85.

479. *Johnston*, pp. 54–55; *Le Jau*, p. 82.

480. The second earl of Shaftesbury—commonly regarded, even by his father, as unfit for public life—died in 1699. His sons, the third earl and the philosopher, Maurice Ashley, each succeeded to their grandfather's share. Both had died by 1726. Lesser, pp. 42–55, provides an account of the last years of the proprietorship.

481. Lords Proprietors to Deputies and Council, April 9, 1709, CO 5/289/196–98 at 198, PRO.

482. Lords Proprietors to the government of South Carolina, April 9, 1709, CO 5/289/200, PRO.

483. The Crown approved Nicholson's commission on February 25, 1713, CO 5/1292/189, PRO. Cf. Sirmans, *Colonial South Carolina*, p. 105.

484. Will [copy] of Rebecca, Lady Granville, July 7, 1711, P 10/1, Badminton Muniments.

485. Craven was appointed on November 30, 1710, proprietary minute book, CO 5/292/34, PRO.

486. Proprietary minute book, January 23, 1711, CO 5/292/40, PRO.

487. Lords Proprietors to Charles Craven, September 3, 1709, CO 5/289/227–28, PRO; Lords Proprietors to Governor Tynte, January 5, 1710, CO 5/289/236, PRO; Lords Proprietors to Charlestown, February 2, 1710, CO 5/289/240, PRO. Again, the proprietors did not use quitrents as "revenue" but to pay the salaries of officers. Cf. Robert K. Ackerman, *South Carolina Colonial Land Policies* (Columbia, SC: University of South Carolina Press, 1977), pp. 27, 39, whose central thesis maintains that the proprietors sought to "profit" from land grants; Converse D. Clowse, *Economic Beginnings in Colonial South Carolina, 1670–1730* (Columbia, SC: University of South Carolina Press, 1971), p. 157.

488. Lords Proprietors to Edward Harte, Secretary, January 17, 1711, CO 5/290/69, PRO.

489. *Johnston*, p. 36.

490. Will of Henry, second duke of Beaufort, September 19, 1712, P 11/1, Badminton Muniments.

491. *Le Jau*, pp. 113–14.

492. *Le Jau*, pp. 109, 134–35.

493. For the connection between the Indian slave trade and the Yamassee War, see Richard L. Haan, "The Trade Do's not Flourish as Formerly: The Ecological Origins of the Yamassee War of 1715," *Ethnohistory*, 28 (1982), 341–58.

494. *Le Jau*, p. 180.

495. Governor Charles Craven to Board of Trade, May 23, 1715, CO 5/1292/215–18, and Board of Trade to Lords Proprietors of Carolina, July 8, 1715, CO 5/1292/219, both PRO.

496. Lords Proprietors of Carolina to Board of Trade, July 12, 1715, CO 5/1292/220, PRO.

497. Lords Proprietors to Board of Trade, July 14, 1715, CO 5/1292/222–23, PRO.

498. On the significance of Jacobitism for the development of the English state, see J.C.D. Clark, *Revolution and Rebellion: State and society in England in the seventeenth and eighteenth centuries* (Cambridge: Cambridge University Press, 1986), pp. 174–77; Kishlansky, *A Monarchy Transformed*, pp. 287–335.

499. "Memorial from several planters and merchants trading in Carolina to the Board of Trade relating to the miserable Condition of that province by the Insurrection of the Indians & to Relief necessary to be sent thither," July 18, 1715, CO 5/1292/224–28, PRO.

500. Board of Trade to Mr. Secretary Stanhope, July 19, 1715, CO 5/1292/229–31, PRO.

501. Joseph Boone and Richard Beresford to the Board of Trade, June 28, 1716, CO 5/1293/3–9, PRO; "A Demonstration of the Present State of South Carolina," [June 28, 1716], CO 5/1293/10, PRO; Joseph Boone and Robert Beresford to Board of Trade, December 5, 1716, CO 5/1293/ 21–25, PRO.

Chapter 10

502. Proprietary entry book, August 10, 1714, CO 5/290/75, PRO. As his will demonstrates, the duke of Beaufort found himself an exceedingly unwilling participant in Carolina. The evidence also reveals continuing proprietary disbelief and annoyance at the inability of their colonists to get along with each other. However, the deaths of Lord Granville and Lord Craven, as well as Beaufort, between 1707 and 1715 really left the proprietorship without a rudder and it is possible to argue that this almost complete lack of experienced leadership among the Lords on the eve of the Yamassee War contributed as much as anything to the limp response to that crisis and the corresponding end of proprietary government.

503. The land issue constituted a major grievance of the rebels of 1719 (for which see later). For modern scholarly views that proprietary policies, with respect to these lands, constituted an aspect of their "reckless behavior" over the last three years of their government over South Carolina—while the Assembly purportedly followed rational and appropriate polices, Weir, *Colonial South Carolina*, pp. 98–99.

504. Lords Proprietors to Governor and Council, March 3, 1716, CO 5/290/92, PRO.

505. Proprietary entry book, August 11, 1715, CO 5/290/86–88, PRO; Proprietary minute book, February 19, 1715 and November 3, 1716, CO 5/292/81, 88, PRO.

506. Proprietary minute book, June 1717, CO 5/292/94, PRO. Montgomerie's plan received sponsorship from Landgrave Abel Kettelby, another London merchant who served a term as the colony's agent but who also appeared before the proprietary board relatively frequently, Lesser, p. 186. Kettleby paid the proprietors £100 "purchase money of five thousand acres" in Carolina, proprietary minute book, March 24, 1709, CO 5/292/12–13, PRO.

507. Cf. Weir, *Colonial South Carolina*, pp. 91–92.

508. Andrews, *The Colonial Period of American History*, III, p. 138n.

509. The Cherokees, the most powerful people in the region and vital allies of the Carolinians, now controlled access to the interior and seem to have been less tractable (and, anyway, further away from Charles Town) than the Yamassees had been. The twin realities of greater distance to prospective slaves and uncertainty about Cherokee co-operation suggest that enslaving Indians became a less attractive proposition economically although the Catawbas continued to be involved to a limited degree. Tom Hatley, *The Dividing Paths: Cherokees and South Carolinians through the Era of Revolution* (New York: Oxford University Press, 1993), pp. 32–41, provides a discussion of the Indian trade, which the Indians seem to have controlled, during this period after the Yamassee War; Merrell, *The Indians' New World*, pp. 104–06.

510. Craven's role in the Yamassee War made him a heroic figure—alone of the colonial governors of the province—into the nineteenth century. He is the hero of William Gilmore Simms' largely forgotten antebellum novel, *The Yamassee*.

511. The cynic could argue that this directive would encourage the payment of rents—and, hence, further proprietary authority or that the language had no real meaning. However, we should note that this order also included revenue derived from land sales that ordinarily was supposed to go to England, ostensibly to pay proprietary obligations there.

512. Proprietary minute book, November 3, 1716, CO 5/292/92–93, PRO.

513. Lords Proprietors to Board of Trade, May 8, 1717, CO 5/1293/46, PRO.

514. Lords Proprietors to Board of Trade, May, 1717, CO 5/1293/49–51, PRO.

515. Cf. Sirmans, *Colonial South Carolina*, p. 105; Weir, *Colonial South Carolina*, pp. 97–98.

516. Lords Proprietors to William Rhett, January 17, 1711, CO 5/290/62, PRO. Sirmans based his argument on the proprietary claim of 1728 that they had not received a settled quitrent account for 20 years. Considering this claim was made at the end of the parliamentary negotiations to buy out the proprietorship, it is quite possible the Lords were exaggerating in order to secure a better deal for themselves from the Crown.

517. The rent-roll may be found in the proprietary minute book, March 19, 1714, CO 5/292/73, PRO.

518. Proprietary minute book, September 8, 1714, CO 5/292/76–79, PRO.

519. Proprietary minute book, (undated), CO 5/292/61–62, PRO.

520. Proprietary minute book, January 29, 1708, CO 5/292/2, PRO.

521. Lords Proprietors to Governor and Council, March 3, 1716, CO 5/290/93–94, PRO.

522. We do not know much about Shelton, who became secretary on February 3, 1709 and retained the office until the end of the proprietorship in 1729, but it seems he gained his place through a connection with the Craven family, Lesser, pp. 49–55.

523. It is also possible that the Carolina rebels used Trott and Rhett as pretexts—"evil counsellors"—for their move against the proprietors. Such a stratagem would fit with what we know of early modern rebellions from the Peasants' Revolt of 1525 and the Pilgrimage of Grace (1536) to the Great Fear (1789) at the dawn of the French Revolution, Zagorin, *Rebels and Rulers*, passim.

524. [Francis Yonge], *A Narrative of the Proceedings of the People of South-Carolina in the Year 1719: And of The True Causes and Motives that induced them to Renounce their Obedience to the Lords Proprietors, as their Governors, and to put themselves under the immediate Government of the Crown* (London, 1726) and [Joseph Boone?], *The Liberty and Property of British Subjects Asserted: In a Letter from an Assemblyman in Carolina to his Friend in London* (London, 1726). Yonge even dedicated his account to his patron, the Palatine. Cf. Sirmans, *Colonial South Carolina*, p. 116.

525. Rhett either never bothered to prepare the rent-roll referred to above or the rebellion interfered with his efforts to do so.

526. Lords Proprietors to Governor and Council, September 11, 1718, CO 5/290/124–25, PRO. Cf. Weir, *Colonial South Carolina*, pp. 98–99. Acting in part on orders from the crown, the proprietors disallowed the legislation, an act, as we shall see, that triggered alarm bells in the colony. However, as we shall also see, it can be argued that their corresponding order to lay out fifteen baronies in the Yamassee lands reflected more than a desire to augment their holdings and their incomes from the province. Cf. Clowse, *Economic Beginning of Colonial South Carolina*, pp. 192–94.

527. Proprietary minute book, October 31, 1718, CO 5/292/106, PRO.

528. Lords Proprietors to Governor and Council, September 4, 1719, CO 5/290/155–57, PRO.

529. Lords Proprietors to Governor and Council of South Carolina, July 22, 1718, CO 5/290/115–17 at 116, PRO.

530. Lords Proprietors to Governor Robert Johnson, July 24, 1719, CO 5/290/150–52 at 151–52, PRO.

531. Proprietary minute book, July 31, 1719, CO 5/292/130, PRO. It should be noted that the Lords need not have entertained any petition from the unfortunate Mr. Wilson, another unwitting victim of the politics of proprietary South Carolina, since he had acted on the Assembly's unilateral "Encouragement."

532. Proprietary minute book, November 14, 1718 and November 21, 1718, CO 5/1292/108, 110, PRO.

533. Lords Proprietors to Francis Yonge, Surveyor General, April 17, 1719, CO 5/290/139–40, PRO.

534. Yonge, *A Narrative of the Proceedings of the People of South-Carolina*, pp. 16–17; Sirmans, *Colonial South Carolina*, pp. 123–24.

535. Lords Proprietors to Privy Council, March 5, 1728, CO 5/290/261, PRO. Cf. Weir, *Colonial South Carolina*, pp. 75–103.

536. Lords Proprietors to Governor, Council and General Assembly of South Carolina, January 27, 1719, CO 5/290, 132–35, PRO; proprietary minute book, February 13, 1719 and February 27, 1719, CO 5/292/113, 115–16, PRO.

537. Lords Proprietors to Governor and Council of South Carolina, July 22, 1718, CO 5/290/115, PRO.

538. Lords Proprietors to Governor, Council and General Assembly of South Carolina, January 27, 1719, CO 5/290/132, PRO; proprietary minute book, February 27, 1719, CO 5/292/115, PRO.

539. Lords Proprietors to Governor, Council and General Assembly of South Carolina, January 27, 1719, CO 5/290/134–35, PRO; proprietary minute book, February 13, 1719, CO 5/292/113, PRO.

540. Cf. Sirmans, *Colonial South Carolina*, pp. 115–17, Weir, *Colonial South Carolina*, pp. 100–01.

541. Lords Proprietors to Governor Robert Johnson, July 24, 1719 [two letters], CO 5/290/147–49 and 150–52, PRO.

542. Lords Proprietors to Governor and Council of South Carolina, July 22, 1718, CO 5/290/118–19, PRO.

543. Lords Proprietors to Governor Robert Johnson, July 24, 1719, CO 5/290/151, PRO; Lords Proprietors to Chief Justice Trott, July 24, 1719, CO 5/290/154, PRO; Yonge, *A Narrative of the Proceedings*, pp. 9–10.

544. Lords Proprietors to Governor Johnson, June 19, 1719, CO 5/290/142–43, PRO.

545. Members of the Convention to the Governor [Moore], December 19, 1719, Papers of the Convention of the People/Commons House of Assembly, SCDAH. The convention members included Middleton, George Logan, John Fenwick, Landgrave Joseph Morton Jr., Bernard Schenkingh, George Chicken, and John Beresford, a cross-section of the colony's political perspectives.

546. "The most humble Petition of his Council and Assembly of the Settlement in South Carolina to the Kings most Excellent Majesty," December 24, 1719, Papers of the Convention of the People/Commons House of Assembly, SCDAH.

547. The proprietors disallowed the laws, as we have seen after warning that no laws on trade could be in force without proprietary ratification pursuant to the king's instructions. It is unclear why the colonists objected to this state of affairs at this time since the Lords had always exercised a "double negative," as in the case of the 1704 Test. The 1698 Fundamental Constitutions, as discussed earlier, codified the concept.

548. Preamble and Resolutions [December 17, 1719], Papers of the Convention of the People/Commons House of Assembly. The charter, as it happens, provided no guidelines on the selection of deputies nor did it limit their number.

549. "The humble Petition of the Commons house of Assembly of the present Settlement in South Carolina to the Kings Most Excellent Majesty," February 3, 1720, Papers of the Convention of the People/Commons House of Assembly, SCDAH.

550. Yonge, *A Narrative of the Proceedings*, pp. 37–38.

551. Both sides furnished reports to the Board of Trade on the state of the colony, "Address to the Lords Commissioner for Trade and the Assembly's answers to their Lordships' Queries," January 29, 1720, 11/569/4, William R. Coe Papers, SCHS; Governor Robert Johnson to Board of Trade, January 12, 1720, in Merrens, *Colonial South Carolina Scene*, 57–66; "Queries [for Mr Boone] from the Board of Trade abt Carolina," August 10, 1720, 11/569/7, Coe Papers, SCHS.

552. "Memorandum between the Lords Proprietors and John Falconer, David Barclay, and Thomas Hyam," May 25, 1720, 11/569/12, Coe Papers, SCHS.

553. Yonge, *A Narrative of the Proceedings*, pp. 37–38.

554. James Bertie to Lord Carlton, President of the Council, August 14, 1724, CO 5/290/165, PRO.

555. Ibid.

556. Lords Proprietors to William Rhett, January 21, 1725, CO 5/290/168, PRO.

557. Treasury to Lords Proprietors, February 2, 1726, CO 5/290/171, PRO.

558. Lords Proprietors to the Privy Council [1725/26], CO 5/290/170; Lords Proprietors to Privy Council, June 14, 1726, CO 5/290/175–76, PRO; Lords Proprietors to Privy Council [1726], CO 5/290/178–80, PRO.

559. Thomas Lowndes received the title along with a barony for himself and three others, July 1, 1726, CO 5/290/238–40, PRO.

560. Sir James Tyrell purchased Maurice Ashley's share, proprietary minute book, December 1, 1725, CO 5/292/152, PRO.

561. Lords Proprietors grant to Thomas Taylor, November 1, 1726, CO 5/290/251–52, PRO.

562. Lords Proprietors to Privy Council [March 1728], CO 5/290/263, PRO.

563. Proprietary minute book, January 24, 1725, CO 5/292/149, PRO.

564. The leading modern study is Arlin C. Migliazzo, "Ethnic Diversity on the southern frontier: a social history of Purrysburgh, South Carolina, 1732–1792" (Ph.D. diss., Washington State University, 1982) and see, also, idem, "A tarnished legacy revisited: Jean-Pierre Purry and the settlement of the Southern Frontier, 1718–1736," *SCHM*, 92 (1991), 232–52. Albert B. Faust, "Swiss Emigration to the American Colonies in the Eighteenth Century," *American Historical Review*, 22 (1916–17), 21–44, provides a hagiographic account. Purry published a *Memorial presented to His Grace, the Duke of Newcastle upon the condition of Carolina and the means of its amelioration* (London, 1724) and, subsequently, a promotional pamphlet that copied the tone of efforts that appeared in the proprietary period, *Proposals by Mr. Peter Purry of Newfchatel, for Encouragement of such Swiss Protestants as should agree to accompany him to Carolina, to settle a new colony, and, also, A Description of the Province of South Carolina* (London, 1731).

565. [Joseph Boone], *The Liberty and Property of British Subjects Asserted: In a Letter from an Assemblyman in Carolina to his Friend in London* (London, 1726), pp. 32–38. This pamphleteer saw the need to go over the entire history of the proprietary period.

566. Lords Proprietors to Privy Council, [1726], CO 5/290/178–80, PRO; "Brief for Council, South Carolina Assembly against Lords Proprietors," [1726], Add. MS. 35,090, ff. 8–9, BL. This document, of course, makes a neat example of the Dissenting perspective within the Convention. Yonge, *A Narrative of the Proceedings.*

567. Lords Proprietors to Privy Council, May 31, 1727, CO 5/290/181, PRO.

568. Lords Proprietors to Privy Council, October 12, 1727, CO 5/290/182–84, PRO; "Some few reasons to shew the Absolute Necessity for the Crown's buying the Propriety of the Carolinas as also the Advantagiuosness of that Purchase to the Publick," [1729], PA 1/9, Badminton Muniments.

569. CO 5/290/257–258, PRO.

570. Cf. Sirmans, *Colonial South Carolina*, pp. 120–28.

571. Alan D. Watson, "The Quitrent System in Royal South Carolina," *William and Mary Quarterly*, 3rd ser., 33 (1976), 183–211.

572. The major study remains Meriwether, *The Expansion of South Carolina*. See also H. Roy Merrens, "'Camden's turrets pierce the skies!' The Urban Process in the Southern Colonies during the Eighteenth Century," *William and Mary Quarterly*, 3rd ser., 30 (1973), 549–74.

573. Weir, *Colonial South Carolina*, pp. 102–03.

574. Cf. T.H. Breen, "An Empire of Goods: The Anglicization of Colonial America, 1690–1776" in Stanley N. Katz, John M. Murrin, and Douglas Greenberg, eds., *Colonial America* (New York: McGraw-Hill, 1993), pp. 367–98. Weir's classic account of pre-independence South Carolina politics notes that the "country ideal" of the Fundamental Constitutions— "rule by an elite composed of public-spirited men of independent mien"— had "figured in the political life of the colony from its founding." However, "squabbling over religious differences and contending for the perquisites of power" by the factious Carolinians delayed its implementation until "during the first four decades of the eighteenth century economic and social developments provided the prerequisites necessary for the growth of Shaftesbury's ideal." Huge increases in the production of rice and indigo between 1730 and 1760 encouraged political harmony among the planters, Robert M. Weir, "'The Harmony We Were Famous For': An Interpretation of Pre-Revolutionary South Carolina Politics" in Stanley N. Katz and John M. Murrin, eds., *Colonial America: Essays in Politics and Social Development* (New York: Alfred A. Knopf, 1983), pp. 421–46 at 427–28. Considered in the context of all of Britain's American colonies, South Carolina's "black majority" does not make it distinctive.

575. Cf. Elizabeth Mancke, "Empire and State" in Armitage and Braddick, eds., *The British Atlantic World*, pp. 175–95; idem, "Negotiating an Empire" in Christine Daniels and Michael V. Kennedy, eds., *Negotiated Empires: Centers and Peripheries in the Americas*, (New York: Routledge, 2002), pp. 235–65.

Index

Albemarle (North Carolina), 15, 20

Amy, Thomas, proprietor, 128, 138, 146

Anglo-Dutch Wars
   1664–67, 20
   1672–74, 46–7

Archdale, John, proprietor and
   governor, 70, 72, 115–18, 124,
   125

Ash, John, Carolina settler and
   Dissenter, 129–30, 134

Ashley, Maurice, third earl of
   Shaftesbury, 201n

Ashley Cooper, Sir Anthony, first earl
   of Shaftesbury, 16–17, 19–20

   and attempt to bar James, duke of
      York, from the succession, 52,
      69–82

   negotiations between and Scots to
      settle in Carolina, 73–82; see
      also Sir George Campbell of
      Cessnock, Sir Hugh Campbell,
      Sir John Cochrane of Ochiltree,
      Scottish Carolina Company

   plans for Carolina of, 21–40; see also
      Fundamental Constitutions of
      Carolina

Ashley River colony
   see Carolina

Atlantic history, 1–3

Axtell, Daniel, landgrave, 36, 70, 72,
   78, 88, 92, 93, 94, 97, 120

Axtell, Lady Rebecca, Carolina settler
   and Dissenter, 72, 134

Bacon, Sir Francis, colonization
   theorist, 28, 77, 116

Bacon's Rebellion, 10

Bahamas, 43, 46, 93, 124, 141, 189n,
   190n

Baillie of Jerviswood, Robert, 79

Baird, Sir Robert, Scottish merchant,
   76, 80, 81
   see also Scottish Carolina Company

Barbados, 4, 5, 6, 8, 10, 15, 16, 17, 18,
   20, 27, 29, 41, 43, 44, 45, 47, 49,
   59, 85, 95, 106
   see also Barbados Adventurers and Sir
      John Yeamans

Barbados Adventurers
   Articles of Agreement between Lords
      Proprietors and, 18–19, 29

Barclay, David, prospective proprietary
   purchaser, 153

Barnwell, John, Carolina military leader
   against Tuscaroras, 140

Belfast, Ireland, 39, 70, 88, 148

Bellinger, Edmund, landgrave, 118,
   120, 121

Benham Valente, Berkshire, manor of,
   21–2, 26, 40

Beresford, John, Carolina settler, 97

Beresford, Richard, Carolina agent, 142

Berkeley, Sir John, Baron Berkeley of
   Stratton, proprietor, 16, 17, 28

Berkeley, Sir William, governor of
   Virginia and proprietor, 15, 16,
   18, 20, 28, 46

Berkeley County, Carolina, 57, 87, 106

Blake, Benjamin, Carolina settler and
   Dissenter, 72

Blake, Joseph, proprietor and governor,
   72, 117–18, 120–1, 123, 124, 125

Blake, Mrs. Benjamin, Carolina settler
   and Dissenter, 134

Boone, John, Goose Creek man, 63,
   64, 65, 88, 95, 97

Boone, Joseph, Carolina Dissenter and
   lobbyist, 130, 142, 146, 147, 152

Boone, Mrs. Joseph, Carolina settler and Dissenter, 134

Bothwell Bridge, Scottish rebellion (1679), 75

Broughton, Thomas, Indian trader and contender for governor of Carolina, 135–8, 149

Bull, Stephen, Carolina surveyor, 46, 49, 107

Burnet, Gilbert, bishop of Salisbury, historian, 79, 80

Butler, James, second duke of Ormonde, lord-lieutenant of Ireland, 39, 82, 86

Campbell, Archibald, ninth earl of Argyll and anti-government conspirator, 75, 78, 80, 81, 82

Campbell, Sir Hugh, father of Sir George Campbell of Cessnock, 76, 79

Campbell of Cessnock, Sir George, Scottish colonizer and conspirator, 73, 76–7, 79, 80, 83, 94

Carolina
    Church of England in, 117–32; *see also* Rev. Gideon Johnston, Rev. Francis Le Jau, Rev. Edward Marston
    Dissenters in, 83–132
    Indian slave trade in; *see* Goose Creek men, Westo War, Yamassee War
    politics in, 69–158
    rebellion against Lords Proprietors (1719), 150–6
    religion in; *see* Church of England, Dissenters
    see also Fundamental Constitutions of

Carolina Coffee-House, 60, 71, 72

Carstares, William, Scottish minister and conspirator, 137, 140, 143, 155

Carteret, John, first earl of Granville, proprietor, 137, 140, 143, 155

Carteret, Sir George, proprietor, 15, 72, 178n

Charles I, king of England, Scotland, and Ireland (1625–49), 17

Charles II, king of England, Scotland, and Ireland (1660–85), 17, 22, 46, 47, 53, 56, 58, 70, 75, 141

Charters, Charles, Scottish merchant and colonizer, 76

Cochrane of Ochiltree, Sir John, Scottish colonizer and conspirator, 73, 75–80, 83

Colleton, James, Carolina governor, 122–5

Colleton, Sir John (d. 1667), proprietor, 15, 18, 20, 29

Colleton, Sir John, first earl of Granville, proprietor, 122, 141, 158

Colleton, Sir Peter, proprietor, 45, 47, 49, 50, 53, 55, 60, 62, 70, 72, 78, 88, 92, 93, 96, 97, 100, 104, 117, 119, 170n, 173n, 192n

Colleton County, Carolina, 87, 121, 135, 136, 198n

Conigsmark, Count, murder trial of, 58, 61, 129, 181n
    see also Sir Nathaniel Johnson

Crawford, Patrick, Scottish seaman, 81

Crawford of Crawfordland, John, Scottish colonizer and anti-government conspirator, 76, 77, 78, 79, 80, 81

Craven, Charles, Carolina governor, 138, 139, 140, 144, 145, 146, 149

Craven, William, first earl of, proprietor, 16, 17, 19, 21, 71, 72, 73, 86, 108, 137, 175n

Daniel, Robert, Carolina politician, 97, 118, 120, 121, 126

Defoe, Daniel, controversialist, 129

Dick, John, Scottish prisoner "of conscience," 81, 83

Dunlop, William, Stuarts Town leader, 77, 80, 83, 94, 96, 106, 144

English, William, Carolina settler, 149

Erskine of Carnock, John, Presbyterian diarist, 82

Erskine, Henry, third Baron Cardross, 7, 76, 82–94, 116, 144
  see also Stuarts Town

Falconer, John, prospective proprietary purchaser, 153
Farr, John, Carolina settler, 107
Ferguson, Robert (the "Plotter"), controversialist and Carolina promoter, 70, 72, 78, 79
Ferguson, Thomas, Irish colonizer, 83
Fleet prison, 129
Fundamental Constitutions of Carolina, 4, 8, 9, 11, 29–50, 56, 98, 99–109, 114, 116
  and Scots (1682 versions), 73–5, 77–9, 84–5, 88–9, 94
  1697 version, 116

Gibbes, Robert, Carolina settler, 137–8
Gibbes, Thomas, Goose Creek man, 90
Gibson, James, Glasgow merchant and sea captain, 83, 84
Gibson, Walter, Glasgow merchant, 76, 77, 83, 186n
Godfrey, John, Carolina settler, 45, 63, 65, 90
  see also Sir John Yeamans
Goose Creek men
  see also Job How, Ralph Izard, Sir Nathaniel Johnson, George Logan, Maurice Mathews, James Moore, Andrew Percival, Robert Quarry
  and Indian slave trade, 51–68
  and Carolina politics, 69–142
  and religion in Carolina, 117–32
Gordon, George, earl of Aberdeen, lord chancellor of Scotland, 78, 80
Granville, John, Lord, proprietor, 7, 121, 128, 129, 131, 133
Granville, John, earl of Bath, proprietor, 72, 73, 120
Granville, Rebecca, Lady, proprietor, 136
Gray, Thomas, Carolina settler, 45
Griffiths, James, proprietary secretary, 138

Grimball, Paul, provincial secretary and Goose Creek opponent, 89, 92, 97, 98, 102, 106, 108, 112, 114, 115

Harley, Sir Robert, 15
Hart, Charles, 151, 156
Heath, Sir Robert, Attorney-General and early Carolina patentee, 17
Hilton, William, sea captain, 18
Hodgson, William, 144
Horsey, Samuel, proprietary nominee for governor, 154–5
Hog, Thomas, Scottish minister, 81
How, Job, Goose Creek man, 7, 60, 97, 99, 100, 101, 102, 117, 120, 129
Huguenots, 39, 69, 91, 97, 102, 114, 118, 127, 130, 151
Hyam, Thomas, prospective proprietary purchaser, 153
Hyde, Sir Edward, first earl of Clarendon, 16, 17, 18, 20, 28, 170n

Ireland, 2, 11, 22, 39, 40, 43, 46, 57, 69, 79, 80, 82, 83, 86, 141, 149
Izard, Ralph, Goose Creek man, 97, 102, 107, 151

James, II king of England, VII king of Scotland, duke of York and Albany, 46, 49, 53, 58, 60, 69, 72, 77, 93, 97, 99, 102, 130, 141, 176n
Jamaica, 16, 43, 126
Jenkins, Sir Leoline, secretary of state, 71
Johnson, Sir Nathaniel, Carolina governor, 7, 32, 57–61, 99–102, 106, 115, 117, 120, 124, 128–31, 134–7, 143
Johnson, Robert, Carolina governor, 143, 145–6, 150–4, 156
Johnston, Rev. Gideon, Church of England commissary in Carolina, 139
Johnston, Patrick, Scottish colonizer, 76

Kettleby, Abel, landgrave and London merchant, 203n

Kinsale, Ireland, 41
Kyrle, Sir Richard, Carolina governor and
    Irish army officer, 86–7, 95, 136

Laurens, Henry, 40
Leeward Islands, 58–9, 106, 178n
    see also Sir Nathaniel Johnson
Legge, George, earl of Dartmouth, 93,
    97, 99
Le Jau, Rev. Francis, Church of
    England minister in Carolina,
    133–4, 137, 199–200n, 201n
Leisler's Rebellion, 10
Linning, Elizabeth, Scottish kidnap
    victim, 83
Locke, John, 4, 32–5, 41–3, 47, 49, 56,
    69–70, 169n, 175n, 180n, 183n
    see also Fundamental Constitutions of
    Carolina, Huguenots
Lockhart, Sir George, Scottish
    colonizer, 76
Logan, George, Carolina settler, 145, 147
London
    population of, 22–4, 36–7
Lords proprietors
    see individual proprietors,
        Fundamental Constitutions of
        Carolina
Ludwell, Philip, Carolina governor,
    107–15
Lynch, Sir Thomas, Jamaica governor,
    43, 190n

Marsden, Rev. Richard, Carolina
    minister, 134
Marshall, Rev. Samuel, Carolina
    minister, 130
Marston, Rev. Edward, Carolina
    minister, 130, 134
Maryland, 108, 134, 164n, 165n
Mathews, Maurice, proprietary official
    and Goose Creek man, 6–7, 14,
    45, 52–3, 55–7, 60–3, 65–7,
    86–8, 90–4, 96–103, 105–8,
    114–15, 116, 118, 121, 124, 156
    see also Goose Creek men

Middleton, Arthur, Goose Creek man,
    88, 145, 147
Modyford, Sir Thomas, 16
Monck, George, first duke of
    Albemarle, proprietor, 15, 16, 17,
    19, 20, 28, 137
Monmouth, James, duke of, 58, 75, 177n
Montgomery, Sir Robert, colonizer,
    144, 154
Moore, James, Goose Creek man, 7,
    56–7, 63–5, 88, 93, 97, 99, 102,
    112, 114–15, 117, 120–30, 135,
    150, 173n, 175n, 196n
Moore, James, Jr., Carolina governor,
    140, 145, 147, 151–3
Moore, John, Goose Creek man, 90
Morton, Joseph, Carolina governor and
    opponent of Goose Creek men, 7,
    36, 57, 72, 77–8, 84, 87–8, 91–5,
    97, 110, 118, 120, 184n, 187n,
    192n
Morton, Joseph, Jr., 120–1, 125, 144
Mosman, George, Scottish merchant
    and colonizer, 76, 81
Munro, Alexander, commissary, 80

Nairne, Thomas, Carolina promoter
    and Indian agent, 7, 121, 134–6,
    200n
New England, 2, 15, 18, 37, 38, 55,
    81, 108, 130, 137, 141, 173n
New York, 10, 47, 77, 108, 138, 140,
    141, 190n
Newe, Thomas, Carolina settler, 65
Nicholson, Francis, Carolina governor
    and proprietary advisor, 138, 140,
    153–4

occasional conformity, 128–30
Osborne, Thomas, earl of Danby, 38,
    46, 49, 71, 73
Owen, William, Carolina settler, 45–6
Oxford Parliament (1681), 58, 70

Pennsylvania, 4, 10, 36, 37, 39, 164n,
    165n

Pepys, Samuel, Admiralty secretary, 38, 93, 97, 99

Percival, Andrew, proprietary agent and Goose Creek man, 7, 47, 48, 56–7, 60–5, 84, 88–9, 97, 101, 103, 107–8, 112, 114–15, 179n, 180n, 181n

Plunket, Oliver, Roman Catholic archbishop of Armagh, 38

Purry, Jean-Pierre, Swiss colonizer, 154, 206n

Quarry, Robert, Carolina official and Goose Creek man, 7, 57, 86–7, 90, 95, 97, 99, 102–3, 106–7, 110, 112, 114–15, 126–8, 187n

quitrents, 4, 7, 18–19, 27, 56–7, 86, 88, 98, 105, 110–11, 114–16, 118, 146–8, 153–5

Randolph, Edward, imperial official, 7, 57, 122–6, 196n

Ramsay, David, historian, 12

Rhett, William, Carolina politician, 7, 117–18, 129, 143, 145–7, 151–2, 154, 198n, 204n

Rivers, William J., historian, 103

Rye-House Plot, 3, 75–6, 81, 183n
see also, Robert Ferguson, Algernon Sidney, Aaron Smith, Robert West, and Samuel Wilson

St. Augustine, 7–8, 66, 89–92, 94, 96, 104, 113, 123, 125, 133, 142, 144, 189n
Carolinian attack on (1702), 126–30, 135, 150, 155

Sandford, Robert, Carolina promoter, 20

Sayle, William, governor of Carolina, 44

Schenkingh, Bernard, Carolina settler and Goose Creek opponent, 57, 88, 98, 106

Scotland, 22, 39, 94, 142
see also Stuarts Town, Archibald Campbell, Sir John Cochrane of Ochiltree, Sir Hugh Campbell,

Sir George Campbell of Cessnock, William Dunlop, John Erskine, third Baron Cardross, Alexander Munro, Scottish Carolina Company, John Dick, Thomas Hog, Elizabeth Linning, Archibald Stewart, William Veitch, Mrs. William Veitch

Scottish Carolina Company, 73, 80–1, 83
see also William Dunlop, Sir Robert Baird, Sir John Cochrane of Ochiltree, Sir Hugh Campbell, Sir George Campbell of Cessnock, John Crawford of Crawfordland, Charles Charters, William Dunlop, John Erskine, third Baron Cardross, Walter Gibson, Sir George Lockhart, and George Mosman

Scrivener, William, Carolina settler, 45

Shelton, Robert, proprietary secretary, 146–7

Shaftesbury, Anthony Ashley Cooper, first earl of,
see Anthony Ashley Cooper

Sidney, Algernon, republican, 75, 79
see also Rye-House Plot

Somerset, Henry, second duke of Beaufort, Carolina proprietor, 8, 138–9, 143, 202n

Smith, Aaron, lawyer and Rye-House plotter, 70, 75, 176n, 184n

Smith, Thomas, landgrave, 36, 72, 92, 107, 114–15, 117, 120

Smith, Jr., Thomas, 120

Sothell, Seth, Carolina governor and proprietor, 7, 55, 57, 73, 97, 103–6, 111, 113–15, 117, 122, 124, 127, 187n

South Carolina
see Carolina

Spragg, Thomas, captain, HMS Drake, 7, 60, 93, 190n

Stewart, Archibald, Scottish prisoner "of conscience," 82

Stewart, John, Carolina settler and controversialist, 58, 60–61, 92–94, 96–102, 104–6, 191n
Stuarts Town, 60, 75, 83–94, 97, 188n, 189n
see also Stuarts Town, William Dunlop, John Erskine, third Baron Cardross, Sir John Cochrane of Ochiltree, Sir Hugh Campbell, Sir George Campbell of Cessnock, Scottish Carolina Company, Stewart, John
Surinam, 20

Taylor, Thomas, Irish colonizer, 154
Thornburgh, William, proprietor, 120, 138, 195n
Thynne, Thomas, murder of (1682), 58, 177n
Trott, Nicholas, chief justice of Carolina and politician, 7, 117–18, 121, 133–6, 143, 145–7, 151, 152, 204n
True Protestant Mercury, Whig gazette, 72, 79
Tuscarora Indians,
war between Carolina and, 139–40, 200n
Tynte, Edward, Carolina governor, 136–8

Vassall, Samuel, merchant, 17
Veitch, William, Scottish minister, 80–1
Veitch, Mrs. William, 82
Virginia, 2, 8, 10, 15, 16, 18, 20, 28, 165n

Walcot, Thomas, Rye-House plotter, 79
West, Joseph, governor of Carolina, 41, 44–5, 47–8, 54, 87, 89, 187n
West, Robert, lawyer and Rye-House informant, 70, 78, 184–5n
Westbrook, Caleb, Indian trader and Goose Creek man, 89–90, 115
Westo Indians, 7, 61–3, 66–7, 86, 90–1, 125, 173n
see also Westo War
Westo War, 63–5, 99, 121, 179n
Wilkinson, Henry, sea captain, 70, 181n
Williamson, Atkin, Carolina "minister," 175n
Willoughby of Parham, Lord, 17
Wilson, Samuel, proprietary secretary, 31, 35, 56, 70–2, 170n, 176n
Wodrow, Robert, Presbyterian historian, 75, 76, 186n
Woodward, Dr. Henry, Carolina Indian agent and trader, 7, 61–6, 88, 90, 121

Yamassee Indians, 8, 89–90, 92, 96, 104, 113, 121, 126
see also Yamassee War
Yamassee Settlement (1717–18), 144–52
Yamassee War (1715–16), 5, 133, 140–2, 155
Yeamans, Sir John, governor of Carolina and Barbadian Adventurer, 7, 18, 20, 42, 44–5, 47–9
Yonge, Francis, Carolina official, 147, 149, 151–2, 155